Beverley Farmer was born and grew up in Melbourne. She has worked as a teacher of French and English and in the restaurant trade in Australia and overseas. In 1965 she married a Greek immigrant and for some years, during which she worked on her first book, *Alone* (1980), they lived in his village in the north of Greece. She has drawn on the experience of Greek life in several of the stories in the collections *Milk* (1983) and *Home Time* (1985), and in the novel *The House in the Light* (1995). She lives on the Victorian coast at Point Lonsdale and has one son.

Other books by Beverley Farmer

Alone
Milk
Home Time
Place of Birth
A Body of Water
The Seal Woman
The House in the Light
Collected Stories

The bone house

GIRA –
MOND
O

The bone house

Essays **Beverley Farmer**

First published 2005
by the Giramondo Publishing Company
for the Writing and Society Research Group
in the University of Western Sydney

Giramondo Publishing Company
PO Box 752
Artarmon NSW 1570 Australia
www.giramondopublishing.com

Designed by Harry Williamson
Typeset by Andrew Davies
in 11.25/14 pt Garamond 3 & Italia bold
Printed and bound by Southwood Press
Distributed in Australia by Tower Books

National Library of Australia
Cataloguing-in-Publication data:

Farmer, Beverley, 1941- .
The bone house.

Bibiography.
ISBN 1 920882 06 5.

I. Title.

A824.3

Cover photograph by the author

To Barry Hill

Contents

All photographs are by the author.
The banyan images in 'Seeing in the dark', all of the one old tree in Queenscliff, Victoria, are from a longer sequence, *Metamorphosis–banyan*. The stone in the photograph on p.248 is in the Avebury Circle in Wiltshire.

Illustrations

MOUTHS OF GOLD

Water has no memory

EILÉAN NÍ CHUILLEANÁIN

All winter, for half an hour after sunrise on any clear morning, a stalk of sun will burn along the edge of my blind on to the wardrobe door. It will spread a tall flame across the matchstick blind, like a church candle. Then the whole blind will be fire and shadow, cast by the tree outside. A print, a lion face.

A slice of blood orange is a wheel of fire. The skin surrounds a smudged pith and ten radiating white veins sodden with dark red: ten segmented translucencies of red gold like a dragonfly wing, and filaments like combed hair. A segment of blood orange is a red gold mouth pressed thick on the mouth, bitter as pomegranate. Two hands hold it, hands that drip blood.

Low tide and a waveline of jellyfish like ice on the thaw, clearer than water, so clear even the sand is alight.

Ship smoke hangs over the garden of this house on the edge of journeys. Some of the older houses around the foreshore have a widow tower where women whose menfolk were at sea in the days of sail – this having been one of the shipwreck coasts of the world – would watch for a ship on its way in and out through the Rip. All of the older houses have a tin roof and narrow windows in wooden walls, hooded to keep the summer out. The rooms have tall sash windows that run on ropes and the boxed panes are made of thin flawed glass that ripples away from you like a sheet of water. The boxes of window are all six feet by three, the dimensions of a single bed, Grania notes, and for that matter of a casket. A street of caskets with glass lids. And the light flowing through day after day as shallow and tawny and cold as creek water.

Fig leaves hanging in magpie patches. Threads, veins. A high chalice of light.

This story in the making: more and more self-effaced, lapped in folds of itself, as water is, and shadow on water, developing in loops rather than along a story line, and therefore devoid – free – of narrative tension. The surface tension of water. It involves Grania and her daughter on the day and night that the family sustains, at a remove, in

Greece – they live in Australia – the shock, the aftershock, of a violent death. To be true to its organic form, any tension there is can only be that between the current of lived time and the reverberating rings of wave made by the stone that has broken through.

Attention to what is. Because whatever is added to the image hoard of one mind is an addition to the world. Not a permanent one, needless to say. What is permanent about a grain of fire in space?

We believe in anything rather than accept that a whole world emblazoned inside the eggshell of the skull is fated for extinction. We must be more than sparks of matter, atoms of finite being. We bind ourselves to our world in the three dimensions of time with silken threads of soul stuff, threads of light, extrusions of the self into the void, webs of our meaning that we anchor where we may and hang there. The hope of the soul is tenacious. It is inborn, in our bones.

White wings, rags, moths flapping out in the garden are irises, for the first time in years, a clump of winter irises on the cusp of spring, self-sown in a blue-flickering darkness of rosemary.

In the cellophane of morning, the shift of gravity, the wave of mirage in the aftermath of a bad dream, he is stumbling down a place of ruin to the hooded platform of a railway station, stricken with pangs of remorse and shame out of a life he is not leading and has never led. Blades of sun stab him. In the blocks of dark air between façades of vast stone he sees the dust falling.

The tawny days of autumn, burning out by mid-afternoon. The garden growing wetter and wilder by the day. Grania's hair catches and snaps on stray twigs as she passes, filaments of her hair flow out in the light. She squats down under the loquat tree with a fork and grubs up weeds, old bones, chicken drumsticks knotted at both ends and baked a wooden brown, a fish spine like a white fern, washed up with stones and roots and covered again, tides of the soil and rain. The place is a midden. Year after year laid down and slowly coming to light again, a lifetime of summers, of winters closing in like nightfall, other lives, compost spread out as mulch, black potatoes, some sprouting, avocado pits and their leather skins – fork over the soil anywhere along the dunes of this coast – ashes, knucklebones, eggshells, cuttle bones, a seabird's head all beak and eyehole, oyster and mussel shells, the antiquities of untold generations of a light-footed race, all the dark dead, their bones and blood and flow of hair.

The woman in the dream room faces the two men and shakes the water off her hands, but it spots the floor at their feet, dark blood, bad blood.

Flapping at her back all the afternoon, the sheets on the lines as they fill out with wind and sun, four sheets like square sails airing for the family, two double for the parents, two single for the boy. About time to haul them down and bring them in, confronting her own self caught in the sun shining through green gold fig leaves, a stranger in the glass, a fleece of hair hung among branches, one black-sleeved arm stretched out as if casting a spell while the other hugs her bundle and pulls the French window shut at her back. Four sheets to untangle and fold, thin old cotton sheets, warm now, and yellow in the creases, like sheets off a sick bed – but no, the yellow goes away once the cloth is hung out flat, it was only the late light pooled in them. For once no orb spider is huddled flat to the weave. Arms stretched and lifted, she takes it slowly, joining up the four corners, matching hem and selvedge in the dance that mothers used to take their partners for when she was a girl, a step forward, a step back, bringing up their hands in slow pat-a-cake unison. If a corner drags on the floor and I tread on it, well, it's sandy, this soil, it'll rub off. So what if I'm not the housewife my mother was. My sheets fill the room with a summer breath of salt, hay.

Out picking the last tomatoes, shaking leaves and webs she finds a hair or two of her head woven into the bushes. Tomatoes she has overlooked are leaking a fuzz of white. Water drops on her arms magnify the weave of flesh. And in the bowl, a puddle, a sag of tomato, a menstrual smell.

A red memory, a bitten fig and a bitten rat's comb of spine.

A stored image can broadcast itself when conditions are favourable, taking form in words, in ink and paint, film, clay, stone. Images are seeds. They have latency and the power to endure. They are like stored shadows burnt on to film for a fraction of a second, decades ago, the long lost negative in the family Bible, the black child in the black dress with the sun in her eyes, seen for the first time in the child's old age. She sits squinting white-eyed in a pram. Her eyes are crescents in a jelly of black flesh, albuminous, as if candlelit from inside. O, let me not be blind, not blind.

Paul Eluard: *Il y a un autre monde mais il est dans celui-ci.* What other world is in this one (is it Death)?

The brass lamp on the mantelpiece has no shade and the globe casts a yellow wash on the pair of photos Grania has propped against the wall at its back, two photos already in the key of yellow. In the first one, the sun through the darkness of a cavernous ruin strikes a brass candle as tall as a man and melts it; on either side of it stand her daughter and grandson, each posed half in shadow, half light, Elinor and Mikey in Greece. In the other one two stocky men are smiling out of the haze. The one dusty with sunlight, his mane of hair alight, is Tomo, older and heavier than the other at his side, in his shade: Tomo and his brother Theo

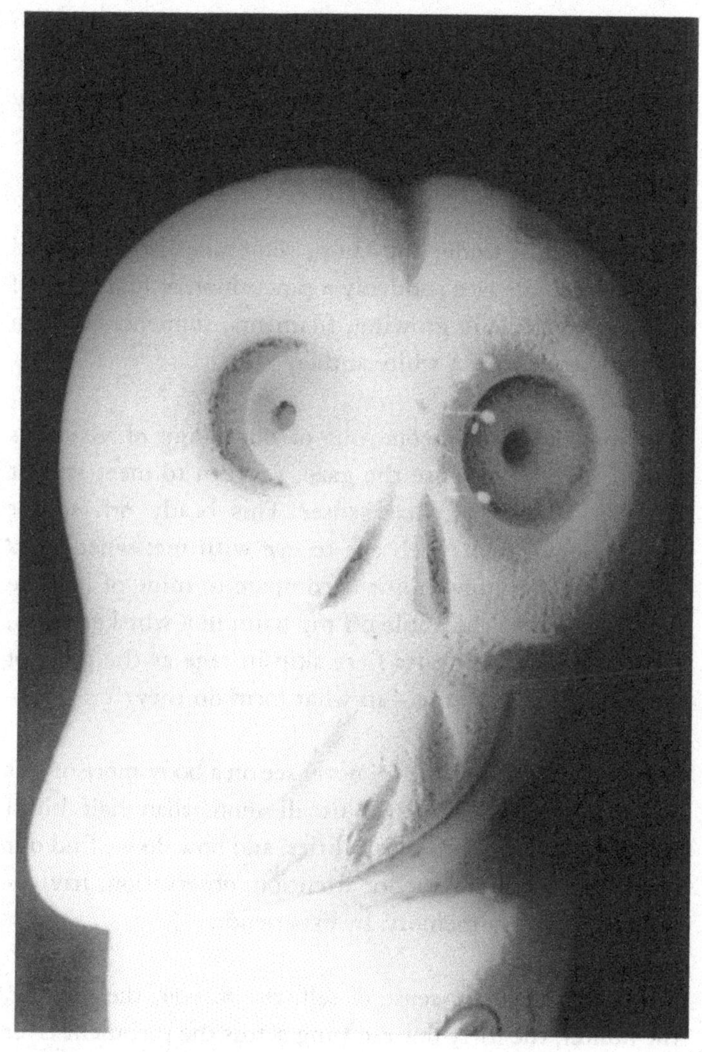

home from Australia on a visit. Not identical, but alike: so close all the same that they might as well be twins. On the back in her daughter's watery blue black script, their lofty names. Chrysostomos, he of the golden mouth, whose speech is golden. Theodoros, gift of God.

Gathering dust under the lamp, the crude little clay owl from Greece, its face suddenly a pincushion of fuzz – hairs! – it has white hairs growing, filaments, stamens, between the eyes, each with a white anther.

We know when someone out of our range of vision is staring at us. We sense the gaze, we turn to meet it: but how do we, using what sense? This beady orb spider upside down in the web eye to eye with me: what is its idea of me and how might it compare to mine of it? The horse as it takes the apple off my palm in a whiskery kiss, the octopus writhing its fiery skin in rage at the glass of its prison, perceive me – in what form do they?

Our eyes live in a head they never see on a body more or less out of sight. What drives us all more than half blind through this world of invisibilities, and how do we find our way? The wayfarer's way of attention, observation, navigation by signs, by memory, by experience.

The spider's self, or sense of self: the weaver, the hoarder, the hunter, the furry one escaping across the turbulent river with strong strokes, and the fine one swinging itself and hanging up its geometric harness, so brittle, jointed with dark beads. How well they know their body's way.

You must have been seeing things, the saying goes, there's nothing there. (Where, then?)

We know, from experience, how all experience has its meaning beyond the moment, a meaning which is only ever gradually revealed and grows with the revelation. The process is always incomplete. The meaning goes on growing, like desire, like memory, in the dark. The fullness of the meaning is only to be known by its weight, its power of displacement. It is at once intimately and exclusively ours and universal; as unknowable as the dark side of the moon or, for that matter, the brain.

It is 1991. No sooner have they driven off the ferry and unpacked than they are off again to look in on a Greek friend holidaying nearby, leaving Grania and Mikey to walk down through the tea trees to the beach for a paddle. They have it to themselves until a man and a woman Grania's age come by with two dogs that take off for the shallows. Strangers, they are picking up drift-wood, whole armfuls of grey logs and branches laced with seaweed, firewood. And there is a feel of winter in the air, the sunlight weighed down by its own density, the blue shadow already advancing on the wet sand, the year gone to seed early, the light thickening by the day and growing a new damp skin, of moss and slime, whiskers of lichen, spider-webbing. The dogs are plunging in after seagulls, lashing their leashes and their tails, propping to shake off a silvery plume of wet. I wish – Nan? – Nan, I wished we had a dog, Mikey is saying thigh-deep in rocky water.

No narrative, so no current of lived time, not so much as an undercurrent. The moment itself, stopped, as in the camera, isolated, shuffled, strung – beads on a rosary.

Ancient time went round and round as visibly as the moon, earth time and sky time unwinding, a cosmic harmony. All time in a spool.

Or see the story as spun out of the self, spread it out as fine and wide and as close to invisible as may be, since it is meant to be seen through, not seen.

One day in late autumn we walked up the winding road to Mykines. We crossed the threshold of the inner chamber under a hood of stone bathed in a cold darkness; outside was a whole hill of hewn stone graves that simmered in the sun, the stronghold of the kings and queens, red-handed Mykines. We had been warned about snakes, but if there were any they were lying low. Into a long-hallowed shrine, here was I, blindly carrying – fast asleep, unquickened –

a child. The hollow stone wound as light as a shell around us, a cobble of honeycomb, a cocoon.

A story is seen by its listener or reader through a lens. This lens is the secret of narration. In every story the lens is ground anew, ground between the temporal and the timeless.
JOHN BERGER

Yes, given that the one and only lens will be flawed, wavy, and will see true.

Someone calling out in the caravan park, Are you by yourself? – the strangeness of this double exposure. I know by inference that another self does inhabit me, live side by side with me, as ever present as the skeleton and no less hidden. It is this other who keeps the flame of my life as flesh, in a dimension outside the mind's reach where it is at home, silent and unerring, a smooth animal. I and my self, the invisible twin: shade and water to each other in a dry land.

A presence accompanies him, keeping pace, moving where he moves, reflecting his every movement, not his brother. It shrinks from the light and is himself alone, his body, transparent, all its complexities of flesh woven on bone, the image and intensification of his dread. It looks like his brother, the image, and is not him at all, nor is it the soul of one or the other of them wrenched or shocked out of the body, an emanation with a seeming life of its own. It is a self-image. What he sees is his undeniable self flayed and infused with light.

Low tide this afternoon again, and there is such a sense of access, plenitude, now that the reef – a stone reef here in the south, not coral – is lying out sweaty in the sun and we can walk out over the seabed. The lips of the pools studded with limpets, hung with skeins of grapeweed, blue black, brown and pale gold, rimmed with wet, so often hidden, are bare. The surf is a long way out and its booming rise and fall muffled. A hot northerly is working itself up. Sun-sodden, the sand spreads. Its creases gather and run under the rocks, like a sheet going thin and yellow, translucent with age, weighed down with stones, sand caking and feathering, drying.

Sun-lacquered, a long live red scorpion tail coiled to strike, a hot chilli.

Talk has never come easy even at the table when they are all together. Theo opens and pours the wine. Grania has baked a tray of potatoes in lemon and garlic and on another tray the single sumptuous great fish they have brought, the red silk of the skin all blisters, swaddling a white body. She can sit back now and let her daughter take over. As always, Mikey picks his fish apart with his fork to pull out the long bones and spike the rim of his plate with them. Theo fumbles in the skull for the cheek meat. Delicious, he says, holding out a white chunk to Grania, who smiles and shakes her head, warily, it is getting so heavy now, not sore, more a beehive of blur and buzz. She is out of her depth. Theo and Elinor have this way of lapsing, anyway, not meaning to be rude, into a hybrid language of their own, Greek with a larding of English, that Mikey seems to follow, though she has never known him to use it himself, and tonight he has nothing to say. She is lucky to take in one word in ten. Visits are few and far between. If there are undercurrents here and there, of ill will, they wash over her.

The wine is yellow and so cold there are crystals of frost, wine diamonds: yellow wine with an aftertaste of quince in a bottle of deep old gold. It has a hollow bottom, a mound swelling up into the wine, a *punted* bottle, as they say, with the punt embossed in beaded rings, a glass beehive inside out. Empty, it has the silky gloss of a rock pool at sunset. Her fingers up close through the bowl of her glass are pale-bellied fish, limbs moving in sea water, starry with mica.

What we know about anything is what the mind knows. Our death, for example: we pay lip service to the impending fact. As for the wisdom of the body by which we live, it keeps its own counsel, which amounts to a working disbelief in death. Let the mind know what it knows, the dreamer in the flesh will turn a blind eye.

A yellow room brimming, a moth pattering at the lampshade like spots of rain, in a high shadow of wings. Mikey has taken himself off to the sleepout. Dinner is over and they are down to the cheese and apples at the end of the second bottle, a black Greek wine, Elinor dropping slivers of apple into each glass to soak until they bleed, blood apples, as Mikey calls them, Grania nodding off now in the embers of the talk when the phone jerks her awake, a call out of a Greek day for – who? Thodoro? Theo, it's for you. The first of many. There has been an accident. A car crash. On the mountain, and his brother Tomo is in hospital. And the boys? Cuts and bruises, shock. The mother is in a coma. And then Tomo is dead. Yes, he died in the arms of his son Michali, died, yes, instantly – it was just that no one could say so straight out. Theo and Elinor burst out crying: they have known all along, Grania sees, since the first call. The funeral is tomorrow, according to custom. Theo calls back, beside himself, and says to wait, to put it off until he can get a flight. It's up to the son now as next of kin and he says no, tomorrow. Where? In Thessaloniki. No, shrieks Theo, in the village of his birth! My father lived here in Thessaloniki, Michali says, with us, and hangs up on him. A quarrel ignites and burns on into the night across the world, the family taking sides: fighting, her daughter tells Grania, like dogs over a bone.

By this time Theo has retreated to the front room. Grania has her coat on. Whiskey? she murmurs, getting out the bottle and glasses, and Elinor nods, blank with shock.

Go on, love. Take it in with you. This too, unplugging the phone and slipping it under her daughter's arm. Plug it in, you never know. Now off you go and try and get some rest – I need a walk. And they hug and kiss goodnight.

Ποιησις was 'making' to the Greeks, not our 'poetry' but the plain act of making. As in honey, as in web – imparting form to whatever a given self may yield. All metaphor is ποιησις. Μεταφορα. One is transported, taken beyond. Where? All gods are metaphors, all religions. We grasp at meaning, for an insecure foothold on truth. Dream is metaphoric. Metamorphic. Visitants, spirits and the occult, the near-death experience, angels, devils, are flickers in the cave of the skull, brain events as real as the fiery afterimages of contrary colour – negative colour – that visit the eye are real. Perception itself comes down to metaphor.

For in Homeric days a restlessness seems to have possessed the Mediterranean basin, and ancient races began shaking ships like seeds over the sea.

D H LAWRENCE

My father, Michali insists to everyone over and over, my father. He was not from the city but he made his life here and here is where he founded his household. It is for the wife to see to her man's grave. The widow, you mean. All right, the widow, my mother if she is to live. Hah! If she is to live! She! – Tomo is the one who is not to live! She is the one who has eaten him alive! Listen to me. My mother if she lives will light his candles and look after him in death as in life.

Once when Saint Chrysostomos was a little boy, so the story goes, the Panagia of the ikon told him to kiss her on the mouth and he dared to and he had his mouth brimful of golden words ever after. He had the Virgin Mary for his muse.

Did you get through?

No. No one answer.

Theo, listen, it's the same earth all over, the self-same earth.

Here too, Linora, is same earth you think?

Listen to me!

So much you know. Nothing. You know nothing!

There are scraps of paper all in the grate that he must have torn up, a head, a speck of candle flame, the photos from the mantelpiece, from the monastery. Elinor is stooping to pick them up when he utters a hoarse cry at her back and swings the empty bottle. It smashes on the hearthstone in a spray of light – she has sprung back only just in time, and terror invades her. She watches, still throbbing all over, as at a great distance as he throws himself face down on the floor, blood in the black hairs of his arm, and on the hearth, no, no, only red ochre and drops of glass. Grania has gone for a walk. If Mikey wakes up and comes in – what's wrong? – it's all right, only a lamp, she will say, it fell and broke, now you go back to sleep. Go on. Listening in to the silent house.

Relics, memorials, the tide's leavings and ours, humanity's, so few, bones and driftwood, shells, crab casts and scrawls on the sand that were wave traces and the broader ones that end in a limpet or a periwinkle, threads each with a knot at one end. Standing stones and rune stones, crosses, middens, ruins, shards and shreds as haphazard and rifted with meaning as the elements of a dream.

Magic began it, resurrection magic to thwart death: hence the gods. Death is the secret name of God. Death, the destroyer of worlds. Religion, science, art, love, as one they body forth the eternal human longing to go on being. What has made us human, *homo sapiens*, if not this most ancient dream of all? So, the rebellion against death – this is our *sapientia*? Such as it is, I think so. What sort of wisdom is that! The wisdom of folly. Paradox.

The poetry is in the falsehood as the portrait is in the unlikeness. There must be just enough falsehood, neither too much nor too little. The most faithful reflection amounts to less in the end than the reflection that is only almost, a reaching always falling short, looping, coalescing, alive.

By all the Greeks the honours due to the images of the gods were paid to unwrought stones.
PAUSANIAS

The pure white marble goddesses in the temples, starry with mica, were works less of faith than of art and all too human. It was in massive battered and crumbling shapeless rocks that our forebears had worshipped the Mother. The more worn and weathered out of recognition, the more the power. Why so? Was it a latent afterimage from the depths of the past, of the shapeless – amorphous – looming blur of flesh we all clung to with lips and hands for dear life?

To the ancient consciousness, Matter, Materia, or Substantial things are God. A pool of water is god. And why not? The longer we live the more we return to the oldest of all visions. A great rock is *god. I can touch it. It is undeniable. It is god.*
D H LAWRENCE

Deep in stone, some of the physicists say now, is where life began. Stone was the womb of being on earth. Microcosms, life-spawn, the constellations of beings.

'Mother' and 'mud' may be one and the same at root, only those roots go too deep into the past to be sure – the mother as soft matter, slime, lees. So we have the mother of vinegar and of bread at work, as in the golden ferment of the chrysalis, to give birth to new forms. Mother of pearl, mother of grapes, and of thyme: *Wild time is called in English... Mother of Time, and our Ladies Bedstrawe.* And the wellspring, η νερομαννα, is the mother of water.

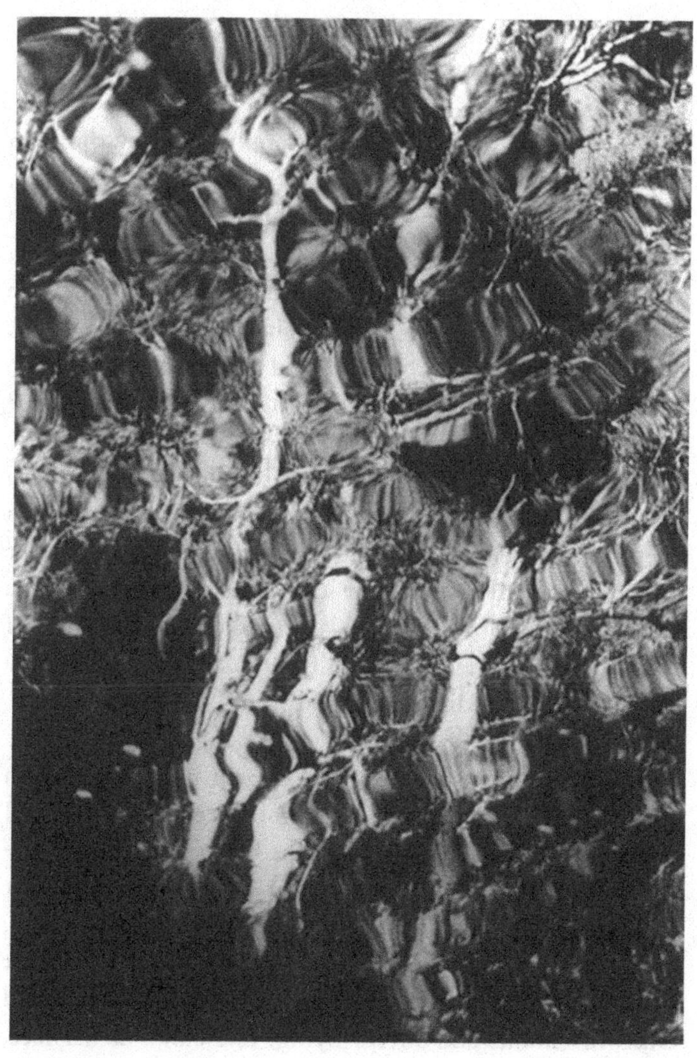

The physicists have known sin, the void. Why are they looking to stone now?

There are those who all their lives are haunted by the twin lost in the womb, the *Doppelgänger* treading a world of water, afloat in dreams. We know that many more twins are conceived than born – identical and non-identical twins, mirror-twins and twins joined together, flesh fused, separable and inseparable. Why so many? What traces do they leave, those others lost in the waters? And is it true, as some say, that a singleton born left-handed is a surviving mirror-twin?

A clear day of high surf is scroll on scroll of wave flying in fuming at a long slant from the horizon, translucent, each a deep blue green shell wall of ice. And yet the water is not moving, not advancing, only the wave is. The pulse, the breath, the soul of the water – is it like this, the pulse of being in and through matter, lifting us up through watery coil after coil and dissolving, reforming, rise and fall?

She gathers water in her palms, dipping her stung face in with a hiss of pain. One eye throbs. Each cold handful warms and ebbs away through her fingers into the washbasin. Dripping in the mirror is her usual face, but bloating as if from a flaw in the glass, and quaking, breathing hard, bursting open in a silent wail. To lash out like that, not so much as caring if he smashes her head in! Glass in chunks and slivers flying! She claws at her face, drops it in her hands, her sore face, holds her breath to listen, she is shrinking in too much light.

A rasp has woken Mikey, a wind, hoarse and steady, which is not the wind, or not only the wind, more the sea and of course he is down at his Nan's in the pitch-dark sleepout. He lies with his hands folded in the heat of his armpits, not daring to pull on the cord over the head of his bed and flood the walls with the salvation of yellow light. Not for anything will he open his eyes or push a hand up out of the blankets to grope in the dark for the cord.

He still has the last traces of a dream in his head. They were all back at the monastery, everyone, even his Nan who has never been to Greece. It was old and crumbling, like a giant loaf of bread with a cracked red crust, and inside it was more like a cave than a church. A saint's bones were in there. Not all of her bones. There was a queue waiting to kiss the glass case and make the cross, all old women in black monks' hoods who looked like they'd seen a ghost, like his other grandmother, but when it was his turn all he saw was himself, an underwater self afloat over a little skull the size of a monkey's in a silver helmet, until he saw its eyes move, and his gasp of breath hid it in a mist.

The instant of the death, the thunderbolt. And the crux, comprehension. At the snowline halfway up the mountain on a Sunday morning in the late winter of his seventeenth year Michali in the front seat of the car sees out of the corner of his eye a truck veer into their path and grind through the windscreen. There follows a long moment like flight, of freedom from all sensation, before he can free an arm, a leg, another, his own and his father's, and drag them both out of the creaking wreckage that may explode at any moment, and over on to the gravel. The head against his shoulder is stove in. It wants to speak. He leans close but no words come out. He presses a shuddering kiss on the wry mouth. When he lifts his head away the jaws fall open. A mask of blood crackles on his face. A screaming in the air, his little brother, alive, and now boots crunch and voices call out but he is too cold to respond, cold and heavy in the snow with the burden in his arms crushing down with the weight of rock. Then he is afloat in clammy air. Cold, dim. Printed on the white of his shirt, a red head of hair.

Calyx, καλυξ, chalice. These are the tall white irises, fleurs-de-lis, white and gold. They have an elaborate structure of six long outer petals, three of which stand up, alternating with three that fold down, pouting bottom lips each with a beard, a thin yellow brush from the tip to the throat. Three beards, three caterpillars heading down to where the light is pooled like wine in porcelain, in a breath of vanilla sugar. The six outer petals rise from a pod enclosing a green gold throat, freckled, mackerel-skinned, to become broad and filmy white with a fan of glassy veins. The inner petals are pure white with a seam down the middle, along which they are humped and thick, but pointed at the tip; after a time the tip may split into two horns. From underneath, this hump of the inner petal is divided along the seam into two lobes, overlapped by a flange at the edge of the horned tip, as if two thicknesses of skin have fused. The hood thus formed shelters the strip of beard where it begins in the depths as the rich gold of egg yolk; out in the open, where the petal spreads, the beard fades to pale lemon, almost white. The hood has a name, *calyptra*, from the Greek καλυπτρα, veil. What does it veil? Nothing, it seems, until you pinch open one or other of the hooded inner petals, like a snapdragon's jaws, and there it is: a little needle, with an eye and a fuzzy skin, quivering out over the bristle of beard, a stamen, so shielded and screened in folds of white as to be invisible. The outer folds are translucent, long-veined under a silky glaze, with a fine sprinkling of moisture, like mica in marble, that is not dew or rain but their own drenched flesh. They cast shapes of shadow on and through their own translucencies.

The petals spill from a green pod, itself translucent, which is one of two at the top of the stalk. The other, lost in the folds of its open twin, remains a closely packed bud, but frilled and already white, while those further down are still the faint indigo of the skin around an underslept eye. In two or three days the twin opens up, just a chink, like a cockle shell, and then wide; the lower, smaller ones follow. Each one as it withers turns cobwebby and shrinks down to a ball in a green fist.

The closing of the eyes and mouth at death was and is

καλυπτειν, to veil. Αποκαλυψις, unveiling, revelation, has the same root.

A hoot sounds in the bay, resounds as if underwater, a ship on its way past, or the lighthouse. Under the water is rock, so Nan said, the seabed is rock underneath, limestone, bone stone, full of caves and tunnels, and under the town as well, caves and tunnels of air and water and not one way in or out that anyone knows of. There might even be a secret passage under the Rip. Because he knows how the old fort on this headland and the other one across the Rip both have underground passages that were lit by oil lamps in the days before electricity, boxed in behind glass in the stone walls well away from the gunpowder and his mind glows with a maze of walls, geometric, in the buttery sooty hiss of the lanterns.

Close up, white on black, this is a sea being, a fat tongue with a ridge of bristles, white caverns, a bonnet and mantle, shadowy membranes. Underneath is a naked woman with her back turned, a tuft of soft hair in a blur where the head should be – a shoulder and breast half in shadow, a long flank and beyond, against the darkness, a white flounce crinkled at the edge like a dancer's fan, a jellyfish mantle. Or it is her front, the second breast in shadow, and she is bent back like a ship's figurehead, a mermaid, the flesh grainy like scales on one haunch: fused thighs and an open fantail. And rising out of her is the white hood, a split tongue of white flame, nose of a white whale. Vast blurred pale convolutions of flesh, they drift at the edge of

vision in water as fathomless as sleep. They look like nothing so much as the deep sea creatures born in the dark around fissures in the seabed that vent volcanic smoke – the fire drake, the kraken, ancient prefigurings – white, blind, gathered at the hearth fire on the ocean floor.

A child crying has woken me. I listen into the silence. I have been dreaming. No, a wail on the wind, sobbing, a child – whose? Mine, mine, the unborn.

It has never seemed to me that 'agnostic' need be a negative, except grammatically. The concept of αγνωσια posits a lack, a limitation and not, or not necessarily, a void. Unlike 'ignorance', whose Greek root it shares, it is a stance. A judicious suspension of belief is implied, a verdict of not proven. There has to be an element of defiance in any wilful embrace of limitation. It is like the absence of perspective in so-called 'primitive' art, which is a dynamic absence, not simply a lack, as of something missing. The beauty is in the distortion, disproportion, of the flat figures that cast no shadow and hardly seem to touch the ground; in attitudes that are timeless, not natural, not caught in passing, not static either, in the illusion of movement just on the point of coming to life.

Like the absence of perspective and proportion, the absence of colour – the refusal, the defiance of colour – is a further freedom. Monochrome is the beauty of the bare bones stripped of flesh. The framework, pure form. The Greek word for 'beauty', for that matter, ομορφια, stems from 'form', μορφη – not so the English.

Ομορφο is 'beautiful'. Αμορφο – one letter away – like its synonym, ασχημο, is 'formless', 'ugly' as if they were one and the same. Only where does 'form' begin to be?

Grania on the jetty sees two torches moving, one near the shore and one on the outer edge of the rockshelf, and shifting in a wide flare or candling underneath or awash for a moment in a pale swill; every line of light in the sea underneath is a fold over lines of shadow drawn in the sand and water, all running the same way; the moon is high and white, already half-full, like the slow lantern spinning in the lighthouse, on off, on off. There is a word for this, it has its own strange word, what? – occult. An occulting lighthouse. Light, dark, and red gold, the heave and loud flaking over a wave.

Low tide, flat water in silver flanges and creasings all along the water line east and west. She turns her face to home, her cloak wrapped around her like wings, and picks her way east under the cliff, through the limestone ledges that throw fans of shadow on the sand and the pools, dragging her feet more the closer she comes. The house is under occupation. Light and noise and turmoil, the shock of death, the near miss, like lightning, for all that it has struck on the far side of the world, burst out at her through its skin of silvery wood. She shrinks from going back in.

And they are her own people, all she has in the world, dear to her. Wishing them away all the same, wishing them anywhere but here, she stares across the winking black bay.

Clavicle, scapula, cranium, Mikey mouths into the dark. Occiput. Maxilla. His palm closes over ribs, over hot heartbeats.

From the beginning, like a coral reef, the old cities have grown on old layers of themselves. Any lost old city is a time capsule. Any old city that is still alive will go on finding ancestors, earlier selves, whenever the foundations are disturbed.

In the buried heart of Thessaloniki not long ago a temple was unearthed and found to be a Serapion containing a marble statue of the goddess Isis, now in the Museum, as the mother holding the child Horus. Isis, Au Set of Egypt, the Blessed Queen of Heaven, was the all-holy of her day, the παναγια, all the goddesses of the world in one – and foremost, in antiquity, in that part of the world, the old one, Demeter who was death's door into the earth and out again. Before there were settlements, let alone temples, a goddess had her shrines in caves and farmhouses and tombs and at the crossroads, much as the Panagia Maria today has her wayside chapels and blue shrine-cabinets like bee boxes with glass doors, containing an ikon, candles and matches and a glass of water with a wick like a toy wheel afloat in dark oil. The plains were sown with graves first, and goddesses, any number of holy mothers, their names lost, and those from the time before they had human names, the great black and grey and sandy golden stones that are still standing, the mother stones, their skin weathered and raddled with oil and wine, milk and honey and blood; and a multitude of little stone or clay ones, fat with child, broken or whole, often only the head, formed in baked clay and left in graves to be turned up one day under the plough. A brown egg laid out here in the furrow, terracotta, a doll's head, a limpid little face almost smiling, her hair braided up in a wreath, a poppet for a granddaughter – the ploughman halts the horse and stoops over the clods, his shadow slithering at his feet in a silence like water and in the hollow of his hand a stored heat, crusty out of the oven of summer.

The earth! In this great temple deserted by the gods all my idols have feet of clay.
ALBERT CAMUS

Soft hootings in the night, a white whoosh and plummet, spread like a wave of the sea and vanished, an owl. Hunching in the dark over what it has snatched up. Χαροπουλι, bird of Charos.

On the floor under the lamp Theo stirs and groans. He is shiny and cold, bathed in a smell of whiskey. Blood is smeared on one arm and Elinor lifts it full of foreboding, but there is only the one slit, so shallow it has stopped bleeding. She sponges it and then his breathing face, taking care not to wake him, avoiding his eyes squashed shut in sweaty wrinkles, squeezing the sponge into the bowl of darkening water and wiping him dry. Ελα, she says, ελα να ξαπλωσεις, come and lie down. Παιδι μου, ελα, and at that he props himself up in his sleep and lets himself be rolled on to the futon and tucked in, it was her saying παιδι μου like that, my child, she knows, my boy, my son. She gathers up the bowl and the towel, the broken glass, the shredded photos, and leaves him to sleep it off.

The dead were always in the keeping of the goddess, in token of which trust, corn was sown on graves. The dead were the Δημητρειοι. To this day the autumn festivals of the Δημητρια are held in Thessaloniki, in the name of a murdered patron saint and martyr known as Demetrios. Dry grains are as always traded in the market as δημητριακα. The river-flat country north of Thessaloniki is one of the rare granaries in a land of dry rock. Here as in Attica, Demeter, Δημητρα, was providence incarnate in arable land, the ample motherly home of corn and barley and sesame. She gave mankind the plough and the threshing floor, and to all those who kept the rites she granted in the flesh the fruits of the field and beyond the flesh, immortal life.

Ceremony is embodiment. Ceremony's hands break the hard-shelled loaf as warm as an egg and pour out the black wine.

Blood of the womb was fed to the cornfields; a ritual coupling sowed them and a girdle of spilt blood kept them from harm. The Mysteries were in the keeping of women. The Mysteries, μυστηρια, are simply the rites and sacraments that make a door open into the godhead: baptism, the Lord's Supper, are ancient μυστηρια. The initiates are μυστες, as they were when they walked to Demeter's shrine bearing a winnowing basket made of wicker and filled with the fruits of the earth, a lighted candle, a phallos; and the candidates for initiation carried a piglet to Eleusis at harvest time, purified along with themselves in the sea in slippery squealing masses of flesh, to be sacrificed to the goddess, as the old sow who eats her farrow. Once, beyond memory, the victim was human, as was still the case until much longer in the cold north, Denmark, Ireland, where they would feed a man his ritual meal of all the grains that wanted blessing, throttle him or cut his throat and thrust him down into her lap of bog. At Eleusis pigs were thrown into snakepits and what was left, well-rotted carrion, bone and ordure, was mixed with the seed corn for laying on the altar. Earth magic, birth magic.

Did Kore appear in the temple, risen again, reborn, in the candlelight of the midnight sun like Christ at Eastertide?

Λικνον, harvest basket, manger, cradle and curragh and winnowing fan. And μυστης, one whose mouth or eyes are closed, from μυω, an everyday word for closing also used of oysters and mussels, of wounds, and flowers whether folding at nightfall or withering.

The past walks at night all over the earth, but in Greece in broad daylight.

In Greek the bee is μελισσα, feminine, as is the honeycomb, κηρηθρα, or μελοπιττα, whose other meaning is honeycake; and honeycake's other name is ψυχοπιττα, soulcake, when offered to the dead. The hives collectively are τα μελισσια. The single hive is η κυψελη; the French is *la ruche*; the Latin is the vast and earthy *alvus*, all feminine.

alvus...*the belly, the paunch, the bowels*...II. A. *The womb*...B. *The stomach, the digestive organs*...C. *A beehive*...D. *Of the basin of the molten sea in the Jewish temple*...

The snake was always holy to the mother of earth in whose dark places he lives and on whom he flings himself winding belly-to-belly. He whose sting is death is also the master of death, sliding out of his old skin ablaze with new life not once, like the bee or the butterfly, but over and over leaving another pale self like a rolled honeycomb in his place. Under the skin, besides, the snake is doubleness itself from the forks of the tongue to the genitals; and, like earth, a store of seed, in that the female can still lay fertile eggs months, and sometimes years, after mating. And the snake is the shelter of the household that gives it shelter and feeds it bowls of milk.

The bee was also holy to the goddess, whose priestesses were the μελισσαι, bees. Like snakes, bees made their home in clefts and caves, passages to the underworld. Bees were winged souls awaiting rebirth. The goddess was offered honey, as were brides, and the dead, and the newborn who still belonged to the earth they had come from, and would only be fully human, no longer liable to be exposed or killed, once their mouths were smeared with honey. The pomegranate belonged to the goddess, and also the fig, a fruit that bears its blood red seeds, its flowers in fact, in the lining of the skin, like a womb. Like a teat as well, the way figs grow plumply, darkly ripe, and they drip milk. The fig tree is hardy, taking root in rockfaces and ancient crumbling walls, drawing up what earth it can to turn into itself, and red honey and milk.

Her flower was the tall and golden-tongued, late-winter-flowering purple iris.

But then, like children, and cities, new gods grow by feeding off the old, and she went to earth, the goddess, earth to earth, biding her time.

Νυκτιπολοις, μαγοις, βακχοις, ληναις, μυσταις – *nightwalking magicians, bacchantes, revellers, initiates in the mysteries...*
HERAKLEITOS, *FRAGMENTS*

Where in the body is the eye that keeps the sleepwalker safe on track?

Iris above all is the rainbow, the high flare and skein that is mirrored in every eye, the bridge of the gods between worlds – *le spectre solaire*, for Leonardo, *arco iris*, and for Lawrence *the rainbow, the iridescence which is darkness at once and light, the two-in-one.*

The widow is a Greek of different stock, tall and milkwhite with a glossy black swathe of hair to her waist. They met through her cousin, a shipmate of Tomo's, when she was eighteen to his thirty and had nothing to offer but herself as she was, με τα ολα της, in all her bland fresh girlhood. More than satisfied – head over heels – Tomo allowed a marriage to be arranged by her people against the will of his. His nickname for her was proud, gently mocking, self-mocking too: Μυζηθρα, cottage cheese. He looked forward to a lifetime of moulding her to his taste. As she was bound to do, however, she matured according to her own nature, regardless of him, growing in strength: a strength rooted in sullen resistance. Her native village is not inland on the plains of Paionia but due east of Thessaloniki, near the top of the dark mountain that overlooks the sea on the haft of the trident of the Halkidiki peninsula. Her family has eked out a living there for generations. The village is goats and stone, dry stone walls and mud streets, icicles, deep in fog the one hot eye of an oven, a smithy. On the way to visit them Tomo would pull up at the old monastery, its wooden bones more and more exposed with time – sooty cupolas and the sun thrusting in, great fallen rafters of smoky sun. Pilgrims would troop in and light candles to poke into plates of sand. In a glass casket was displayed, set in silver, the skull of Saint Anastasia, Holy Resurrection, brought here reverently after the fall of Constantinople, tiny in a lace bonnet of silver like muddy melting ice.

Χειμων, *Winter*. In a book of prints, a set of four small silk-screens on silver by a modern master, Tsarouchis, now dead: four figures, two lads and a lass and one grave woman. Poised between icon and folk art, they are the spirits, daimons, of the seasons, with wings to match: silver for Spring, blue for Summer, tawny gold for Autumn, and for the woman who is Winter, Mother Death, glossy black tufted with white, like swans' wings. Behind her, the faint name Χειμων traced with a finger in frost on the window. She is hooded and robed in saffron, threadbare, or shot with gold, her hair down in two black braids, her gaze inward. Her hands are held open over an amber basin that appears to be melting, containing what could be broken water, or white ash and charcoal; at her back is a deep red net or basket, or a quilted chair or grated fire, She may be enacting a ritual, or a spell or a household task, or washing her hands, or warming them. The border is a frosty pattern of black boughs forked like the leaping deer in a Stone Age cave. Χειμων, χειμωνας, has always embraced *storm* and *turmoil*, *madness*, *hardship*, *devastation*. Whatever else, she is Winter's housewife, she is the kernel.

It sat on vine leaves in the bowl all winter, a durable

pomegranate, its red cask weathering like paint, no stain on it though, no black spots, intact – only that it felt light when I picked it up idly on a spring day, as light as a shell, and when I cut it in half there was only here and there a glow of red, no more than three seeds left alive in what was otherwise earth, soft, acrid, brown, full of clots the size of sheep droppings, a dusting of pale green mould.

The innermost rites of the Mysteries were held underground bathed in fire. The initiates took an oath of secrecy, which was kept. The doorway was a waterfall of hidden light. Only a chink or two has come down to us.

I approached the very gates of death and set one foot on Proserpine's threshold yet was permitted to return, borne through all the elements. At midnight I saw the sun shining as if it were noon: I entered the presence of the gods of the underworld and the gods of the upper world, stood near and worshipped them.
APULEIUS

In space it is always midnight. Space is a vast net of pure light, the divine fire, invisible, until some matter breaks its fall: and then what is caught in it is what we see.

The all-mother Isis is sister, wife and widow to Osiris, the dying god. After his murder she gathers his remains together, all but the phallos, which she remodels in clay, and brings him to life, bones and carrion and clay, a whole man again and again. By his own seed she conceives him and as his mother she brings him back into the world, a baby boy, and washes him and cuts the cord. She opens his mouth first with her finger, as must be done for anyone pulled out of deep water who is close to drowning, to clear the airways: then with her nipple.

Elinor knocks and pushes her mother's door open into the dark. The bed is empty. She undresses and slips in under the covers on the far side, her father's side. But her mother's side is no less empty, no less cold. Where is she? A widow and her double bed. No one is saying a word about the widow who is fast asleep in Greece, the widow who doesn't even know, who is wrestling with Charos, as they say, and will wake up only to be told that her man is dead and in his grave. And the boys? she will cry out and, reassured, will undergo the first spasm, as in labour, of her bereavement. How will she bear it? Much like all the village women who have gone on keeping house and planting, hoeing, milking all week and on Saturdays seeing to the family graves. Bent over their work, their heads are shaded under a white cloth, a τσεμπερι, and under the hot fabric and the glaze of sweat their faces take on an intense frail pallor, a transparency in the sunlight reflected off the dry soil, as if by candlelight. Frail, and yet even the oldest, the ones whose τσεμπερι is brown or full black, for widowhood, burn with a naked strength. A black strength in a milkwhite body. The sisterhood of the bereaved.

The eclipsed moon in its totality, all its scabs and burnish clear against an inner coppery light, as in a hand held open, filling with sun, over the eye. In a deepening silence, dimmed, making its way across the stars in a flush of blood.

The brother of the dead man lies torpid as shapes of light swim up under his eyelids, red shot with blue. The bed smells of hay and something acrid and sweet, wine in the basin. Two women are hovering over the doughy mass on the bed, one a darkness, his mother, and the other in a rim of yellow. One lifts the scrubby grey head in both hands while the other fastens a bandage under the chin, knotting it at the nape. He hears the soft lick and slop of the sponge as they lift one limp arm and then the other, one leg and the other, a line of drips as yellow as oil strung out shimmering. He is as cold as the sea. The strokes of the sponge leave a varnish of water scribbled with black hairs.

A rumble in the bay and in the wooden walls, then a soft hooting, a ship far out to sea, echoing. Sleeping alone although I am not asleep. The widow, how she hated the sea. She always refused to go in. Day after day of the holiday she would pull on her new bathers and, in spite of the heat and our teasing, never get them wet. All she wanted was to lie under the pines with a towel over her to keep the wasps off. One day of flat calm, though, she changed her mind, she stood and coiled up her long hair and took my hand. Look after me, sister-in-law, she said as we strode in step by step, knees, thighs, bellies ravelling in water light. But a little wave, from a passing boat, reared up suddenly out of nowhere and slapped at our breasts. With a shriek she was on top of me and we went under, the white bulk of her ramming me down on stones and shell grit, blind, choking, thrashing, until she got to her feet and thundered out, and I washed the blood and fury off in the green underworld, shaking depths, masses, densities, the lit green gold.

Name the widow Zoe. Ζωη, Life.

The moths are dying off, the brown moths that came flocking out of their caves and clefts in the mountains to the lights of houses, dusty husks beating at lampshades, piling up in corners. The more you put them outside the more they gather. One has crept on to the page under the lamp, head bowed. A bent amber feeler, a sumptuous ruff, a cockade of fine hairs like the stamens of a dark flower. Her wings are patterned black and brown with a scribble of white paint, and pleating, quilting with a nap of plush, wings like weathered bark. Her shadow on the page is warped as if underwater.

Unless the sun were enveloped in the body of darkness, would a cast shadow run with me as I walk? Unless the night lay within the embrace of light, would the fish gleam phosphorescent in the

sea, would the light break out of the black coals of the hearth, would the electricity gleam out of itself, suddenly declaring an opposite being?
D H LAWRENCE

The fool in the fable who sells his shadow like a black skin he can peel off and hand over, is it his soul – do we have a soul in much the same way as we 'have' a shadow? I and my shadow are alike and not alike, my image without my substance, pure, a shape of air and darkness, a flickering, unstable other self. Was it our shadow that gave us a soul, our idea of a disembodied soul? But doesn't everything have a shadow? When candles began to be lit for the dead, was it to call them up in the flame, as the flame calls up the shadow? – and the moth? Was the flame the soul? Or the attendant shadow? Or the moth, fine-winged and passionate? All of these?

If the soul is in the body as the skeleton is, fused, for the time being, that makes skeleton and soul the lees of death.

Mikey will have to be told when he wakes up. The task will fall to Grania. It seems no time at all to her since they brought him home, a newborn, and she gave up her bed to the three of them. In the morning sun she watched her daughter lift him out of the bath and hold him up to the light, a rim like milky glass all around him as she turned him into the sun like some great soft-shelled egg, and his moon-face, his planetary poise – there, see? – and there was no flaw in any of him.

Who will have to tell the widow? The son. The mother.

There was a poster up at school that had an orb spider, ruby red, carrying a white egg on her back, her own egg, they all thought, until they found out it was a mud wasp's egg and when it hatched the larva was going to eat her alive. The spider had no idea what was in store. Now he can't get it out of his mind.

The child Demeter lost was Kore, image of her mother. Greek names take the article – *the* Maria, *the* Thessaloniki – the same as common nouns. Κορη is the everyday word for a daughter, as well as the mirroring pupil, apple, of the eye. It used to encompass girl, virgin, maiden, doll, so that the κοροπλαστης was the moulder of κορες, figurines for the grave, dolls of clay or wax that came fully formed out of the plaster shell. Spoken of by name, Kore is just 'the daughter', any daughter, at the same time as she is the Kore whose womb is yet to shed blood in the moon's good time and, on her resurrection, the Persephone whose blood has run cold.

Kore in her green girlhood is picking crocuses and lilies one day in the fine haze of a waterfall when the earth opens at her feet, black horses whinnying, stamping, sun-dazzled: one wild scream and she is gone. When no one alive can tell the mother where her Kore is, she takes the form of an old widow in black and, fasting, searches the land lamenting for nine days and nights on end by the flare of two fennel brands held high, until she comes to Eleusis, 'advent': and so pilgrims would fast and carry burning brands to the temple. The priestess of Demeter would play both parts, Kore and Demeter, the daughter raped by Death, and the *mater dolorosa*. She would play all three parts, it might be truer to say, since Kore as a girl torn from the sunlit fields is a world away from her Persephone self. The figures of Kore and Persephone stand as the two halves of the matrix split apart, two shells and in their clasp the moulded figure of the mother, Demeter – a plaster negative and its mirror twin, Day-in-Night and Night-in-Day, the one white as milk and the other white as bone, enclosing the red gold clay of Birth, Life. Or – since Persephone replaces Kore, they are never both present at once – she is the sliver of cusp, first on one side then the other, that clasps the dark ball of the moon. She is to the figure of the Mother what the glow is to a source of light, the equivalent of the penumbra around the shadow, *umbra*: she is its fullness. All three are the one goddess, as the full moon and the two halves are the one moon; and each of the three is all three, fusing and splitting like flames over water.

The moon, the mother of time. The first men marked her passing in stone, as their women did in the flesh, bleeding in time with her, in time with each other.

What does it mean to have a sense of time? Or no sense of time? Is time a sense at all in the sense that sight is, and hearing and the other three (or four, if, as some traditions hold, the mind is also a sense)? Our senses bind us to a world built by the mind out of the illusions imprinted on it by the senses. Is time itself an illusion – or only our sense of time? And the mind? Dark to itself, it lives out our life in a time capsule, a consciousness, a pinhole of being.

I slip out of bed leaving a dark dream behind in the bedclothes.

As long as they live, cults also grow in layers of themselves, augmented by influxes, grafts, fusions, reincarnations. The holy ones of old Europe and the Mediterranean basin (which has no tides, or only human ones), the goddesses first, and then the gods spreading war, all migrated, divided and coalesced, shifting shape through story after story. In an oral culture they are presences as immanent as breath, having their whole being in the lived ceremony, the sacrifice, the oracle and the old wives' tale by the hearth fire. They live on in the word, while given breath. Sooner or later art turns them to stone. Writing is the death of them.

We, on the contrary, say: In the beginning was the Word! – and deny the physical universe true existence. We exist only in the Word, which is beaten out thin to cover, gild, and hide all things.

D H LAWRENCE

Μυθος, myth, originally meant whatever was spoken, delivered by word of mouth, including the spoken part, the wording of a ritual.

Rather than bring myself to eat the three sound pomegranate seeds I had potted them in their skinful of earth. Now one was in leaf. I was digging a hole in the garden for it when the spade found a blob of mud, two water drops that were slit, were eyes, alive, a frog! Keeping very still. I carried it caged in my fingers to the safety of the long grass, knelt, opened my hands. It sat on in my palm staring out for some time, spun jelly fingers strung out on mine, pulsing, before it could gather itself for the leap. Then I was free to plant my death fruit in its well of earth.

Unseen horses, a chariot, the pale god of the dead, had come bursting out of the earth and seized Kore. Demeter appealed to Zeus, the god of gods. He was her own brother, as was Hades, and dark-maned Poseidon, three lords of sky, earth and sea: like the sea god's trident, a three-in-one, a three-pronged godhead. Zeus had fathered Kore. Now he turned a deaf ear. Ruthless in her rage and despair, Demeter let the land fall into waste until at last he gave in and told Hades to let the girl go, as long as she had not eaten in the land of the dead. But Kore had. As she was leaving, Hades, the blind god, had forced down her throat one seed, or three, or seven seeds, some say, of a pomegranate, to bind her to him, and for that she was doomed as his wife to pass one third of the year underground ever after. In the summer of her absence the land would lie bare under the sun as if dead. At the time of the autumn sowing of the stored seed corn – the old crop, and the new – it, and she, would come back to green life.

Kore was the offering, the perfect one trussed up, torn open and eaten, the sacrifice who would come back to life in glory and feed the people. In Attica her time of absence began as the furnace of summer after the harvest. Later it changed to the winter of ice and snow.

In the myth she has nothing to say. One scream rings out through the earth and sea and then silence. The silence of Persephone is the silence of the grave. Did she know what would happen if she ate? Hades knew. Did the serpent beguile her? Was it brute force? The lily maid pure as the snow, and the apple of venom, meaning death – or was it for the glow of red in it, for love of a far sun? There in the underworld gloom she finds a tree hung with faded carapaces, ruddy little clay pots left out in the rain. She remembers. She knows these battered balls of red, a weight in them and a pulse of seeds, on the verge of a hatching. A sure birth. One has a crack in the bottom, a red darkness. She pulls it open and there are the snowy lobes of honeycomb full of shiny red beads – she picks one out, bites down with a shudder. What has she done? She stares. A thread of blood runs down her arm.

The skin of a face quaking like milk on the boil, before collapsing, and on its mouth the blood drop of a pomegranate seed. And this is what it takes to prove the right of Hades to his bride, his seal of ownership? Yes, if it stands for the show of blood between her thighs.

Σκοτος, σκοταδι, is darkness, the dark in every aspect. As death, Hades, as the unborn state, as blindness, as unknowing. The verb is σκοτωνω, I kill.

A fine-boned profile floating, rusty, translucent, a parchment head, *sfumato* – a wispy cheek half eaten away with shadows, Μαννα? Whispering. Μαννα? Πες! Speak! The ink is a red wash all down her face, dark, a stain spreading in the dark and vanishing.

The agonised lament of the Mother of God, Θεοτοκος, Godbearer, at the foot of the Cross in the Good Friday liturgy in Greece was a seed, a pomegranate seed, of the lament of Demeter the foremother. *Woe is me, divine child! woe is me, light of the world! Why didst thou vanish from mine eyes, thou lamb of God?*

His father's older sister and her husband are looking after the details of the funeral and his mother's hospital for him. They are paying because there is no money anywhere at home, only small change. The younger one is looking after Michali's little brother. She and the uncles urge on Michali the anguish of his old grandmother, who can visit the grave any time as long as it's in the village,

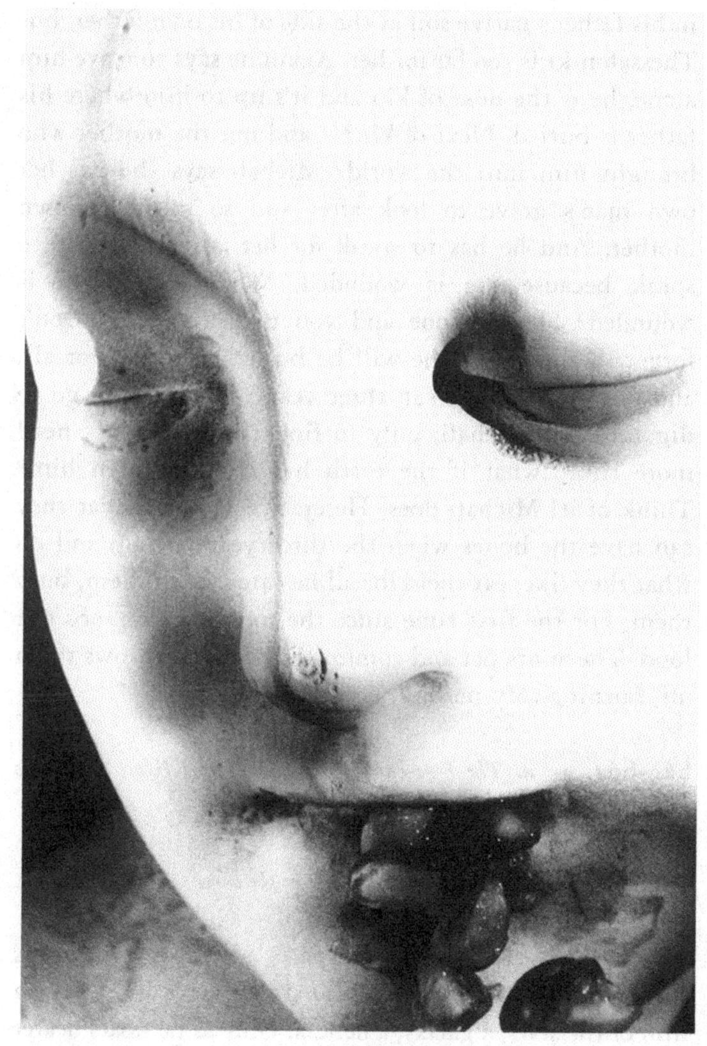

in his father's native soil at the side of his own father, but Thessaloniki is too far for her. Again he says to leave him alone, he is the next of kin and it's up to him where his father is buried. Next of kin? – and not the mother who brought him into the world? Michali says she has her own man's grave to look after and so must his own mother. And he has to speak for her who is unable to speak because she is wounded. Wounded? – she is wounded? She is stone and you take after her! Don't forget in the village he will be buried once and for all, and not dug up again in three years. What if you go to dig him up, Michali, only to find that the bones need more time, what if the earth has not yet eaten him? Think of it! Michali does. He cracks. He yells that they can have the bones when the three years are up and do what they like, eat them for all he cares, burn them, bury them. For the first time since the mountain he sobs out loud. The aunts pet and comfort him and he throws them off, burning. My mother, he prays, wake up.

bán-hús, es; *n. The bone-house, the chest, body...Hence* bánhúses weard, *the body's guard, the mind*

bán-wærc, es; *n. Grief, pain,* or *ache in the bones...*

Mikey looms in a clouded space, a red cavern, walls spangled with pinpricks and bursts of white light, like a film of the stars, a galaxy, a nebula. Only as he floats nearer can he see how the stars shrink down into ice crystals and the walls stiffen, turn hollow, turn into stiff meat and bone.

Spindling down, Elinor is pleased to see Tomo where he belongs on the outskirts of a green city where the kelp hangs swinging, a forest of great loose ropes of weed rolling and swilling under the mirror panes of the sea. Domes and globes and silver disks hang in midwater, flat fish on edge, one silver eye tilting. At the edge of the dark there is turbulence, a vortex. Tomo is hanging in a bubble of water, his eyes squeezed shut, now probing the water with bony fingers, now clutching his head, now beating his arms like wings in slow gestures of appeal, blessing, embrace, absolution.

Through the waters of his widow's deepest sleep a black death's head, the last god, Charos, shimmered in her man's wake, never losing sight of him.

Blessing, Old English *blóedsian*, *blédsian*, *blétsian*, from *blód*, blood. It began as consecration with a sprinkling of still living blood. Blood, bloom, blossom are from the same root, each a silken outflaring of life from a core of being. By the same token the Greek σταυρωνω, from σταυρος, cross, means both 'I crucify' and 'I make the sign of the cross over'. No blessing without sacrifice.

Hacked into wood, cherry wood, and printed out thick and black on paper is a naked man, so brutally naked that he looks flayed, arching up in agony out of the earth where he is buried to the loins. One hand clamps his brow, forcing the head back and baring the sinews of the throat. The other clutches a wound in his breast, out of which a blackness seeps through the fingers and down into the soil. Rearing over him is a dark lily, open-mouthed, swaying, whose roots grope in his flesh, his genitals, to suck his flow of blood. For all the torturous extremity of the image there is a balance. They are at one, the flower and the man, as are the figures and the master who carved them and named them *Allegory (Hemanthus)*. The flower is the αιμανθος, from αιμα, blood and ανθος, flower, an amaryllis, a belladonna lily. The man is the artist himself. The fatal flower, the vampire, is his art and counterpart.

Art must be created with your heart's blood.
EDVARD MUNCH

He is not all dead, not all over. Parts of us will stave off dying as long as they can. I believe it. The fruit you pick green ripens. The pumpkin vine you uproot shrivels into dust and yet every day for weeks it has its handful of green leaves, and a new crumpled golden flower opening wide. Tomo they will have wrapped in a shroud with the face of the Christ printed on it, with the holy face over his heart. His mirror heart – will anyone have remembered how his heart is back to front, on his right side? Η μαννα μας! Of course, our mother will.

Something heavy is going thump on the waves of the tin roof. Mikey lies still with his eyes shut remembering baking days in Greece, his other grandmother thumping dough to make bread. It swelled up after, with just air, she said, bowing at the oven, sliding the trays in. He wonders again what made the difference between her tough dark bread and bread that was a soft white honeycomb of air and whether the air stayed inside or flowed in and out, a hot wind, cooling, the breath of the bread. She had a round wooden stamp like a pancake for printing the crust of some of the raw loaves with and making them holy for soaking in the wine at church and afterwards any leftover bits got handed out at the gate. She let him have a go of the stamp. The pattern was a cross with two columns of letters down it that she said meant *Jesus Christ conquers*. What, Grandmother? – conquers what? The death, Maki, she said. He was Maki for short and his cousin was Michali, after their grandfather, as the firstborn sons of his sons. Because the lord is the death of the death, she said. Or that was what he thought she said.

The pyre, the bonfire, bonefire. Let the last sight of the dead be as a lantern in a bone cage, as long as the fire lasts. Anything but hidden. Aflame at full length, a chambered shell of fire on a fire raft in midair falling to ashes. Anything but the slow grave.

As for the bridegroom, he had loved the sea. The sea was my first love, he liked to say, before my wife was even born.

At her urging, however, on the birth of their first boy he had found work onshore, at a tyre factory on the outskirts of Thessaloniki, at Sindos. Σινδος – the 'δ', δελτα, is as thick and soft as silt on the tongue, *Sindhos*, a sibilant name, like Thessaloniki, like θαλασσα, a watery name for a place so near the old coastline, on the flat seabed of the delta and the low slopes of shore land since turned into an industrial zone by American dollars. He got on well enough with the bosses there, having spent his working life in the engine rooms of freighters and picked up some English in his time in Australia. It was American bulldozers that nosed out the tombs, stone-lined single tombs and lidded stone crates holding the bones and gravegoods of a people who had farmed and fought and grown their dry black wines in the sun. Mostly when you drove in and out of the city past the turn-off to Sindos in those days it was sunk in fumes, a deep greyish mist with a hint of rottenness that clung and shone on the skin and choked the lungs. He sickened. Once he was well again he threw in the job, insisting the sea was where he belonged, to his wife's despair – in my dreams he is always drowning, she told the family, he can be home in bed with me and still be drowning – and went back to sea, shuttling to North Africa and back while ship after ship of the line went down and he slipped through the sea's fingers.

In suspense in isolation, the widows of the world, like every spider spun in a leaf cocoon, in a sphere of net, who spreads out naked and watchful under the moon, herself the anchor of her own craft, enduring time.

In the ruins of Eleusis Demeter went on being worshipped under Roman, Byzantine and Ottoman rule, only now as a saint, an old mother, Agia Demetra, who kept the land fruitful, until one day her beautiful daughter was kidnapped by a brutal Turk on a black horse that breathed fire. Calling, lamenting, Demetra pleaded with all the world to help her find the girl, but only the stork on the rooftop dared to stand by her, and in her fury and despair she laid waste to the land.

As the coffin is carried past, where the customs are kept up, crockery is smashed in the houses and any standing water emptied out. Women in mourning toss pomegranates, apples, quinces, and sometimes walnuts, and almonds, in with the corpse as gifts to their own loved ones underground from the wives and mothers who had fed them living. Like the pomegranate, apples and quinces ripen late and keep through winter; besides which, cut across the core they have a star, a soul, embedded in each fleshy hemisphere, a token of immortality, bearing in its five arms the seeds of a life to come. As for the nuts, they are richer still and more filling and more durable: and there is something human about them too, the long-lipped almond in the shell, a mouth, a vulva, and the walnut kernel, a folded brain. Along the way and at the graveside raw passions are let fly, pleas and reproaches, screams of rage and despair aimed at the corpse by way of a dirge, a μοιρολογι. At the end of the service, red wine and κολλυβα, wheat grains boiled with honey, sesame and pomegranate seeds, the food of the dead, are shared out among the mourners and tossed on the earth grave.

Tholos, θολος, the drystone dome. Θολος, the ink the cuttlefish pumps out, darkness, the unravelling veil.

The widow wakes. She opens her eyes, only to be clamped in her mother's arms and told the missing chapter of her story. Her mouth howls and she claps her hands to her head, arching back. Her mother, whose black widow-scarf and bun of hair have come loose, fights to hold her down in a flood of words, all the old childhood endearments while she, bereft of speech, flails and chokes and wets the bed. My eyes, my joy, my golden one, be still, my darling, my soul. The nurse comes running with something to help her sleep. Her mother lies down at her side.

I pulled the lid off the compost bin the other day and recoiled from a pale animal nestled inside, a ball of spun white fur, long and spangled with dew, the size of a kitten, but not moving and its body, as I peered into the silvery pelt, one raw wound. I lifted it on a stick only to see it fall mushily apart, sending up a sharp smell of what on earth? – I know – fermenting figs.

Almost morning when a body sinks on the bed and she gasps, but it is only her mother saying go back to sleep, and so she does, they both do, fitfully, in the quiet bed breathing in her blood smell. The shuffle of the sea in their sleep and now and then a thud, hollow, on ribs of water.

The spun fur, faintly incandescent, of mould on the figs, a smell, an exhalation, of alcohol – the veil that spins itself around death is what art is.

Who goes to Eleusis anymore? The shrine is still there, plundered, a ruin in an industrial wasteland, but no Demeter, no Agia Demetra. She was a raw lump of marble, almost flesh, and faceless (they knew who she was). More than two hundred years ago she was carried off, like her daughter before her, by two Englishmen who had bribed a Turk. They bundled her off in the teeth of the screeching, wailing women of Eleusis, peasants, who knew what was in store now for them and for the land.

On her side with her legs and her arms drawn up, so, she sleeps cuddled up like me still. And when were you last in bed with me, my own one, breath full of tears? Sssh, I know, I know, sleep tight now there's a good girl. Now what has he done? He will go too far. Love is it, the body in the bed, the presence, bulk and body heat and the gravity of to have and to hold? But the bond of the body wears out and that only leaves the bond of the child. Mikey. Maki. His mother's boy. No, be fair, he has a Greek life too, by right of birth, a sort of mirror self – a distorting mirror, mind you, if it turns an Elinor into a Linora (though who am I to say?). The way the roots of a tree mirror the branches in a different dimension, the life of earth, and its shade in another, which is air, and its reflection in water, in yet another. And a marriage spends a third of its time out of the light of day, at least a third sunk to the waist, a marriage has a night life of its own, and ebbs and flows. (For all I know she may thrive on being the two in one, Linora, Elinor.) A twofold birth. As for Mikey – he was conceived over there, if that counts, though she had him here – how will Mikey know his true life when he sees it?

The widow's first words. Nil by mouth. Her head swarms. Fate. My house is poleaxed and riven and black with blood. And I. And I. My fate to live on inside the carcase.

The widow has nothing to say. All her being is unsaying, unravelling, unwinding life back. What strength she has goes into calling her man back to bed, not here, at home, and there they will be, asprawl across the sheet, his head on her breast as heavy as a baby full of milk, his man's wetness clinging to hers, his heat cooling, cold, without breath, her drowned man huddled on a sheet of sand, loose, lost. Found. With her loss cuddled in close belly to belly she is sobbing aloud at last, long burning rhythmic sobs, spellbound, luxuriant, falling asleep.

Three years from today, the day of the funeral – still evening in Greece and here not yet first light, will the dark never end? – the whole family will gather on the lip of the grave, all hostilities suspended for the time being, the women shrilling around the young widow, the old mother, and the priest intoning, all eyes on the shroud of dark flesh on the bones. The head on its hinge will be a broken shell too heavy for its stem of neck, like a baby's. The sexton will put aside the spade and step in to lift out the skull, greeting it by name and wrapping it in a cloth. Headfirst he came into the world: now the mother, not the widow, will open her hands for it and they will look on while she stands numbly turning and turning her hands in their black sleeves as if it were a lost school cap and she looking for the name, who up until this last moment of the unearthing has hoped for a miracle, a new Lazarus, opening his eyes into the sun.

In a recurrent dream she is at a crowded beach on a hot night, a child, when an apron of water, having hollowed out a lap between knees of lifted sand, surges high up over the wave line to where she is lying, alone, she must have fallen asleep, and she wakes up to find a black wave breathing in her ear, in the nick of time.

Down the road from the graveyard of the Evangelistria –

another title of the Holy Mother – is the Archaeological Museum. We in here, the two of us, mother and son, on a day of baking heat have found, if not coolness, dimness, footsteps echoing in room after room, a glow on a blade of glass taking shape as fine leaves, goldfish, on a shelf, mouth-masks of pure gold – gravegoods of a kind unknown elsewhere, in an abundance so far only found in the ancient tombs of this region, from a settlement at what is now Sindos that went back long before there was any city on the gulf. The mouth-masks were for wearing once, in death, when they were tied on with threads passed through two small holes and knotted at the back of the head, and how they call up even in here the silence of the deathbed! – the shadows of women moving around the corpse, the head lifted briefly up, as if for feeding, while the knot is tied, two working together, or else one working alone with the head held to her breasts. What were they for, these mouths? They swim in the heat and gloom with the dense liquidity of honey, but they are finely detailed, made out of hammered sheets of a soft red gold, plain or embossed with rosettes, waves, spirals, even a little ship with oars and a bellying sail, its owl eyes wide, a ship of death among dolphins. Most of them have crumpled under their weight of earth, some with an impression of the teeth. No lid for the eyes, except for one skull that had a gold butterfly in the sockets, and only a few masks where the whole face was embedded in the gold: otherwise, just this mouth of gold closed on the mouth of flesh. Was it that the dead would still need to see – they had oil lamps – but not speak? All the same, food and drink were offered, as they are today at the funeral and every memorial day to follow. Was it meant like a baby's dummy, dipped in honey, for solace? Or a coin for Charos, more like it? – which they wore over the mouth rather than in it, οι χρυσοστομοι οι νεκροι, the golden-mouthed corpses of Sindos, each a plumb weight of silence at the gravemouth, gagged under this kiss.

The mourners had left them with clay figurines of a seated goddess and such keepsakes as birds in the shape of luminous globes of sea blue glass, beads and rings and amber drops, small golden suspended worlds, to be a light in the dark; phials of perfume; little black iron models of household goods, pans, cauldrons and tripods, wine cups for the black wines of memory, sieves and copper lanterns pricked like sieves, green as mould, that must have thrown a net of light over the stone walls until the oil ran out. Souvenirs of a life above ground – much as if I had come face to face with a battered little tin fire stove out of the dust of my own life, with tin-lidded pots and pans to match, or a doll's tea set. Here children were given playthings of clay, barnyard animals as plain as the dough ones of baking days, some still with a queer blind spark of life in them, a puppy, a pigeon, a craning tortoise small enough to close a fist on, worn as smooth as river stones. The soldiers had on the green mask of a helmet, bronze trimmed with three strips of gold leaf, a little golden doorway into the void. They had their rusty armour and weapons.

A clay goddess had a red stain from her breasts to her lap.

More lamps burn down on the pride of the Museum, the relics of a king murdered over two thousand years ago, and on his ivory and gold shield that they found in flakes like fish scales, and on his gold wreaths. He was inside a casket of gold, a jumble of bones, brown blotched with indigo, and a crushed wreath of oak leaves and acorns, pure gold, on the skull. One eye socket was stove in. The corpse had been burnt and the bones washed in wine, or the flames doused in wine as in Troy at Hector's funeral, so many days into his death and still as sweet of flesh as a man asleep when they lit his pyre; and at the funeral of Achilles in turn, when he was washed and burnt *in raiment of the gods, and honey and oil in abundance* and his bones were taken up, as Odysseus tells his shade in the underworld. So they went by the book when they buried this murdered king in the casket in the marble tomb under the mound, whose purple silks had evaporated like smoke leaving only a blue stain on the bone. Now he lies in a glass case at full length, cracked spindles of long bone, a smashed grin in a brown shell. This case is all my son has eyes for. Outside is a blinding sun. In here in the marine sombreness of the hall the objects shine through the glass in drops and pools of irregular brightness like the sun through cracks in a cave, and along one wall swim speckled fish with gold-ringed eyes.

Unless – what if they had another meaning altogether? That speech, not silence, is golden? In which case the mouth, being the organ of the soul's truth, turns to gold;

and the mouth-mask is more like the warrior's bronze armour in a tomb in Etruria that looked to Lawrence to be *beautiful and sensitive as if it had grown in life for the living body, sunk on his dust.*

Souls are weighed in silence, as gold and silver are weighed in pure water...
MAURICE MAETERLINCK

The women in black who traditionally wailed the dirges, μοιρολογια, 'fate-tellings', so bitterly and formally worded, over the dead, were not family as a rule, not from among the mourners at all. The μοιρολογιστρα was a hired singer, a poet. She had her own dead, on whose fate she would hold her tongue. All her keening was for the corpse on the bier. And yet as the harsh words came shrilling out – her enveloping voice, her breath in the air, its screech and dive and soar – and the other women joined in one by one, each privately wailing for her own loved ones, as the *Iliad* tells us, the singer's heart was also opened in a universal sorrow.

A girl who has died unmarried is dressed as a bride for the grave. Does Kore wear black or white for her wedding underground? The bitter warlike men in the ballads who take the black earth for a bride – Kore is that bride, the mythic bride already sown with the seed of death. In the rites, men would break the earth open each year with mattocks to let her out, green and fluent as the spring water, to ripen in the sun, abundance itself, barren though she remains. Death and his queen have no children.

The last rite of the Egyptian burying ceremony was the opening of the mouth. The son of the deceased, or a priest, solemnly opened the mouth, and this act allowed the dead person who was in the other world to speak, to hear, to move, to see. In Henry Moore's last great work the mouth has become the mother's nipple.
JOHN BERGER

Ζωη σε σας, say the mourners one by one to the members of the family, *Life to you*, and ζωη σε μας, say the family to each other, strophe and antistrophe, στροφη, αντιστροφη, ζωη, ζωη.

In the house the lingering presence, singed, voluptuous, of the baked fish, its fins and white eyes and spine calling to mind the harp of bones she has under folded arms and a bowed and smiling skull, unearthed more than a century ago from a Bronze Age barrow on the chalk downs in Bedfordshire. Half bird, half human being, so open, a webbing of bare fretworks and long claws, crouched in such an attitude of tender intimacy – and yes, there in the nest of the ribcage is a second skull, smashed like an egg, a little one, stillborn, or still not weaned, on a spine curled up in a ball. They must have been wrapped up just so into the one shroud, one flesh swaddled, Mother and Child like a sculpture, inside

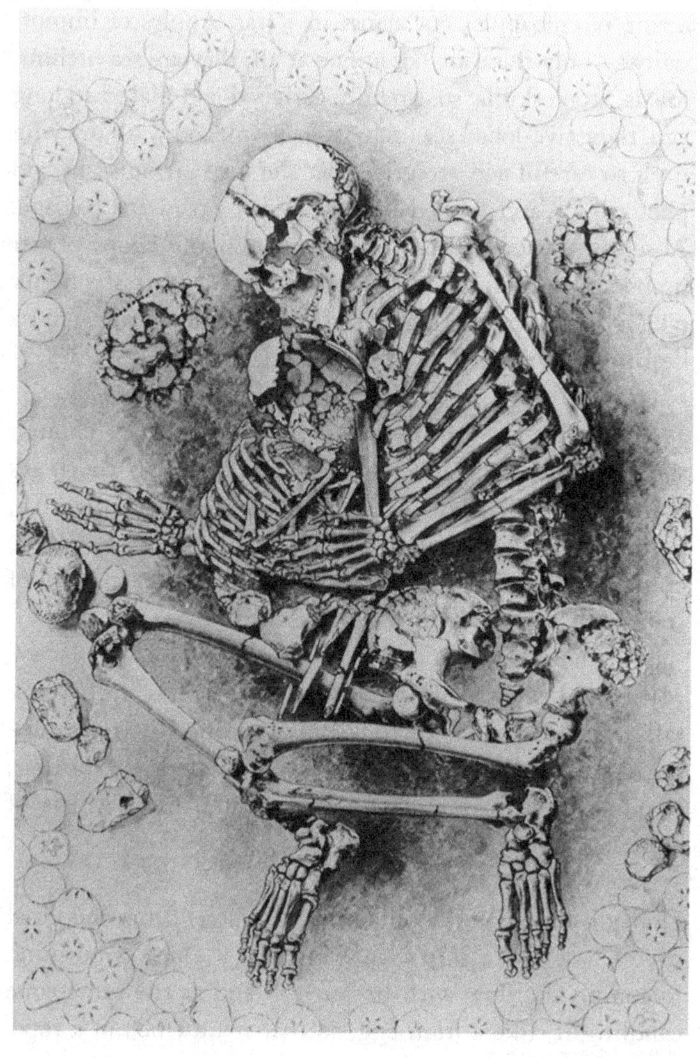

a ring of crabapples cut across in a star. Apples of immortality? – only these are not apples at all, they are sea urchins, fossils, stone skulls, so carefully gathered and placed so long ago, these five-lobed sea urchins, in an ink and wash drawing itself so careful and attentive that she loved it on sight and photocopied and framed it and hung it up in the passage. Absently she presses her open hands on the hoops of her hipbones, thinking, bone-tired, sighing – hadn't she better take it down, considering? Like shrouding the mirrors after a death in the house? No, what on earth for.

We never see the soul inside, we take it on trust. Though some, on the contrary, see it as outside, with the body being inside the soul. Why not, if its life, its being alive, animate – where soul, *anima*, is implicit in the word, enfolded and enfolding – is its soul? This mantle of livingness we move in, whose tissue is pulse, breath.

My friend who is dying of cancer has fits and blank falls and visitations. Struck down in the bathroom one night she stared into the light and saw her own mother, long dead, lean out of the mirror mouthing words of encouragement.

Honey is on tap at the bulk store, in a steel drum mounted over a base like a ship's lantern where a globe is burning, loosening the flow with its warmth and at the same time candling it, like a fresh egg, so that it unwinds in a rope, every speck visible, dust motes, pollen, a white trail of bubbles, a galaxy. In the jar it lapses, red gold. Here is the truth of honey laid bare in liquid fire. Grania closes the lever and a last wisp hangs like blond hairs down a little boy's nape. When it shrinks up into a neb she wipes it off with her finger and sucks a sweetness that chokes, of winter honey. Iris honey, for all she knows, though not everyone has irises this time of the year. In Greece they grow wild, ιριδες, or simply κρινα, lilies, the death flower, and αγριοκρινα, wild lilies. Winter-flowering icy efflorescences. Essence of fleurs-de-lis.

So that the Nectar *or liquid hony is of tvvo sorts: one hard and white even like vnto sugar, which is therfore called stone-hony, or corne-hony: the other so soft that it will runne, which therefore is called liue-hony.*

CHARLES BUTLER, *THE FEMININE MONARCHIE*

Here and there all over Europe are small ruined graves left over from the Stone Age in the long grass or snow. On a day between winter and spring, after the thaw, in a meadow like matted tobacco from the months under snow, I came across two such graves in a mound inside a ring of rocks overlooking a bright sea. In the belly of the mound they were two gashes lipped with stones and lined with splintering snow, and in the shadow of the tall rocks were huddled clots and shreds, the last snow in sight, as if where stone was, and only there, winter still was. A low tomb lay out on its own further inland at the edge of the bare beechwood. This was in Denmark once, not far from where the Tollund Man had lain two thousand years in the peat, his face crushed to the earth, like the full-fed baby to the breast. The tomb had legs of stone edging a rough lintel blotched with lichen. The pillow in its lap was the last snowdrift, blue with deep shadow. A dark hole, a breath of ice.

A Virginia creeper handweaving itself in red on a wall.

That time in Denmark when I watched the red gold sun rise clear as honey in my window first thing in the morning, I was making for the shower – it was late March, on Lady Day – when a shaft of sun fell full on my bare back like a great hand and the power of it took my breath away.

We wake up swaddled in warm wellbeing. Over the day it wears thin. Night time renews it. So it will be in this house, in time. Day breaks and the sun comes in.

The cave was the first temple, the cavity with a tight entrance, reborn as the stone beehive with its mouth to the sunrise, the tholos tomb, an egg, a belly and an oven in one: magic lay in the grave raised in the shape of the mother's womb, stone-smooth or furry with grass. Then as now, the bereaved set up the wail at the graveside that we all made as babies for our lost mother. The dead were folded in the foetal position, hollowed out and tarred, cured, pickled, reduced to ash or jugged in the honey of immortality, set adrift in a ship of death at sea or in the earth, or in between, in bogs that were her womb. They were bathed in red ochre, the blood of rebirth, for nurture and for safeguard, so she would know them for her own. They were given oil, grain and wine, milk and honey, kitchen tools, armour and gold; a good dog, slaughtered to lead the way, horses in fine harness, a slave girl to bed; a siren to fly them to the isles of the blessed; freshly painted scenes on the inner walls of sarcophagi, paradises, the soul's habitation.

In flat tones but coarsely brushed on
in a thick impasto the walls pale lilac
the floor a broken and faded red, the
chairs and the bed chrome yellow the pillows
and the sheet very pale citron green the blanket
blood red the washstand orange
the washbasin blue the window green
I was wanting to express an absolute
repose *through all these very different shades*
you see...
VINCENT VAN GOGH

Un repos absolu...

Water is molten, permeable, mirror and threshold of the soul.

I see now that the story will never unfold, in the form of waves of living opening water or any other form. It was a freezeframe all along, fixed in the moment, the explosion at the core, the cauldron, the death pang – not so much loosening water as the stone that has broken through its ceiling, repercussing, is the story. Not even water but frost growing like coral, crystal by slow crystal. A marbling of blood on snow, on cloth as cold as stone – a death mask, a red nimbus.

The dead were as running water once, say the marble steles, they were as living springs, and the tears of the bereaved, say the mourning songs, trickle down to the underworld to quench the fierce thirst of the dead.

A gap over the lintel of the megalithic howe of Newgrange in Ireland was so angled that the sun rising on the winter solstice would penetrate in a lightning thrust, a blade of gold, a glaze like candlelight along the stone walls, the reanimating fire.

Heavy lips, articulating words of honey, in the dream, the golden flow of words I understand without hearing and wake up having forgotten. I am at a window watching snowflakes, slow and heavy, rising, blurring, a flight of white bees, some so close and slow I see the glaze of their wings. Now I am pacing along a cloister, a caged quadrangle under snow, a vault of silence. The snow is unmarked except for folds of shadow and a few dry stems poking up, each in its hollow of melt. The columns of the cloister shimmer and then fade like the skin of a caught fish. I open my eyes on a sword of light emblazoned on a door.

SEEING IN THE DARK

Eros came into being as an eye filled with its vision

PLOTINOS OF ALEXANDRIA

Over Swan Bay are two wings of fire on the point of parting, the lips of a vast wound. To the far rim of slopes and bushes the water skin is red, striped with gold in the inlet where the swans are moving; here and there the trickle of a lamp, a post like a dead match. Long wings, gold, vermilion, tufts of plumage, becoming ash.

In the stillness of a rock pool, no fish until one silver belly turns to the light, an oxyacetylene flash, a whitebait. It moves on in a shoal, gunmetal needles all on one level above the dim floor, its weedy lime and sand. A storm is about to break. The world, sky and sea and shore, holds its breath. Another fish flashes – the shower of whitebait, dark rain, flash.

The lighthouse lantern is fieriest at sunset when the sun lights it.

The canopy is high overhead, evergreen, half gold, always shifting. Under the tree is a muffled stillness among trunks like figures carved on a drowned *wat*, watertorn, but they are rock solid, they are limestone, or sandstone, naked gods, rudimentary, tentative, who take shape only to lose it in the shadows.

Take a blood orange cut into segments and arranged upright on their slivers of skin. Drops and trickles of juice have stained the white plate. In the low slant of afternoon light the segments are eight boats full of bloodlit water. I screw on a close-up filter and focus on one point of light, a drop in the sun, the veins below it seeping red into the gold. The sun is sinking in the window: the flow of the light changes in the time it takes to peer, to adjust the tripod and press the shutter; each half-second of dense black is filled with a clutter of blue prows. When the sun has slid off for the day I press each warm red gold lozenge of skin on to my mouth and suck hard. I am stiff from all the crouching. My eyes are stinging. When I shut them all I see is these eight slivers of fire glowing in my belly, hot coals in a stove.

The sun has never seen a shadow.

LEONARDO DA VINCI

The sea cave of awakenings in a wash of water, salt air, the half dark, the room taking shape as a vague powdering as of dust falling, or snow at a distance, every object, a wardrobe door, a lampshade, having the eroded penumbra of edges in a grainy photograph. If I shut my eyes, the mottle of light and dark remains, only without form or graduation, a grey inner skin out of which there slowly develops a series of radiant crystalline forms of the densest blue that well up from the depths of my field of vision, warping and fading, pulsing, sometimes forming a hole in the mass, a well, an eye, and dissolving. They have nothing to do with dreams, still less, I gather, I hope, with failing eyesight, but an optical illusion, called in Sanskrit the *nimitta*, known to haunt the minds of those practising insight meditation, who are told to disregard the passing show and to dwell instead on the engendering emptiness. The forms may appear after orgasm as well, the body lying stunned in its own radiant heat, blood fluttering in the earlobes, to make long sweeps of the inner eye like radar, like a lighthouse beam under the sea. In what sense can they be said to exist? Why are they always blue? Since they appear only to closed eyes, do the blind see them? *Looking on darkness which the blind do see.* Both those blind from birth and those who go blind later, or would it depend on the root cause of their blindness? As for the powdery shifting, it surrounds me in every light now, weak or strong, an aspect of whatever I see with the naked eye; even with lenses in and everything sharply in focus it is there in suspension, the fabric of my world.

But this is the exposition given in the commentaries: it appears to some like a star or a cluster of gems or a cluster of pearls, to others with a rough touch like that of silk-cotton seeds or a peg made of heartwood, to others like a long braid string or a wreath of flowers or a puff of smoke, to others like a stretched-out cobweb or a film or a cloud or a lotus flower or a chariot-wheel or the moon's disk or the sun's disk.
VISUDDHIMAGGA

I question not my Corporeal or Vegetative Eye any more than I would Question a Window concerning a Sight. I look thro' it & not with it.
WILLIAM BLAKE

The deep truth is imageless.
PERCY BYSSHE SHELLEY

BLUE.
778.
As yellow is always accompanied with light, so it may be said that blue still brings a principle of darkness with it.

779.
This colour has a peculiar and almost indescribable effect on the eye. As a hue it is powerful, but it is on the negative side, and in its highest purity is, as it were, a stimulating negation. Its appearance, then, is a kind of contradiction between excitement and repose.

780.
As the upper sky and distant mountains appear blue, so a blue surface seen to retire from us.

781.
But as we readily follow an agreeable object that flies from us, so we love to contemplate blue, not because it advances to us, but because it draws us after it.

782.
Blue gives us an impression of cold, and thus, again, reminds us of shade. We have before spoken of its affinity with black.

783.
Rooms which are hung with pure blue, appear in some degree larger, but at the same time empty and cold

784.
The appearance of objects seen through a blue glass is gloomy and melancholy.
GOETHE

A long-familiar image or word-picture suddenly comes alive as if for the first time: how – why? At low tide under the lighthouse I stop and look for whitebait stranded in a rock pool; a skin of cloud and mirrored rock, or grey lead, smooth, ruffled and underneath, dark water, rock, limpets, seaweed, a starfish, no whitebait until a glint like the strike of a silver match, a fish! And by its light the whole shoal – they were there all the time – is clear against the bottom, a mass of dark spines moving as one. The same goes for the word-picture. A trick of the light one day and before you know it – once you know it the moment is over – you are seeing through the words to the meaning. Not by any act of will. A flash of insight. Revelation.

Light's mode of being, in the absence of light's body, in the language of optics: *luminance* is the light that an object is reflecting or emitting; *illuminance*, on the other hand, is the light incident, falling, on the object (and not, as it might seem, the negative of *luminance*). Then there are the units of light, a lumen, a candela. Illuminance. Luminance. 'Black' or 'invisible' infrared and ultraviolet light. Iridescence, phosphorescence, luminescence. *Brightness*, defined as the subjective 'what is seen' by a living eye, as against *luminance* as recorded by photometric instruments. Coherent and incoherent light.

Nature is not only what is visible to the eye – it is also the inner visions of the soul – pictures on the other side of the eye.
EDVARD MUNCH

Living out their lives in the perpetual icy slow-moving darkness of the deep ocean among the Archaea, the oldest of beings, are fish that light up at will, to see and be seen, flash and flare and glow – the lantern fish and others whose huge eyes are far from blind, in no way vestigial.

The brown shade, shuttered heat of the room, the glass bowl inside a wooden bowl on the table, brown tones and the one red incandescence of the camellia. The dance of winding down the head of the tripod, snapping its leg locks open, swinging it in closer, locking the camera into the head. Sun flare on the rim of the bowl, on the flat surfaces of the water in it, and in the drops of water on fleshy untouchable petals, swollen, luminous, over the staring veins, their loom and warp. Blades and vanes, the scarlet mantle and a yellow spattering of seed.

Last light on the boggy shore between red masses of cloud, lines of swans at a lazy distance, their mews and whimpers loud over the sandbanks and reaches of water – a sudden splash at my feet, a whorl of water shakes open, swallowing, and a double ridge of black juts out, a dorsal fin, a banjo shark, spinning. Another whorl opens further down, and another, more knots of turbulence in a net that spans half the bay. The red has drained out. Only fold on fold of silver and black beating at the reflection of the hill, pierced by a pine and two streetlamps, far apart, dragged in like fishing lines.

Sinuosities sibilances tenacities repercussions

A winter tree, one of a row of slender plane trees waving their bobbles of fuzz against the sun in the mirror of a long pool: but I have made a mirror image of her instead, black for white, a print of her incandescent writhings in dark water – an apparition, a milkwhite spirit.

A soft drizzle on the lens, black boughs fading to grey, a yellow streak of sky over the old Melbourne Cemetery, the broken headstones and long grass around the graves of my mother's Irish forebears. Born in Dublin, Cork, Mountrath, they sailed over in the famine years. But she died knowing nothing about them as far as I know, not so much as a face in an old photo. Even their names had been kept dark, a family secret, a secret family. Her father and mother were both dead by the time I was born. But her father's own mother Fanny was still alive in Melbourne until I turned eleven and my mother never said a word. Did she know? Surely she must have known Fanny, born in Richmond, seventh and last child of a London chimneysweep and his washerwoman wife – my great-grandmother-to-be, Fanny, who earned her keep as a 'mantle-maker', as it says with pride on her marriage certificate, and bore a son at twenty to a married Irish bootmaker who had married her as well under a false name and landed in jail for bigamy. Fanny lost her man and her good name overnight: and she lived it down, and she held on for dear life to Will, her son. She married again, a Welsh blacksmith this time, a widower. Will got his stepfather's surname and perhaps over time his own true history, since he became the family wild Irishman under a bland Welsh name. His blood father, the bigamist, the black sheep, is not on the list of names cut in the stone, streaky with wet, or on the separate headstone alongside, of a younger brother dead in France in the Great War. Will himself, the grandfather I never knew, fought in France; a comrade-in-arms, for all I know, of these unknown uncles and cousins, dead and buried, tracked down at last, my people, like it or not, my relics underfoot, blood of my blood and bone of my bone. What did my mother know of her father's flesh and blood? I know who they were now and when and where they were put down to sleep like babies in the crib.

Long silvery sweeps of sky, sand, rock, water, almost still at the Rip. Black swarms of gnats huddled in the rock faces, spattering with a loud hum and settling back again; a Pacific gull on heavy wings; swallows looping; a heron; wan clarity of the late light, reflections in verges, pools, wrinkling over when a boat passes. A sub-polar clarity and luminosity of Scandinavian distances as clear and faint as Risskov beach in Denmark in the late winter, and Nordstrand, Åsgårdstrand, Kragerø on the Oslofjord where Munch lived, the lonely islands strung out in drizzle, sun, rain.

On a granite crag over the Sagfjord, above the Arctic Circle, is a sculpture made some time during the Stone Age, the images of two reindeer, graven where they can only ever be seen by hanging precariously over the cliff edge on a rope. They must have been made the same way, by men swaying on ropes and crawling from handhold to handhold with their tools slung round their necks, chipping into the rock face the invisible shapes of the great animals – as invisible in the midnight sun as in the winter night, either from above or from a boat out on the fjord. They were never there to be seen. Like the animals painted in the heart of caves, their work was done in the dark. Latent in the rock, spirit presences to draw the living herds to the cliff edge, where until recent times the waiting hunters would drive them over to their deaths.

The moon is visibly on the wane. A bath of silver light for the house last night, and some got into the darkroom through chinks and slits, but not enough to stain the paper. I could make a photogram outside, lay a twig or petals or a leaf skeleton – moongrams, monograms – on a live sheet of paper for the moon to print. How long would that take? You would have to keep a record of which sheets were exposed for how long: having numbered each one on the back first, in the darkroom, you would take it outside in a black sleeve, lay it flat on the grass while you counted the seconds or minutes, and take it back inside in a different sleeve for printing. The subjects would come up stencilled on black according to their relative translucence, rather as the moon does in the night sky.

The kosmos is like a net which takes all its life, as far as ever it stretches, from being wet in the water; and has no act of its own; the sea rolls away and the net with it…
PLOTINOS

On the radio a program about an experiment showing that, left to its own devices, the body adjusts to a 25-hour day, so that without a clock we will wake, eat and sleep about an hour later each day. So it is with the moon and, it follows, with the tides. Is this a sign that the body keeps time by the moon, not only by the sun? A slowly unspooling rhythm of subliminal time.

A figleaf burning in a patch of sun on the path, a ribbed shell like a boat, balanced on its stalk, a crumple of brown on one side, all its freckles and veins clear in a green pool of light.

Sun and a fierce wind, cold from the south, the sea black and white. The corpse of a seal pup is on the beach under the lighthouse, bloated – a plump grey bag of skin with all but one patch of dark fur rubbed off and a blowfly hovering – a shine on the head, the open mouth stringy and crusted with sand, an ear or a pod of seaweed but no visible eye. The black knuckles of its hind flippers stretch out behind. It was very young, newborn, or stillborn. The seals haul up on the wooden pyramids that mark the shipping channel, the ancient river bed, the deepest water in the bay. They fling themselves up and crowd in along the narrow beams, fighting for space. A pup born up there would slip from the womb into the sea before it could draw breath. Pelt on skin on bone, intricately woven. I nudge the flank with the cap of my shoe and it wobbles, a bladder of seawater or gas; the fine gunmetal skin stretches, a net of glints and crinkles, veins, shadow.

Edvard Munch grew up as an artist in Christiania, now Oslo, in a doom-ridden household. *For my inheritance I received two of man's most terrible enemies, the heritage of consumption and madness. Sickness and madness and death were the black angels standing by my cradle.*

Our inheritance is ours to spend. His was spent wrestling with Charos.

How the eye works: the pupil, the apple, *Augenapfel* – and *prunelle*, sloe – opens its dark pool to admit light on to the back wall of flesh which is the retina, flesh awash in veins. The eye, then, as the first camera obscura? – no, there were chinks of light in caves before there was any being on earth with eyes to see. Like the shadow-play of Plato's cave, the phenomenon of the camera obscura may have been common knowledge for millennia before Plato, before the Stone Ages when they made mounds with long passages of rock for the sun to shaft in deep. In a dark place a chink of light appears, a bright point with a halo. The faint visibility that it imparts is weaker the further it spreads away: and the dazzled eye soon narrows its pupil in response to the glare, unless the chink itself is outside its visual field. But the magic lantern show of the camera obscura appears directly opposite the chink. All it would take was someone for once not to be looking through the chink or at it, but at the wall behind, to see a moving image of the world, microscopic, as the gods would see it, and upside down, as they swam overhead. Like a painting made of light, here was a marvel, a vision, a god's doing. The dark place of insight, of outsight, belonged to the god; the image glowing in it like a butter lamp was the sign of presence. Sometimes visible, sometimes not, it was a momentary threshold between the worlds, the domain of the shaman, the mage, μαγος, who was its seer.

Why does the eye see a thing more clearly in dreams than the imagination when awake?
LEONARDO DA VINCI

The *Odyssey* remarks mysteriously that the island of Syrie (Συριη) in the Cyclades is *where are the turnings of the sun.* Might it have had a stone circle like Stonehenge, tracking the solstices, or a cave or beehive temple like Newgrange in Ireland, Maeshowe in Orkney, a stone sundial in the sea? (Might the name be related to the Sanskrit *Surya*, sun?)

Starch white on Swan Bay, a paper nautilus washed up, broken eggshells.

Today I bought myself a red safelight – darkroom lamp, *lampe à chambre noire*, *donkere kamer lamp*, *Dunkelkammerlampe* – and a spare to be safer still. An Arab astronomer over a thousand years ago, I read somewhere and jotted down, was the first to watch the *éclipse du soleil et de la lune dans une chambre noire*; anyway, the first to record the experience. A lovely languid phrase, *une chambre noire*. How would the frail eclipse of the moon show up inside? And why bother, with the whole dark night wide open?

On the other hand the camera lucida – also known at first as the *camera clara* or *camera chiara* – is barely two centuries old, the invention of an Englishman who found inspiration, as did James Joyce, in a cracked mirror; a man so sharp-eyed that he once caught sight of a mirage on the Thames. But a 'light chamber' it was not – no chamber at all, the name being only by way of a match for the camera obscura. The camera lucida is made up of an angled sheet of glass or mirror and a prism mounted on a stand at eye level as an aid to drawing – which the camera obscura itself would become over time, shrinking to a little wooden box with mirrors angled to the paper, a trap to be sprung by images, foreshadowing the modern camera.

The low sun catches in every single lump of jellyfish along the waterline. One is a dome as pure as glass burning along one edge. At the core is a steady yellow glow like a candle in which every grain of the sand underneath is steeped, more or less enlarged.

The seal pup has washed back up. Hand and eye, the seeing eye, the right eye, magnified in the lens, extended, turned monochrome red, or orange, or yellow green. Flattened. The film is infrared and I take each shot with and then without the red filter. Only with the red filter does the infrared band of light register on the film, and on these shots when I print them I hope to find this invisible, metavisible light exposed, made manifest: the caul of radiance in which the seal pup was delivered out of the sea. Mirages and miracles, auras of breath, heat, decomposition.

The early photographers kept a cat in the studio to act as a light meter, going by the subtle swell and shrink of its changing eyes in the changing light. How did they keep it awake?

In a dim room, the only source of light a little oil lamp, a dish of thin glass on a black iron tripod, with a candle holder in the base. First a layer of water, then a match touched to the wick, a few drops of oil – lemon grass and rose – that clot and sway and coalesce – rings, orbits, galaxies – in the heat and light. The flame wavers on a bed of white wax – these are close-ups, long exposures from above through oily water to the moving flame; the gold rim on darkness of the glass dish, the fume coiling up off a surface of spotted water.

The sea is silver, sheets of gelatin, silver scales melting in green lumps as I wade in hot, iced, my thighs swelling in meshes of silver, and sink myself down to the gloom, through the silver and under, eyes swollen in greening shredding and reforming cold forms reflected under the silver lid of the sea, all in this one translucent rolling, tearing and reforming, cloudy flesh alight over a small green shadow, so bounded in water I am the water, I am the water's wide eye.

It is a significant fact that even in man...the beautiful crystalline lens is formed in the embryo by an accumulation of epidermic cells, lying in a sack-like fold of the skin; and the vitreous body is formed from embryonic sub-cutaneous tissue.

If we must compare the eye to an optical instrument, we ought in imagination to take a thick layer of transparent tissue, with spaces filled with fluid, and with a nerve sensitive to light beneath, and then suppose every part of this layer to be continually changing slowly in density, so as to separate into layers of different densities and thicknesses, placed at different distances from each other, and with the surfaces of each layer slowly changing in form.

CHARLES DARWIN

Outside all afternoon, the windy sun and sleepy sounds of the hens in their shed one wall away, a sudden squawk or a rhythmic outburst torn from the throat of one in the pain of laying. Inside in a borrowed shed, airtight, *une chambre rouge*, night air with a last glow of red and soft sounds of water as it washes through the tub where my prints float face up. A womb, a retreat.

A school of philosophers in the early Greek world held that the blood is the thought of man, where the heart lives, *in the sea of blood which surges back and forth* – blood, for its hot fluency being the part of us most like fire, like pure spirit.

The changing of Bodies into Light, and Light into Bodies, is very conformable to the Course of Nature, which seems delighted with Transmutations.
ISAAC NEWTON, *OPTICKS*

Science is spectrum analysis: Art is photosynthesis.
KARL KRAUS

On the dry Aegean island of his political prison the poet Yannis Ritsos, now dead, wrote his poems in the privy, bottled and buried them. He found smooth stones and gave them faces, embodying Eros. He sowed his images where nothing else would grow, an island with no water. *Here no water exists,* wrote the poet into the silence. *Only light.* Εδω δεν υπαρχει νερο. Μοναχα φως.

(In giving birth a Greek mother is giving the light, φως, to her child.)

Ghosts were shades, shadows – they were black in old Europe. How did they go white?

I am no more than a humming-bird blur of being to the banyan tree as I move through the hanks of roots and silvery multiple trunks catching on film images far beyond my bare eyes, revelations. Since any tree lives by its own time, and for us the growth and writhings of a banyan are so glacially slow that it might as well be stone...Now if a timelapse camera could only be set up to take one shot a year for a hundred years, hundreds, even. How wonderful then, to see the long dance of the banyan, braided and clean-limbed in all its vast grey self rolling itself out through time as if through water.

Timelapses, timescapes. My father's old bellows camera unfolds on tracks like a toy train engine and for a viewfinder it has a swivelling glass eye with a dusty mirror set at a slant inside. It made grey little prints like this one at the lake in a rim of trees, two figures in a rowboat. The child in the stern emerges as a white fuzz of head and dress against a mass of darkness, trees in full leaf; she is hanging on hard with both hands, doing as she is told, sitting so tight she doesn't dare wave to her mother on the far shore, feet apart, head down over the viewfinder. Her father has his back to the camera, facing the trees, facing away, oars lifted. But the child's face, her blank flare of light, might still be made visible even now, by burning in, if the negative had not disappeared: as have the father and mother, gone to ashes long ago, ashes and dust and air. Fifty years on in the last of an autumn sunset, the lakeside is deserted and I am the one holding a camera as I walk through stillness under trees that are filtering down yellow on yellow, light on light, through the caravan park, past the boats in stacks, to the leaden water, at my footfall a duck here and there, a waterhen, skittering away and launching itself, gathering at its back all the long bare trees in the lake in a fan of dark folds.

The lake of the holiday is in bushland on the fringe of the goldfields town where we stayed. One afternoon my father took me to see the poppet heads and mullock heaps, relics of its heyday, and we fossicked late into the twilight for knuckles of quartz with specks in the creases that might be gold. Now I know that his own grandfather worked in these mines and his father, John James, was born here and lived here until 1871, when Mary, his mother, died in childbed. Mary, born in Lincolnshire, died here at thirty-seven. The baby – William, after the father – outlived her by ten days, her eleventh child and the fifth of them to die, and joined her in the grave. The widower decamped with the older boy, Levi, to the Queensland goldfields, where he married a mother in distress from Norway and fathered a second brood, an alternative family, only to die his own father's death, by water, so they say – in the Mary River, like his young father so long ago in the Swan. But little John James was packed off with his sisters to his mother Mary's people.

Mary, the grandmother my father would never know, stayed behind. Did he know we had family in this town, bone of our bone? If so he never said a word. Or did he, and did it just wash over the child I was, one with no grandparents of her own? I do know we never went near the cemetery, a tract of flat land on the road out, with tall gums full of wind at the far end, a high, deep, soft roar of windy trees and a hot silence at ground level. A map in the portico has her grave plot inked in, down by the back fence, but there are no graves any more in the grass, the springy couch grass, mown short. There are thick grey stumps in a row along the fence that were saplings in her day and must still have the dead cradled in their roots like so many flies in an old web, Mary, underfoot, embedded, a long shape of bone with a bone child at the breast.

It was on the deck of a steamer on the way up to Queensland to see his old Uncle Levi that my father met my mother. She asked for a light.

He saw the creek drown a playmate, he lived with a deep dread of water.

Images in words, in poems – they float in the mind like so many reflections in the water – in the water, as we say, though what does the water know of its reflections? It takes nothing of them in, not the faintest impression, not so much as a shadow – they float away unmarked, overhead.

In 1640 on Christmas Day in the evening, the turn of the year, the winter Sunnestead, John Donne told the congregation of St Paul's how 'in heaven it is alwaies Autumne'.

Nothing grows in a spot where there is neither sentient, fibrous nor rational life. The feathers grow upon birds and change every year; hair grows upon animals and changes every year except a part such as the hair of the beard in lions and cats and creatures like these. The grass grows in the fields, the leaves upon the trees, and every year these are renewed in great part. So then we may say that the Earth has a spirit of growth, and that its flesh is the soil; its bones are the successive strata of the rocks which form the mountains; its cartilage is the tufa stone; its blood the springs of its waters. The lake of blood that lies about the heart is the ocean. Its breathing is by the increase and decrease of the blood in its pulses, and even so in the earth is the ebb and flow of the sea. And the vital heat of the world is fire which is spread throughout the earth; and the dwelling place of its creative spirit is in the fires, which in divers parts of the earth are breathed out in baths and sulphur mines, and in volcanoes...

LEONARDO DA VINCI

The earth is a daimon with a womb of molten fire.

Autumn light is photographic. Early and late on those still days in mid-autumn that balance on the point between sumptuous and threadbare, the light slants through and across, an element in itself. Every surface steeps in this light already too frail, spread too thin for warmth. The days are shorter, more concentrated, slick with wet, even the buttery light of noon is no more than a glaze that sets in splinters, a fly's wing. Sizzle of gnats, bees, a blowfly's zoom. Leaf smoke striped in the sun, the flesh of autumn burning low. Baggy webs are spun from every tree, invisible once they are out of the sun, blowing in the slightest wind like reflections, all the sun-gathered spider hairs. By day the sun makes lanterns of the webslung dry leaves, each one enfolding a spider who hangs out in the open all night, a clawed amber bead, as still as death by the torchlight.

To any vision must be brought an eye adapted to what is to be seen, and having some likeness to it.
PLOTINOS

At the library I took out *Camera Lucida* by Roland Barthes on impulse, under the spell of the title. The original title is better still, perhaps, all the more resonant for not being Latin: *La chambre claire*. The style is as laborious as I feared, stilted and jerky, rhetorical, bristling with neologisms and parentheses, often obscure, but somehow never seems so just for the sake of it. In fact, having fought my way through the thickets I can hardly bear to take it back now, for love of the man himself whose humanity shines through. This, as it happens, was to be his last work, a meditation on death and photography, on memory and *le temps perdu*.

A trick of vocabulary: we say 'to develop a photograph'; but what the chemical action develops is {the} undevelopable, an essence (of a wound), what cannot be transformed but only repeated under the instances of insistence (of the insistent gaze). This brings the Photograph (certain photographs) close to the Haiku. For the notation of a haiku, too, is undevelopable: everything is given, without provoking the desire for or even the possibility of a rhetorical expansion. In both cases we might (we must) speak of an intense immobility*: linked to a detail (to a detonator), an explosion makes a little star on the pane of the text or of the photograph: neither the Haiku nor the Photograph makes us 'dream.'*
ROLAND BARTHES

Less a development than a making apparent, εμφανεια (and επιφανεια, epiphany, a revelation). Εμφανιζω μια φωτογραφια, in Greek I make a photograph appear. What is latent, pre-fixed, predetermined, is being brought to light. Negative or print, its full being is not attained by growth, organically, as with a painting, nor by the stripping away of whatever is notionally superfluous, as with a sculpture in wood or stone. The photograph has its full being in the instant of exposure. The rest is aftermath.

First the exposed film has to be winkled out of the film cassette, the lips prised open, velvet on metal, and the dry tongue-tip of film pinched out, all inside the sleeved and rustling darkness of the changing bag. The loosened film must be wound on to a reel in total darkness, not exposed to the least crack of light, any more than it was between the dark walls of the camera – so much as the green glimmer of a watchface and the image will vanish as if struck by lightning. But if I could safely have a look, all I would see is a coil of plastic, no trace of the images inscribed.

Once the reel is locked into a light-tight tank like a black jar with a funnel and a lid, I can work in the light, tipping a succession of solutions down the funnel to swill around the film on its reel while I time each one – developer, stop bath, fix, then running water. Now the strips of film can be unwound in the light and pegged up on a length of string to dry like snakeskins, safe to look at now, if not to touch. With a torchlight on them from behind and a magnifying glass in front I can see each little picture, black velvet and clear glass under a last runnel of water.

Εμφανιζω for *develop* is sober, neutral. The German *entwickeln* is to unroll, unfold, from *Wickel*; a *Wickelband* is a swaddling-band. Our *develop* is from the French *voluper*, to wrap. The French also use *développer*:

Ruse du vocabulaire: on dit «développer une photo»; mais ce que l'action chimique développe, c'est l'indéveloppable, une essence

(de blessure), ce qui ne peut se transformer, mais seulement se répéter sous les espèces de l'insistance (du regard insistant). Ceci rapproche la Photographie (certaines photographies) du Haïku. Car la notation d'un haïku, elle aussi, est indéveloppable: tout est donné, sans provoquer l'envie ou même la possibilité d'une expansion rhétorique. Dans les deux cas, on pourrait, on devrait parler d'une immobilité vive: *liée à un détail (à un détonateur), une explosion fait une petite étoile à la vitre du texte ou de la photo: ni le Haïku ni la Photo ne font «rêver».*
ROLAND BARTHES

Another word they have for it is *révéler*, a long step further in the direction of the positive. For the spurt of joy in the process, only *révéler* comes near. *Révéler* brings the effect of the photograph – at least on the photographer who has 'made' it, or in whose hands it has achieved its latent being – far closer than *développer* to the satori, the little star on the pane of the mind, that is the gift of the haiku. The packet of chemical developer names it *le révélateur*, with the clear inference that he or she who presides over the process is a mage, or angel.

Glossy paper, *carta fotografica*, is *lucida*, aspic.

In the dark of the red safelight you push one negative of a strip into place in the enlarger and focus it through a filter, in any one of a dozen shades between yellow-red and blue-red, on to the white baseboard by means of a kind of slanted handheld periscope that magnifies each grain of silver in the negative. A ball of tiny red spores of grain, like a blood orange, a moon in eclipse, swims into view and is focused to the glittering sharpness of mica. Then with the enlarger lamp off (or on, as long as the built-in red safelight is swung over the lens so that the paper sees the light as black, as total darkness) a sheet of photographic paper is put in place, the safelight swung away and the lamp left on for a matter of seconds – how many seconds is guesswork to begin with, print by print – for the sensitive coating of the paper to absorb, invisibly, as yet, the stencil of projected light. Only when immersed in the tray of developer does the paper grow those shadows that spread and darken like a mould, threads and masses of darkness ordained, however long ago, by a fall of light on that section of blank film. Once developed, the print is quickly lifted out with tongs and dropped first in the stop bath, then the fix, then the washtub. The prints lift and furl in the running water, shapes on them warping, rippled blacks and whites as fluid as hot enamel. One after another they are pegged up to dry. By now any impression that the image is fluid, organic and capable of change, of growth, of development, has been dispelled. Its shadows are indelible. A mineral fixity is the truth of it.

Prints in the wash, slow lift and flat flop of tail flukes, of a whitebacked wing.

Black and white prints, though far less volatile than colour, will tarnish over time owing to the silver content. For greater permanence they can be put through a bath of bleach and redeveloped and fixed in gold or selenium toner or in sepia.

The photograph is literally an emanation of the referent. From a real body, which was there, proceed radiations which ultimately touch me, who am here; the duration of the transmission is insignificant; the photograph of the missing being, as Sontag says, will touch me like the delayed rays of a star. A sort of umbilical cord links the body of the photographed thing to my gaze: light, though impalpable, is here a carnal medium, a skin I share with anyone who has been photographed.

It seems that in Latin 'photograph' would be said 'imago lucis opera expressa'; which is to say: image revealed, 'extracted', 'mounted', 'expressed' (like the juice of a lemon) by the action of light. And if Photography belonged to a world with some residual sensitivity to myth, we should exult over the richness of the symbol: the loved body is immortalized by the mediation of a precious metal, silver (monument and luxury); to which we might add the notion that this metal, like all the metals of Alchemy, is alive.

Une sorte de lien ombilical relie le corps de la chose photographiée à mon regard: la lumière, quoique impalpable, est bien ici un milieu charnel, une peau que je partage avec celui ou celle qui a été photographié.

ROLAND BARTHES

The camera lens, a crystal of darkness in blades of glass, concave, convex melded into one. Depth of field – playing it by eye, turning the rings that throw the whole bay now into sharp focus, now into the smudge it appears to my unaccommodated eye. *Flou* is the French for blurred, smudged, *flou*, a lovely word in the mouth, from the Flemish *flauw*; related to *flow*. *Le flou* is the world I wake to underwater every day before I put in my contact lenses.

Hydrophilous? Hydrophilic lenses, drops, rings of light. Photograms made by torchlight on a sheet of glass above the white paper – waterdrops bulbous and dark as a seal's eye, that turn into white rings, once developed, on a dense black gloss of paper.

Soft lenses are water-lovers. Out of the eye or water bath for too long they dry to a flake, a fish scale. Trembling on the ball of a finger they are drops with a blue edge, jellyfish, a watery mantle in a loose ring of blue. They keep folding over of their own accord, or turning inside out and shrinkwrapping my fingertip.

Out of the shower a body, trickled over with blue, and blue-guttered, hairy in the gutters, and marbling as it cools. These limbs, these lipped breasts, white flesh moulded on bone in a haze of steam and sleep. Seaming of mother of pearl on breast and thigh, loosening. Splash water on a dry face and the taut skin dissolves into *silk*, *soie*, *une peau de soie*, *le soir. Une peau de soir.* Skin is hydrophilous. A handful of water opens a face like a paper flower, softly swelling on immersion, dissolving, *une peau floue.* Skin is aqueous, subaqueous. *Peau de soif.*

As a child whose short sight went unsuspected by anyone for years I passed the time when I was alone in my room by looking through a mesh of cloth or along the hard edge of anything solid held up to the eye so that it was almost touching – a pencil, a sheet of paper – until I saw a rim of clarity that was like a halo, an atmosphere, faintly fluid, beyond which lay the usual fuzz of the world. A meniscus, a film, a sheath of clarity like the sheath of ice on a stalk of grass, a twig, a leaf skeleton. I found out in private how the weave of my blanket or my skirt over my head would let me into a darkness of tented breath, a rustling of faceted walls made up of images of a hallucinatory clarity, bulging slightly, so that the cells were rounded in the rectilinear latticework of threads, like so many drops of water, a honeycomb of water.

Myopia, μυωπια, short sight. The μυωψ must close – μυω – the eyes to slits, peering, narrowing the focus (and 'focus' is εστια, hearth).

Why is it that when the sun passes through quadrilaterals, as for instance in wickerwork, it does not produce figures rectangular in shape but circular?

Why is it that in an eclipse of the sun, if one looks at it through a sieve or through leaves, such as a plane-tree or other broad-leaved tree, or if one joins the fingers of one hand over the fingers of the other, the rays are crescent-shaped where they reach the earth? Is it for the same reason as that when light shines through a rectangular peep-hole, it appears circular in the form of a cone?...But they do not come from the moon, neither in eclipse nor when it is either waxing or waning...
ARISTOTLE

Crescent, *cresens*, *croissant*, growing. In the original Greek, μηνισκος (Latin *meniscus*), from μηνη, moon, sickle moon. He means tiny images of the sun cast through pinholes in the foliage, not the everyday dapple of sunlight. It was only an eclipse that made the distinction apparent: as long as the sun was in mid-eclipse, so were the images.

Θαλασσα is sea, πελαγος the open sea; as in French, *la mer*, *le large*.

Τω γριπηει Πελαγωνι πατηρ επεθηκε Μενισκος κυρτον και κωπαν, μναμα κακοζοιας.

To the fisherman Pelagon his father Meniskos has put up a fishing-basket and an oar as a memorial of his hard life.
SAPPHO

One morning a few years ago something black got into

my left eye, not dust or an eyelash, as I first thought, but inside the eye. Suddenly in my blurred, because myopic, left eye a long shape was hanging, stiff-jointed and spidery like a puppet in a shadow-play, high in the visual field as if in outer space, but it was in inner space, a husk, responding slowly to every shift of the eyeball. There was no pain beyond a sharp headache, simple eyestrain, I thought, or fear. It was two days before the optician could see me. He shone a lamp in my eye: yes, there was a shred of membrane, the aqueous – it can detach without warning in an extremely myopic eye. Not vitreous? No, aqueous, and it would not get any worse, nor was my sight going – it could even be good news, the aqueous having come away without taking any of the retina with it. On the wall of the darkened room by some trick of projection, or so I see it now in my mind's eye (it must have been some mirrored kind of ophthalmoscope), he gave me a look into the blood red pit of my own eye. The same, or worse, he said, a detached retina, might happen any day in the other one. The 'floater' could not be got out, though it might be partly absorbed in time and anyway, I could live with it. I was unconvinced. Everywhere I looked it hung, a black shag. But so it is. These days I barely see it. Of its own accord my eye turns a blind eye.

A news flash. For millions of years a pale fish, *Astyanax mexicanus*, has lived and died blind in sea caves off the coast of Mexico. In the egg it grows eyes that are lost, like the human tail, before birth. Others of the same species living near the surface have eyes and do see. When the lens from the eye of one of these fish was implanted in a cave fish, an eye began developing within days under the flap of skin, and in two months it had a pupil, iris and cornea. Yes, but could it *see?*

The stars, invisible in daylight, can be seen from the bottom of a deep well.
'ABD AL-JABBAH

In the hollow eye, a green ball, an afterimage. But in the mind's eye it stays red, an imprint of the inner screen of flesh reflected as a planet afloat in space, the pallor of the full moon in a webbing of red, a microcosm, rivers of blood, replenishing eyesight.

Memorandum that I have first to show the distance of the sun from the earth and by means of one of its rays passing through a small hole into a dark place to discover its exact dimensions, and in addition to this by means of the sphere of water to calculate the size of the earth.

And the size of the moon I shall discover as I discover that of the sun, that is by means of its ray at midnight when it is at the full.
LEONARDO DA VINCI

The *sphere of water, aqueous sphere, la spera dell'acqua.* The aqueous perceived as solid – as in another sense, ripples are in a photograph – patterns whose whole being is movement, caught and fixed like waves, water and sand fixed in flows of rock. The aqueous seen through, seen past, no longer seen at all.

Quoi qu'elle donne à voir et quelle que soit sa manière, une photo est toujours invisible: ce n'est pas elle qu'on voit.

Whatever it grants to vision and whatever its manner, a photograph is always invisible: it is not it that we see.
ROLAND BARTHES

(Ceci n'est pas une photographie.)

Our visual world hardly ever appears to us in pure black and white – in 'grayscale', as it says in my printer window, a beautiful new word that calls fish to mind, silverfish. How would it be to see the world with new eyes? Meaning different eyes – as mine are to each other, if it comes to that, the one seeing all cool colours where the other sees warm, never quite seeing eye to eye – but more than that, with entirely other eyes, like those of dogs, amber eyes in a world drained of colour (or is it really only of red?), or honeybees whose faceted eyes – *articulate and latticed eyes*, in Sir Thomas Browne's fine flourish – see the cool colours as far as ultraviolet but no red, which is black to them. Are there eyes that only see in ultraviolet, in a world without shadow where every stone is a jewel? Or infrared, in a world of incandescences? There are any number of beings, like owls, and bats, whose dark-adapted eyes dazzle, as good as blind in daylight. Are the eyes of fast-moving creatures, dragonflies, hummingbirds, kingfishers, adapted as well, so that they see in slow-motion, as on film, what to us is only a blur? If so then the kingfisher will dive headlong and the splash will raise an afterimage of him over the surface on wings of glass, plumage and water flounces falling, until the real bird breaks through with his fish and again a glass bird is left shimmering in a mirror of air, in real time – real to the bird. One bird, repeating.

Throughout the *Iliad* and *Odyssey* the goddess who keeps Odysseus safely on course is γλαυκωπις Αθηνη, as a rule translated as 'flashing-eyed' Athene. But γλαυξ, *glaux*, her votive bird, is 'owl', so surely she is owl-eyed (just as Hera is ox-eyed, βοωπις)? Be that as it may, according to where it lives her little owl, *Athene noctua*, is surnamed *glaux*, *saharae*, *lilith*, *solitudinis*, *spilogastra* or *somaliensis*.

Sun after rain on the bare fig tree silvering spangling cobwebbing.

Grayscale. The grey mottle of fog I see in the dark, we all see, whether our eyes are open or shut. Nothing abnormal. It even has a name of its own, *Eigengrau* – variously, 'brain grey', 'subjective grey', 'dark light' and 'intrinsic dark light' and 'the threshold in the dark'.

Il faut te lever plus tôt, nourrice, si tu veux voir un monde sans couleurs.

You have to get up earlier, Nurse, if you want to see a world without colours.
JEAN ANOUILH, *ANTIGONE*

I shot in blind hope months ago, no, years, into the noon sun, a reel of close-ups of a white fog wreathing through casuarinas along a lake. And now in the darkroom, the apparition of shapes in the red tray, fog webs, reeds and furry needles dusted over with light like pollen, a nest of spangles in a bark armpit – a pale shape I had never noticed was there on the day – it must have been there – a nakedness in the thickening of the shadows, a billow of cloud underwater, faint at first, a quivering of silken flanks opening and closing with each breath of the water, parting on a vision of intricate bone.

Apparition, vision – οπτασια.

Low tide, and the rocks of the cliff at sunset, pale honey in this light, reflect in the pools as dark honey, a little darker than where they are still wet in the air.

On the cover of *Camera Lucida* stands a man in a black hat, a bowler hat, except that for a head he has a bellows camera gazing out of its one lustrous gold-ringed eye. *This is not a camera.* In fact, on the grounds of having no experience with the camera he has ruled out any speculation here about the photographer's way of seeing. Instead he expands on the experience of being the 'Spectator' of certain photographs old and new, taken by others, some of which are in the book in their original black and white: colour he rejects like the wig and rouge on a cadaver, a stain on *la vérité originelle du Noir-et-Blanc*. What is vital is the authenticity. Nothing but those very light rays once reflected off a subject on that given day are to reach out and touch him, the onlooker, in an almost mystical transmission. What one sees in any photograph, he argues, is never the photograph but the subject, the 'referent' (a certitude that we have lost in this day of the digital image). I wonder, though, if there is not more scope than he allows, whether one's response may not be more of a continuum, an awareness that shifts between the subject and the physicality of the made object itself. By becoming a photographer, even once – one photograph – one has lost the innocence of the spectator's eye and become complicit in the photograph-as-such. Not to mention the photograph-to-be, as Idea, latent in the mind's eye, the *gostly eye* of the photographer with a finger on the shutter or red-handed in the darkroom. In a sunset afterglow print after print comes to watery life, not one a perfect incarnation of the photograph in the mind's eye, even after a whole run of prints, infinite variations of the one finite shot – long hours of deepening a shadow here with a cone of light hovering over it, and lightening one there with the shadow, kept moving to avoid sharp edges, of an illuminated hand.

{L}a Photographie a quelque chose à voir avec la résurrection: ne peut-on dire d'elle ce que disaient les Byzantins de l'image du Christ dont le Suaire de Turin est imprégné, à savoir qu'elle n'était pas faite de main d'homme, acheïropoïétos*?*

{P}hotography has something to do with resurrection: might it not be said of it what the Byzantines said of the image of Christ with which the Shroud of Turin is impregnated, namely that it was not made by the hand of man, αχειροποιητος*?*
ROLAND BARTHES

The translation on to solid film and paper – linen, silk – of what has been projected in flight on to the eye's retina. What is changed, either lost or gained, or conceivably both, in these translations into a silent language that the eye – what Barthes might have called *the eye of man* – has had to learn. The eye jibs, then accommodates, learns by what it has learnt, as does the mind.

(*Le Noir-et-Blanc*, 'black-and-white', but in Greek the other way round, ασπρομαυρος. And *pas faite de main d'homme*, not made by the hand of man – but in Greek *not handmade*.)

At a Gauguin centenary exhibition in Auckland, *Pages from the Pacific*, they showed frail works on paper, woodcuts and ink-and-wash, a notebook dismembered and hung up as if to dry leaf by leaf in section in a dim room, *verso* and *recto*, yellowing membranes whose pigments, however faint, burned like stained glass. *Translucide.* A signature in the visitors' book: *Paul Gauguin, Paris*, and a quotation on the wall: *A critic at my house sees some paintings. Greatly perturbed, he asks for my drawings. My drawings! Never! They are my letters, my secrets. The public man – the private man... What if you do often see me quite naked; that is no argument.* These pages, then, were a flayed hide, in lampshade strips.

Mortally ill towards the end of his life Gauguin gave one of his rare visitors on Hiva Oa, a Hungarian fellow-painter, a proof of a woodcut that he printed off for him then and there, as the Hungarian later wrote on the back, *in the most primitive manner*, by lying on it in bed for the whole three hours of the visit. The print, *Nave nave Fenua*, was handed over at midnight still warm, reeking of ink and paper and male sweat on skin, *l'homme public, l'homme intime.* Where is it now, that relic, that last imprint of the living man?

The baleful stoneware statue he had made in France on his brief return – *Oviri*, 'Savage' – had gone unsold. Three years before he died he wrote and asked in vain for it to be sent out to Tahiti to go on his tomb. Now a cast of it guards his stone grave on Hiva Oa: Oviri, goddess of death, a female nude and counterpart, androgynous, an earthen self-portrait with the blank stare of a corpse. She clutches a wolf cub to her belly. At her feet is a fullgrown wolf with its muzzle agape in a blood-stained scream. He was a lone wolf, he liked to say, the lean wolf in Aesop's fable who will suffer no collar – *le Loup maigre, sans collier*. Underfoot he is long bones and a ring of teeth in a white shell.

Dunt and creak of an unseen rowboat, water-drips, hollow sounds, secretive household night sounds out of a blind space, as if the lake were the floor of a dim room.

The silence of the language of the photograph is heavier in black and white than in colour – why? Is it because black and white is that much more remote from the living reality we see? The composure, the depth, transfixity, and graininess, fine or coarse, of photographic surfaces, is like bare skin. Taken back to 'grayscale' these surfaces then reveal a subject, a world, drained of everything but contrast. This is true of slides most of all, transparencies, *diapositives*, whose image as it shafts through the air, not bonded to any surface, comes closest to the essence of sight. There is already a difference in clarity and intensity between the print and the slide looked at as a single frame of film in the hand, the one in a coating of milk and the other in water, in ice. But the slide in action, projected through space as if painted on the air, appears as pure light and shade, transitional, a reflection in the mind's eye.

Diaphanous, διαφανης.

A bottled spider grown to human size, a jinn, a lantern of fire, a Pacific octopus in the Vancouver aquarium – I spent a day there just gazing in at her without so much as putting a camera to my eye, for very shame. She was, or is – it was years ago but they are long-lived – captivity incarnate, and she knows, she is a seaborn creature after all, as fluent in herself as the sea, pouring herself along ahead. And at first, at rest, quite invisible. So that you falter in front of her tank, seeing nothing in there but a rock cave, a drift of little fish, when suddenly a slug is swelling out of a rock, owl-shaggy and horned, long vines studded with grapes for arms and slit eyes rolling in ink, a raptor's beak. She sees you, the shadowy watcher at the window, her eyes lock on – the wily, exploratory mind behind them, the long memory, shrivelled to an actuality of glass. Here she comes oozing up to it and the stony mantle opens in a flare of purple, crimson, crinkling, undulating, and she is lapped in the folds of herself like a sari, Draupadi's everwinding, ever-unwinding sari, in rags of reflection. In her rampage she is clamping tentacles high on the glass and slapping it with her blunt head, butting and butting, bursting open in petals like a tiger lily, molten. She who has not one drop of blood in her, she is awash in blood.

One gold spill of light through low cloud into the water, almost still, twitchings of its fish-skin, a wedge of furrow behind a duck. A pair of herons wading now at my back, now ahead of me, watchful, taking off in another leggy, shawled skim of flight when I go too close.

What if you lost your colour vision gradually, or overnight, as has been known to happen? A universal lack of colour – it would mean that the particular beauty of black and white, no less than that of colour, was lost on you forever. The beauty of black and white is what is strange about it, what is missing, eliminated, laid bare, as in sculpture.

Films and photographic papers have what is called a 'spectral sensitivity' which is measurable. It appears in the form of a graph in the catalogue, as white parabolas on black, loops of filament.

Why is it that light does not pass through anything thick, although it is less substantial and travels farther and more quickly, but sound does pass through? Is it because light travels in a straight line, so that, if anything obstructs its straight course, it is completely shut off, whereas sound can also travel in a line which is not straight because it is breath?
ARISTOTLE

Horn sonorities, a sun fog in the bay, ships syncopations halts.

The variables of the equation are the intensity of the light, the diameter of the lens, the distance of the subject, the length of time of the exposure. The projected image – what passes through the lens – pupil, pinhole – will arrive upside down on the surface because the light enters in a straight line at an angle determined by its height in relation to the pinhole. A circle of light, however minute, is projected from any single point of a subject: a *circle of confusion.* Confusion is a matter of degree, relative to the size of the pinhole. The narrowest pinhole will admit some loosening of the light rays, which reach the wall – retina, roll of film – not as points but spread out into circles. The smaller the hole, the smaller each individual circle of confusion and the sharper the image. The larger the hole, the larger the circles of confusion. If they are so large that they overlap, the effect is fuzzy, a myopic image. Take two diagrams of a man standing outside a room, a man, say, in a black hat, whose image is projected through a small and a large pinhole in a wall on to the back wall of the same room. In each case the lines of light fanning from the crown of his hat to his soles will cross to make two triangles, a double fan joined at the pinhole. Those that enter the small pinhole reassemble the man's image upside down in tight clusters, bubbles of image like frogspawn, on the far wall. The same man projected through the large pinhole is a blur, a mass of bubbles like rain in water, dissolved in his circles of confusion.

Vermeer may well have had the use of a camera obscura.

The only evidence is circumstantial, to the naked eye. Sprinkles of light on the hull of the barge to the far right of *A View of Delft*, for example, look like *pointilles*, circles of confusion, a distinctive dazzle usual in highlights when seen projected in a camera obscura. The strange sense of simultaneous nearness and farness, precision and flimsiness, the presence in it of a body of air, all on a fine skin drawn out tight – even the sprinkles – of this painting would resurface nearly two centuries on in the photos Henry Fox Talbot would take with his box camera obscuras, his 'mousetraps' – the 'Sun Pictures' of Loch Katrine in particular, with their unearthly shimmer, like dragonflies on the water surface, the glassy black of the bank in the shade and its reflection in a wash of ink. Others prefer to think that Vermeer, like da Vinci, used mirrors. Still others deny that he used any optical aids at all.

In May 1930 a bloodvessel burst in Munch's right eye, and caused almost total blindness, as his left eye was already weak...The result was a series of drawings built up with the help of spectral colours grouped together in concentric circles. He portrayed the projection in the interior of his damaged eye on a sheet of paper. In the centre he drew the damaged part, often in the form of a bird.
ARNE EGGUM

Death is pitch black. Colour and light are one. To be a painter is to work with rays of light. To die – perhaps that's like having

your eyes poked out. You can't see anymore – perhaps like being thrown into a cellar.
EDVARD MUNCH

Empedokles of Akragas in Sicily likened the eye in its housing of bone and clear horn to a storm lantern with panes to break the wind: so too was *the elemental fire, the round pupil, confined within membranes and delicate tissues, which are pierced through and through with wondrous passages. They keep out the deep water that surrounds the pupil, but they let through the fire...*

More often than not Munch painted his darkness blue, a deep and enveloping wave-on-wave midnight blue. He was struck, he once told a friend, by the way the Greeks, living life as they did in the full sun, had thought of death as blue and not black as it is in the grey North. *Blue death closed his eyes*, he had read in the *Iliad*. But where? Death after death in the *Iliad* is dark: *the shades of death*, *dark death*, *the darkness of death* that covered the eyes of so many, and death's dark jaws, hands, and shrouds. Unless darkness, σκοτος, and blueness were one and the same (a blue cloak was worn for mourning)? Twilight is blue, after all, a candle, a lamp, a lantern in the night, any red gold flaminess, will draw out the blue in its surroundings. On the other hand, some scholars have doubted that the Greeks even saw blue as we see it. Skies in Homer are metallic and his seas black, or white, purple, or crimson – πορφυρεος –

and wine-dark, not blue, when the obvious word, surely, obvious to us, would have been blue, κυανος, deep dark blue. Then again, a blind man might well see a sky as a furnace, molten, and a jug of wine as a turbulence of acridity – just as a poet might sidestep the obvious. He does have κυανος in the *Iliad*, but this is for the dark veil of Thetis, for Hector's dark mane trailing in the dust of Troy. Blue black, then, midnight blue, blackness and blueness overlapping?

κυανοχαιτης – dark-maned, dark-haired, of the sea god Poseidon
κυανοπεπλος – dark-veiled, of Demeter in mourning for her daughter
κυανος – lapis lazuli
κυανεος θαλαμος – the dark chamber of Persephone (in Sappho)

Sappho, Σαπφω, was so named not after sapphire but lapis lazuli, for her dark skin, eyes, hair. Φεροεφονας κυανεος θαλαμος – *Fersefone's dark chamber* – is from an epitaph of hers: *This is the dust of Timas who before she could be married was led to Fersefone's dark chamber*... Φεροε- is *the one who brings*, and -φονας is the possessive of -φονη. This is not *voice – phone* meaning 'voice' has an omega, ω: φωνη. This is φονη, φονος meaning *death, murder, slaughter*. This chamber is the black earth, the pit, the womb, Sheol, the Hades that Christ harrows at Eastertide.

Is Persephone a counterpart of the Gaelic Cailleach, 'Veiled One', the winter hag embodied in standing stones, with a blue black face under the veil – the Crone who is also the spring Bride?

The 'Crone' is 'carrion', they are one and the same. (*Caille*, 'veil' – calyptra?)

Aristotle's rainbow, ιρις, has κυανος for blue, πορφυρεος for crimson, the Tyrian sea-purple. The *chasms and trenches and blood-red colours*, the *torches and stars* inflaming the sky on clear nights – he must have seen the aurora borealis – are the effect of a dense mass of air against the dark blue, κυανος, or inky black, μελαν, of space, whose fires are hazed over, mirroring. Plato's dark wilderness where the Styx has its source is κυανος. Is death ever κυανος (as in the pallor, cyanosis, of the dying)? In the *Iliad* one death at least is purple – πορφυρεος θανατος.

RED.
792.
We are here to forget everything that borders on yellow or blue. We are to imagine an absolutely pure red, like fine carmine suffered to dry on white porcelain. We have called this colour 'purpur' by way of distinction, although we are quite aware that the purple of the ancients inclined more to blue.
GOETHE

Mehr Licht. Darkness covered his eyes. Τον δε σκοτος οσσε καλυψε.

Not every man has gentians in his house
in soft September, at slow, sad Michaelmas.
Bavarian gentians, tall and dark, but dark
darkening the daytime torch-like with the smoking blueness of
Pluto's gloom,
ribbed hellish flowers erect, with their blaze of darkness spread blue,
blown flat into points, by the heavy white draught of the day.
D H LAWRENCE

Early Chinese sages such as Mo Ti speculated on the pinhole and the way that light scatters, but only ever in straight lines, and why the projected image is inverted. The Egyptians and the contending schools of the Greeks evolved a discipline of optics by a blend of guesswork and blind faith, enquiry and, increasingly, geometry. When the Library of Alexandria, that great Pharos of the mind and storehouse of heathen scholarship, went up in flames, much of Plato survived, along with Aristotle and his school, including, in those lists of puzzles, the *Problems* – δια τι, δια τι, why, why? – the mysteries of light and shadow and the behaviour of the pinhole. And yet those mysteries went unsolved, the pinhole an open secret, all through the Dark Ages and beyond, while the lamp of science was smothered all over Europe.

It shone on in the Middle East, where Arab scholars and scribes, mathematicians and astronomers kept the flame, salvaging what withering relics of Greek thought they could and translating them into Arabic, copying and studying them and going on where they left off. One of the greatest was Abou Ali Al Hassan ('Alhazen') Ibn Al Haytham, a scholar remarkable for his scope and lucidity and his empirical cast of mind. Born in Basra in the ninth century, he lived for most of his long life in Cairo, where he made the first advances in many hundreds of years on both Euclid and Ptolemy of Alexandria. He was to live on in the Islamic world as a genius of an astronomer, a second Ptolemy; but in the West, eventually, as the founding father of the new optics. Few of his manuscripts have survived, and the desert sands might well have buried his *Book of Optics*, *Kitab al-Manazir*, altogether, but for the lucky chance that one came into the hands of a European translator from the Arabic who brought his Latin version west, where it could kindle in a few bold eccentric spirits, Friar Roger Bacon for one.

Bacon was a child of the Middle Ages, a dreamer with a Renaissance thirst for practical knowledge: an alchemist and a tinkerer with lenses, prisms, mirrors, burning-mirrors, fireworks and the pinhole for watching the solar eclipse; a monk who took experiment – not reason, not faith – as his *domina* and marooned himself by night in the Isis at Oxford – by Folly Bridge no less – in his study *invironed with waters and there to take the altitude and distance of stars and make use of it for his own convenience*...For his pains his fellow Franciscans clapped their 'Negromancier' in gaol, where he died after fourteen years, unrepentant.

In a worde, a man may make an infinite sort of such things: as bridges over Rivers without postes or pillers, and instruments and engins never heard of before.

But physicall figurations are far more strange: for in such maner may we frame perspectives and looking-glasses, that one thing shall appeare to be many, as one man shall seeme a whole armie, and divers Sunnes and Moones, yea, as many as wee please, shall appeare at one time: for in such wise sometimes are the vapours figured, that two or three Sunnes, and two Moones appeare together in the ayre...

ROGER BACON, *AN EXCELLENT DISCOURSE OF THE ADMIRABLE FORCE AND EFFICACIE OF ART AND NATURE*

Enough, then, to have kindled the spark, but even so it was a very piecemeal *Kitab al-Manazir*. Compounding the loss was the disappearance of Alhazen's summary of a lost passage in the *Optics* of Ptolemy – itself lost by the ninth century on the way from Greek into Arabic – that might have shed new light. A double loss, loss on loss, as in the vanishing images of mirrors in mirrors in a mirror. And yet, and yet. One long-vanished mirror – a treatise in Greek, *On Mirrors*, by Archimedes, who once used mirrors to burn a whole Roman fleet to ashes in Syracuse harbour – lost, short of a miracle, in antiquity, has recently reappeared. The miracle began in Istanbul in 1906, with the chance discovery of a copy of a copy written in Greek on parchment, parts of it known until then only in Latin translation, and some not at all. It was enshrined in a prayer book, the decaying corpse of a prayer book, written and resewn after the Fourth Crusade sacked Constantinople in 1204, by some resourceful monk who scrounged a relic of parchment and scrubbed off the pagan science in order to veil it in faith, a palimpsest in gall iron ink, and inadvertently preserved it. Invisible under the skin, beyond the reach of his scraper, his herbs and juices and milks, lies the original writing in the same gall iron ink, *On Mirrors,* and much else. The prayer book survived fire and water, six centuries in the desert monastery of Mar Saba, mould, rot, mutilation and war with its secret intact – only to go missing again, sold or stolen, for most of the last century. Now that it has resurfaced, the technologies being brought to bear on it include magnetic and multispectral imaging under infrared and ultraviolet light.

Make the visible invisible, the invisible visible.

Art does not reproduce the visible; rather, it makes visible.
PAUL KLEE

Wir sind die Bienen des Unsichtbaren. Nous butinons éperdument le miel du visible, pour l'accumuler dans la grande ruche d'or de l'Invisible.

We are the bees of the Invisible. We forage frantically for the honey of the visible, to store it in the great golden hive of the Invisible.
RAINER MARIA RILKE, *LETTERS*

In the Byzantine ikons the Christ Child is a grown man in miniature, a doll enthroned in the sombre lap of the Mother of God. Their eyes are sunk in shadow. She is old, he in his first youth, a homunculus with an ageless face, never a baby, let alone a Renaissance *bambino*. What incongruity! Surely the ikonographers knew better? They did, as did the worshippers. They knew that the ikon is for lifting the mind's eye to the mystery beyond our earthly reality, to the divine. To such an eye the chubby *bambino* is the incongruity.

In Christian Europe the intellectual mainstream, steeped in the ancient philosophers, went on living in a visible world that shed multiple self-images, 'idols', 'rinds', 'husks', into the seeing eye, the eye in turn sending out its own rays into the world, an inner fire meeting the outer fire of day, like to like, apprehending the visible. To Galen's eye these rays were threads of light as fine as gossamer; to Euclid's they made a cone whose apex was the eye; to Ptolemy of Alexandria they made – what else? – a pyramid. All wrong,

Alhazen had concluded by the eleventh century: the visual ray was an illusion and the eye a purely receptive organ. He laid its anatomy bare.

Here was a man living and working inside the mazes of light and shadow that were the Cairo of his day, the world of the bazaar and the shadow-play with its jointed puppets, backcloth and lantern, the world of the *Thousand and One Nights*, multiple worlds of illusion, of truth. Were they one and the same? *Optical illusion is optical truth!* – so Goethe, himself short-sighted, would in time, far into the future, come to see. No problem there for Alhazen, busy dissecting, and paying particular attention, besides, to the phenomenon of the afterimage – which Aristotle had ranked with things seen in dreams among the sense impressions that lag behind their cause (without noticing that it was negative, black for white, red for green), and which would inspire Goethe's impassioned forays into optics.

Alhazen had his blind spot even so; and it was on the retina. He believed the crystalline lens to be the seat of vision, because that was the point where the rays that made up an image converged before crossing over to enter the chamber of the eye – upside down and back to front. But that was not how anyone saw the image, so how, where, was it righted? He was willing enough to disbelieve his eyes, if he had proof. He was a meticulous experimenter, a man for whom the 'dark chamber', *al-bayt al-muzlim*, was as familiar as the shadow-play of the bazaar. He had used it to observe the eclipse of the sun by way of tackling the problem

Aristotle saw in the crescent-shaped images; and he knew that the projected image of the sun would not harm the eyes. He also knew that the crescent moon would cast a crescent image, a very faint one. He observed the distinct shapes of light cast through a pinhole at angles by a row of candles and drew his diagrams and conclusions. But if he ever saw that the image – *sura* – was upside down, and a clear picture, not just a shape of dissolving light; and if he ever saw through the crystal of the lens into the secret hidden in the red backcloth of the chamber of the eye, no word has come down to us.

52.

I had entered an inn towards evening, and, as a well-favoured girl, with a brilliantly fair complexion, black hair, and a scarlet bodice, came into the room, I looked attentively at her as she stood before me at some distance in half shadow. As she presently afterwards turned away, I saw on the white wall, which was now before me, a black face surrounded with a bright light, while the dress of the perfectly distinct figure appeared of a beautiful sea-green.

GOETHE

It was as if every image had a latent, ghostly, opposite self only visible once the image was gone, and then only for the blink of an eye. As for that man in the inn with the avid enveloping gaze – when Munch had a similar experience it was with a red-green billiard table – what image does that man leave in the mind'e eye? Isn't it – isn't it Faust?

So it fell to Leonardo, four centuries after Alhazen died, to be the one to declare the eye a living camera obscura. He built a shed to show how the image of the sunlit world was cast, reduced and upside down, through a pinhole on to a translucent screen ready to be traced, remarking, *The same happens inside the pupil.* He gave his device a name, *oculus artificialis*. It went under a variety of names, *conclave obscurum*, *cubiculum tenebricosum*, *camera clausa*, until Kepler – who built a portable one in a little black tent (and knew his Alhazen) – came up with the resonant *camera obscura* – and, at long last, with the role of *the concave reddish surface of the retina* in sight. Bullseye!

An eye filled with its vision. And still, like love in the Chekhov story, *a great mystery.*

Kepler wrote his own epitaph:
Mensus eram coelos, nunc Terrae metior umbras
Mens coelestis erat, corporis umbra jacet.

I scanned all heaven, now I scan the shadows of the Earth.
The mind was of heaven, the body's shadow lies here.

Mens, mensus. And why is this *mens* so often rendered as 'soul' (*anima*)?

(Plotinos was punning too, with ερως, love, ορασις, vision.)

Necromancy, from νεκρο, dead, and μαντης, diviner – the art of conjuring a corpse or skull or a raised ghost to reveal what is safer hidden – changed in Middle English into *nigromancie*, the black art, black magic, from confusion with the Latin *niger*.

We that be citizens of Rome, have a sacred and solemne manner and use among us, To close up their Eies that lie a dying, and are giving up the ghost; and when they be brought to the funerall fire, to open them againe. The reason of this ceremonious custoume, is grounded hereupon, That as it is not meet for men alive to have the last view of a mans Eie in his death, so it is as great an offence to hide them from heaven, unto which this honour is due, & the body now presented.

PLINY, *THE HISTORIE OF THE WORLD*

22 *The light of the body is the eye: if therefore thine eye be single, thy whole body shall be full of light.*
23 *But if thine eye be evil, thy whole body shall be full of darkness. If therefore the light that is in thee be darkness, how great* is *that darkness!*

THE GOSPEL ACCORDING TO SAINT MATTHEW

The rare eclipse of the sun, the shawl of darkness in a slow tide, the alarm of birds and animals, the cringing of plants, the hush as the world stops still: and in the population, along with the danger of going blind, the mounting scream, an urge like vertigo, to take a mad leap into oblivion – a total eclipse of the eyes, forever – and stare, regardless. Mirrors were no use, everyone knew that the sun's face even in a mirror would turn all eyes to stone. In the Middle Ages people made do with stained glass and a dark sun full of bubbles, veins, flecks. Here and there, however, a solitary astronomer – Bacon in Oxford, Saint-Cloud in Paris, Rabbi Levi Ben Gershon (Leon de Bagnois, Gersonides) in Arles, Maurolico ('black wolf') in Messina – was seeing through a pinhole a solar eclipse clear as a mirror on the wall.

Even the Church in Renaissance Italy played its part, in its determination to reform the calendar once and for all and settle the perennial discord over the dating of Easter. A movable feast based on Passover, Easter is worked out by juggling the dates of the full moon and the spring equinox in a given year. The moon of course is inconstant, rising and setting, waxing and waning in a rhythm of its own, just as regular, but not, or not obviously, in time with the sun; and while the moon dances, the sun marches straight ahead. But if every day at noon as the year swings round an image of the sun can be made to fall on a straight line advancing north, retreating south, a living diagram, then its progress is clear to see and record, and the exact date of the spring equinox – and therefore Easter – at that place can be pinpointed for all time.

A high dark vault of space had to be found, and a handful of brilliant astronomers who could put a hole in the roof or lantern or high in the wall of a suitable church or cathedral exactly where it would let the sun throw its clear face on the floor of the nave at noon. The best known example is the limpid rose-russet and ivory basilica of San Petronio in Bologna, stately and lovely in its flesh tones and honeycomb paving, a vast camera obscura, only relatively dark, however, where the one hot shaft of sun lands in an airy tissue of arch and pillar and sifted light and shade, reverberating light. The sunspot would then make its way between midsummer and midwinter along a timeline of noons that would be calibrated, inscribed, illuminated with the signs of the zodiac, inlaid in marble with a seam of gold.

The whole monumentally simple device, hole, sunline and stoneline – as if some god or angel were up there fishing in a dark hole, a well, and had just nailed himself a flounder on a golden spear – is a *meridiana*, a sundial.

The sharp-eyed were quick to see something else: how the sun's image changes in size along the line, a slight waxing and waning as its distance from the earth changes, the further away the smaller. Kepler was right about an elliptical, not circular, orbit in space and here lay the proof the astronomers were after! An epiphany of the sun, lodged in the heart of the church.

As Rodin's secretary, the young poet Rilke went with him one frosty, sunless midwinter morning in 1906 on the train to see Chartres Cathedral, and an angel caught his eye, *L'Ange du Méridien*, as his poem calls it, the Angel of the

Sundial – a stone being, a spirit being as serenely oblivious of human life and time as he was of night or day – while, caught there in an abrupt brawl of wind, buffeted, sculptor and poet *stood like damned souls compared with the angel holding out his dial so blissfully to a sun that he always saw...*

Just the first impression, the way it rises up, as in a great cloak, and the first detail, a slim weatherbeaten angel holding out a sundial exposed to the day's whole round of hours, and above it one sees, infinitely beautiful still in its fading, the deep smile of his joyfully serving face, like sky mirroring itself...

RAINER MARIA RILKE, *LETTERS 1892–1910*

Il sole no si move.
The sun does not move.

In every spot in which the sun sees the water the water also sees the sun, and in each of its parts it can present the sun's image to the eye.

LEONARDO DA VINCI

The only sun in a Greek Orthodox church is in the apex, the dome of heaven, in the form of a man, Χριστος Παντοκρατορας, Christ Almighty, a dark sun.

The mollusc *Nautilus* – ναυτιλος, 'sailor' – floats deep down in a shell of coils, tiger-striped outside, fluted inside with successively vacated chambers that it smooths over in mother in pearl, a living fossil, the last of the ancient order of the nautiloids. It bobs like a severed head. A close relative of the paper nautilus *Argonauta* – and of the cuttlefish *Sepia*, but with no ink sac for throwing out a black veil – the nautilus propels itself rocking, rising and falling in the water column by juggling the air and water in its chambers. It mates face to face, clamping on with some of its ninety-odd tentacles. Its flat eyes tilt on stalks to keep the image steady, and have no lens and no cornea. The eye of the nautilus is the first eye, the earliest living eye, a pinhole so open that the water flows in and out. What does an eye see that has the whole sea for a lens?

One day when they had celebrated their Masses, a pillar in the sea appeared to them that seemed to be not far distant. Still it took them three days to come up to it. When the man of God approached it he tried to see the top of it – but he could not, it was so high. It was higher than the sky. Moreover a wide-meshed net was wrapped around it. The mesh was so wide that the boat could pass through its openings. They could not decide of what substance the net was made. It had the colour of silver, but they thought that it seemed harder than marble. The pillar was of bright crystal…

When they had gone in and looked around here and there, the sea was as clear to them as glass, so that they could see everything that was underneath. They could examine the foundations of

the pillar and also the edge of the net lying on the sea bed. The light of the sun was as bright below as above the water.
NAVIGATIO SANCTI BRENDANI ABBATIS

Chiaroscuro of the full eclipse of the moon, a bronze mirror damascened in its slow procession through the earth's shadow and, yes, its light, because the earth, while blocking the sun, is refracting red sunlight from the atmosphere into the shadow cone and on to the passing moon.

Let us see what facts Megalithic man had as a basis for his cosmology. Men of scientific bent living on the trade routes of north-western Europe were in a position to glean information from far afield. They would hear that from the northern Island of Unst the moon at the major standstill appeared to be circumpolar for a few days. Anyone can make the observation that the shadow of his own head falling on an object, no matter what its shape, appears circular and anyone who has, from the water level, watched a boat receding knows that it eventually vanishes; he knows that if he climbs a hill the boat will come again into view. He would know that eclipses of the moon occur at full moon and that the shadow as it crosses the moon is seen to be circular. This might lead to the thought 'my head is spherical and its shadow is always circular. The sun is behind me. Perhaps I am seeing a shadow of the earth on the moon.' The memory of the vanishing boat and the circumpolar moon could have suggested that the earth was a sphere.
ALEXANDER THOM

Aristotle first put in writing the idea that the crescent shadow that the earth makes on the moon in an eclipse can only mean that the earth is a sphere. Empedokles held that *the sun is not fire in its nature, but a reflection of fire, like that which takes place in water. And he says the moon consists of air that has been shut up by fire, for this becomes solid like hail; and its light it gets from the sun*. Alhazen, in his treatise *On the Mark on the Face of the Moon*, noting that the moon alone among the heavenly bodies has no light of its own, asked whether the dark mass on the surface could be a cloud, a reflection – *sura* – of seas or mountains on earth, the shadow of mountains on the moon, or a sign that the moon is translucent and the dark shape is something dark behind it in space, showing through. Some parts of the moon might be denser than others – *as though one part were alabaster*, as Leonardo put it in his notebooks, *and others like crystal or glass* – and hold and reflect more light. So Aristotle thought; although Leonardo disagreed, on the grounds that in that case the darker and lighter spots would be constantly moving in accordance with the sun and moon. He saw the moon as clothed in water, an *aqueous sphere* that caught the sun and raised clouds, waves darkening in a storm; while the *moon's night* that we see, the old moon inside the crescent of the new, was a reflection off the waters of the earth.

If the eye were as large as the aqueous sphere, it would see the whole water surface shine with the splendour of the solar image.
LEONARDO DA VINCI

Still as a slave before his lord,
The ocean hath no blast;
His great bright eye most silently
Up to the Moon is cast –
SAMUEL TAYLOR COLERIDGE, *THE ANCIENT MARINER*

Lenses to gather and refract light. Philolaos the Pythagorean was another who saw the sun around which the earth revolved not as fire but as rock crystal, a vast lens taking in the ambient ethereal invisible sun of the universe – the true Fire and Hearth of the World, Guardhouse of Zeus and Meeting Place, Mother of the Gods, Altar – and beaming it through space. That outer sun and its burning glass, he said, made two suns – three, if the sunlight refracted down to us in rays counts as 'sun': image of an image, ειδωλον ειδωλου, and a step beyond Plato's Cave, out into a sun beyond visibility. To Aristotle, on the other hand, the cosmos was a fixed earth at the core of revolving crystal spheres studded with sun and moon and stars. Others of his time and earlier saw these as so many lamps kindled and rekindled every day in celestial bowls, σκαφαι, from the smoky luminous exhalations of the sea, so much closer to fire than water – much as the steam must have appeared by torchlight or a shaft of sun, in ritual immersions in stone basins in the dark of caves and stone mounds. Steam, as a fusion of elements in unstable balance, water and air and fire, between states of being, has always been a shamanic threshold, like the rainbow and the rising and setting sun. Unless what the basins were there for was the steaming blood of the sacrifice – that too was a threshold.

And there are living beings of fire among the daimons.
PLOTINOS

Over time Ptolemy of Alexandria's compendium of mathematical astronomy came to be known simply as Ο Μεγας Αστρονομος, *The Great Astronomer.* To his Arab heirs it was the Μεγιστος – *Greatest* – for short, with the Arabic *al-* in front making it *Almagest*, still its name worldwide. *I search with my mind*, wrote Ptolemy, *into the multitudinous revolving spirals of the stars.*

The Ptolemaic cosmos is firmly sphere on sphere, after Aristotle, with the earth at its heart. A rival, Aristarchos of Samos, working at Alexandria, has proposed a solar system, but Ptolemy ignores it. He can: he is the authority. His system, forged into an article of blind faith in the Alexandria of the Patriarchs, clamped on all Europe at the hands of Rome, will shackle astronomy for a thousand years and more. It might have been otherwise, and then, imagine! – one hinge in history, one day a Ptolemy who sees the sun stand still, and the soul of medieval Europe takes shape in an alternative universe.

(A universe with no Dante! No *Inferno*, *Purgatorio*, *Paradiso*.)

Like the Egyptians before them, the Arabs were a people of the desert rather than the sea. Won for the Caliph by the soldier poet Amr, the remains of Alexandria emerged from the conquest intact only to be abandoned when, as Governor, Amr turned his back on the sea in favour of an inland fort, the future Cairo. It was there when he was on the point of death that his friend asked him what he, Amr, had often wished he might ask of a thinking man on the point of death: what does it feel like to die? Amr's reply: *I feel as if the heaven lay close upon the earth and I between the two, breathing through the eye of a needle.*

The Arabs were not the Barbarians. The city was extinguished as a force and her soul ashes in the sands of time – the handiwork of Romans, finished off by the Desert Fathers in their piety – generations before Amr could breach her walls. In Arab hands she was to lie half asleep, half in the sun, half in the sea like so many marble mirror cities, for over a thousand years as if under a spell, a city of dreams out of the *Arabian Nights*.

The city was all white and bright by night as well as by day. By reason of the walls and pavements of white marble the people used to wear black garments; it was the glare of the marble that made the monks wear black. So too it was painful to go out by night…a tailor could see to thread his needle without a lamp. No one entered without a covering over his eyes.

(Now where men go in white from head to foot, the women pass as shadows.)

In no time the great lighthouse, one of the seven ancient wonders, was gone. First the lantern fell into the sea. Then an earthquake crumbled the tower of marble the medieval world would come to look back on as *the work of Jinns*.

The second storey was octagonal and entirely filled by the spiral ascent. Above that was the circular third storey, and above that the lantern. The lighting arrangements are uncertain. Visitors speak of a mysterious 'mirror' on the summit, which was even more wonderful than the building itself. What was this 'mirror'? Was it a polished steel reflector for the fire at night or for heliography by day? Some accounts describe it as made of finely wrought glass or transparent stone, and declare that a man sitting under it could see ships at sea that were invisible to the naked eye. A telescope? Is it possible that the great Alexandrian school of mathematics discovered the lens, and that their discovery was lost and forgotten when the Pharos fell? It is possible.
E M FORSTER, *ALEXANDRIA*

Legends hatched in the ruins. The Emperor of Byzantium, thwarted in his lust to retake the city by the power of the magic mirror, sent a spy to the Caliph to whisper that Alexander's treasure was buried in the foundations, and trick him into pulling it down. The tower stood on a 'glass crab' so huge that once a troop of horsemen rode into a crack in it and disappeared in the sea. *It beaconed to the imagination, not only to ships at sea,* wrote Forster, *and long after its light was extinguished memories of it glowed in the minds of men.* As El Manarah, it gave its name and form to the minaret.

When the tower fell, was the great eye lost in the sea, the silver jewel, the treasure, the mirror? Or was it smuggled away and mounted in some other tower on a far coast?

On its height a dome enshadowed me, and thence I saw my friends like stars.
I thought that the sea below me was a cloud, and that I had set up my tent in the midst of the heavens.
EL DERAOUI

Ο φαρος. *Le phare*, *il faro*, *el faro*, *o farol*. The tower took its name from the harbour island where it stood, passing it on in turn to every lighthouse in the path of the Romance languages. Like the chain of beacons lit from the earliest times on hills and islands and clifftops from the Mediterranean to the Atlantic, it burned wood, as did the light towers that the Romans went on to build in their hundreds, storm lanterns like eyes on the cliffs of the Empire. (Palamedes of Mysia on the Anatolian coast – he fought at Troy on the Greek side – is credited with the invention of the lighthouse.) Was there an arrangement of pulleys? Ramps and long chains of donkeys to lug the logs up and the ashes down? The relics keep their secret. The spiral huddled in its shell – in fact some say the Pharos may have had a double helix – lives on in its descendants worldwide. Over time the fire towers began to be lit with candles and oil lamps in a lantern of glass or horn. Like the Pharos, they were all fixed lights. The flashing, eclipsing or occulting light – *feu à éclipses* – is modern.

A magnificent new Library has been built on the site, the Bibliotheca Alexandrina, to be a window and a lamp for our time. But wouldn't we give the new lamp for the old any day? – it was the old one, wasn't it, that had the *jinni*?

To φαρος? – cloth, bedsheet and winding-sheet, cloak, veil (καλυπτρα) and sail of a ship.

The king of the island of Pharos in the *Odyssey* is Proteos the old sea god, a cave-dweller, shapeshifter and oracle, merged, some say, with the Egyptian god Osiris, as elsewhere with Dionysos – who according to Herakleitos is none other than Hades.

So one of the gods with hidden faces walked out of the water, and climbed the hill...and looked about. He looked up at the sun, and through the sun he saw the dark sun, the same that made the sun and the world, and will swallow it again like a draught of water.

D H LAWRENCE

They are all protean, the gods. On the wheel of the year they rise and fall, flesh into soul into flesh of the world –

this kosmos, lit with many lights, in the words of Plotinos. Dionysos, son of Zeus, was born a horned boy in a wreath of snakes. The Titans dropped a mirror in his lap to snare his other self, his soul and, undaunted by his frantic changes of shape, ripped him to shreds and ate him boiled in a cauldron or, some say, raw: a pomegranate tree sprang up out of his spilt blood. But Rhea, his grandmother, brought him back to life. Plotinos, speculating on why any soul should ever want to take flesh, a lower form of being, blamed Eros, Love, and used the mirror of Dionysos to show how souls, falling in love with their own image reflected in the round mirror of the world below, yearn so ardently to be united with the beloved that they fall to earth. Another kind of Fall, into Eden.

Maximus Tyrius says that Socrates calls Love the wizard, while Sappho uses the term μυθοπλοκος, *'fiction weaving'.*
EDWIN MARION COX

First I saw the mountains in the painting; then I saw the painting in the mountains.
CHINESE PROVERB

A charmed and mystified Chinese scholar during the Sung Dynasty, shortly before Alhazen's day, made the observation that a nearby pagoda was casting its image through a pinhole upside down, and thought it must be because the pagoda was on the seashore, on the model of the reflections in lakes and rivers, until another scholar put him right by demonstrating how the rays of light crossed over at the pinhole, on the model of the oar in the rowlock: when the handle was down, the blade was up.

Dante wrote that visible forms enter the eye *through a diaphanous medium as if it were through transparent glass. It is the water which exists in the pupil of the eye which renders the form visible...rather like a mirror which is glass backed with lead so that the form cannot travel any further but comes up against it like a ball and stops.*

In the sixteenth century, before either the telescope or the microscope was invented – or, it might be, reinvented – a Florentine nobleman did something so simple that anyone might have done it at any time: he magnified a bee in a concave mirror. He published a poem about it – a bee swollen in its silver ball as if in amber – but it sank without trace. No one saw the point. What caught the public's eye was the young Giambattista della Porta's exuberant book of tricks, *Magiae Naturalis*, for such optical arcana as how a convex lens in a pinhole sharpens the focus, good for drawing and even better for spying on the neighbours; and how to regale house-guests asleep *in a tempestuous night* with an apparition in a white sheet, using torches and a pinhole in the wall to make an image *hanging in the middle of the chamber, that will terrify the beholders*. Having caught the fiery eye of Rome besides, Porta was lucky to escape a charge of sorcery.

His second edition, vastly richer and wider in scope, described a mirror – not a lens – in the lantern of the Pharos of Alexandria, known far and wide as the 'glass' or 'telescope' of Ptolemy (Euergetes, not the great astronomer): a reflecting, not a refracting telescope. Arab accounts agree on there having been a great concave mirror that threw the fire of the lantern far out to sea all night and was a spyglass by day.

New lamps for old: but often the truth of new theories is slow to prevail, the old lingering on, afterimages in the mind's eye.

By a ground floor window in the British Museum I came across a case of vases, vessels for light, mosque lamps from Cairo or Damascus, no one can be sure, made of a glass that changes with the day outside, now smoky, now rosy, now a coppery water skin, bearing inscriptions, a flow of blue enamel in Arabic, reflections, uttering light:

Allah is the light of the heavens and earth; His light is like a niche in which is a lamp in glass and the glow like a brilliant star, lit from a blessed tree…

The caption tailed off there, citing the Koran, the Sura of Light, *Al-Nur*; and most wonderful of all, the blessed tree, as the ecstatic line unfolds, turns out to be an olive, yielding a lustrous oil whose very flow is like fire.

Allah is the Light
Of the heavens and the earth.
The parable of His Light
Is as if there were a Niche
And within it a Lamp:
The Lamp enclosed in Glass;
The glass as it were
A brilliant star:
Lit from a blessed Tree,
An Olive, neither of the East
Nor of the West,
Whose Oil is well-nigh
Luminous,
Though fire scarce touched it:
Light upon Light!

So Vincent van Gogh said of his sunflowers in the sun on canvas: *clair sur clair*. And, looking back the following spring from a cell in the Hôtel-Dieu, *the high yellow note* he had reached last summer: *la haute note jaune, a-O-O-O*, easier chanted than said, easier blown than either, a blown phrase, hollow, not brass, not a clarion, more an oboe – only so, though, in the French.

He was working on his sunflowers every morning from sunrise on, he said, as they were quick to fade and had to be done all in one go.

Dark lamps all the same, as dead as matches behind the glass. These days the British Museum is itself a lamp under a new shade, a glass mantle that fills the open forecourt with facets of light, tilted, magnified, the whole great net throwing its shadow as if in shallow water. The meshes twitch at the sun like spider thread. Spokes of shadow swing over walls and columns and the mirroring stone of the floor as the day wears on. How lovely it must be at night, in starlight, in the full moon. The white tower at the centre, the old Library, is a drowned lighthouse: high up in the double arches of the slotted windows is the glimpse of a white rose window, a parasol. Strange how the latent impression carries over into this whole stone maze of relics until every niche of the mind's Museum is a glass beehive.

A drowned lighthouse. *A telescope?...It is possible.* The bell-capped, full-bodied St Paul's of Christopher Wren, raised after the Great Fire of London on the ashes of the old St Paul's, has a clock tower built to house a zenith telescope – poised, this phantom telescope, this wish, like a *meridiana*, on the cusp of science and blind faith.

Walking in my sleep last night along a shore of lily pads made dark with birds and shadows and flares of dazzle I saw a slow quiver, the bulge of a black globe of shine forming, an eye, and another eye, eyes welling up all over the lake, opening, alive.

Rilke's Prodigal Son, mired in the extremity of poverty and hardship, watched as *ulcers broke out all over his body like emergency eyes against the blackness of tribulation* – blind eyes that wept blood.

Ματι, not οφθαλμος, is 'eye' these days, and that covers both the Evil Eye and the blue glass bead or stone to ward it off; and in botany, a bud. An αυγο ματι is a fried egg; ματι της θαλασσας, a whirlpool in the sea; and ματι νερου, a spring welling up, globular, throbbing, fanning water.

Sunset, the full moon over my shoulder and the tide out, the rowboats leaning in a skin of water, all surface, jogged in the wash of motorboats coming in to the ramp in a low percussion of waves. Mudbanks rising, sodden, in cakes, with shards of crockery, glass, shells, sea grass, bird prints, crab holes that well up when you step too near and gulp the air back in when you go. A heron peering, jabs up a struggling shape, a crab, all legs. A cormorant hangs out its wings. The pelicans are drifting off together for the night. A sky burnt to the one red point across the bay, the drag of tree shadows in water, specks of spooling light, dark wings.

One secret {Apelles} had himselfe, which no man was ever able to attaine and reach unto, and that was a certaine blacke vernish which he used to lay upon his painted tables when he had finished them; which was so finely tempered, and withall driven

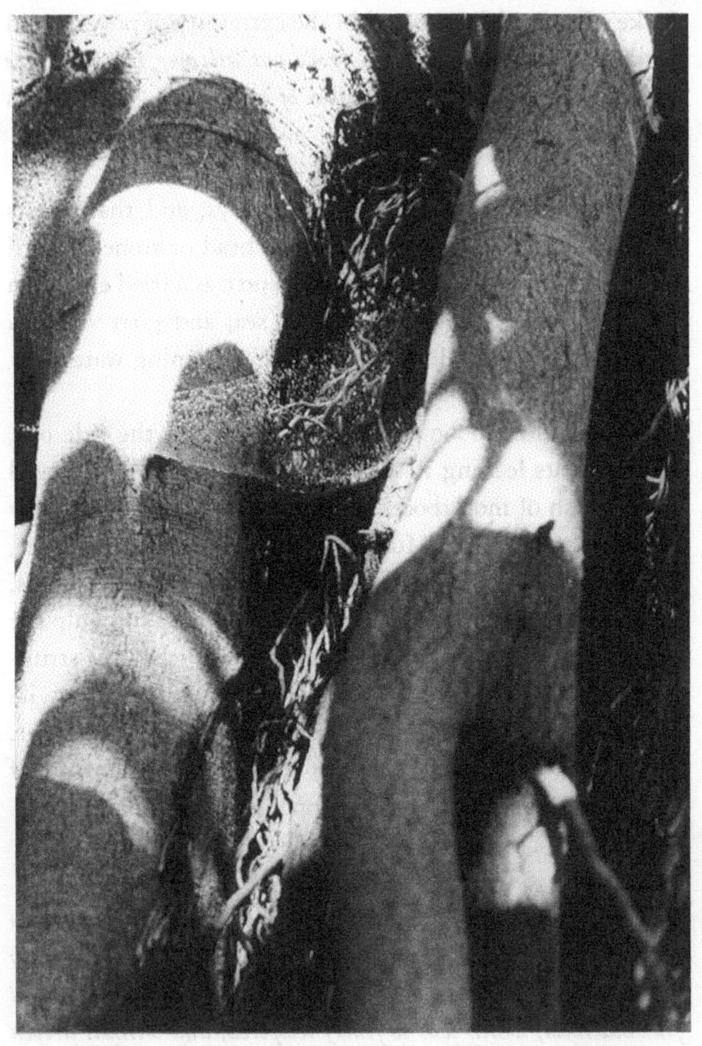

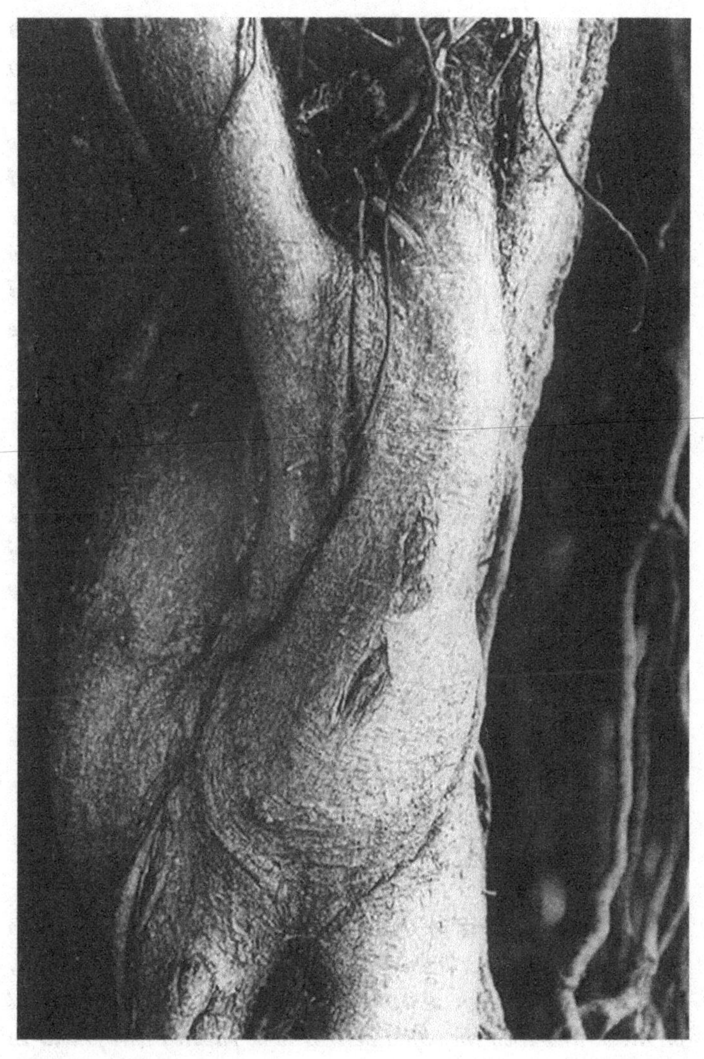

upon the worke so thin, that by the repercussion thereof it gave an excellent glosse and pleasant lustre to the colours; the same also preserved the picture from dust and filthinesse: and yet a man could not perceive any such thing at all, unlesse hee held the table close at hand, and looked verie neare. And great reason hee had besides to use this vernish, namely, least the brightnesse of the colours without it, might offend and dazle the eyes, which now beheld them as it were afarre off through a glass-stone; and withall, the same gave a secret deeping and sadnesse to those colours which were too gay and gallant.

PLINY, *THE HISTORIE OF THE WORLD*

And suddenly, as one approaches the obelisk (around whose granite there is always a glimmering of blond old warmth and in whose hieroglyphic hollows, especially in the repeatedly recurring owl, an ancient Egyptian shadow-blue is preserved, dried up as if in the wells of a paint box), the wonderful Avenue comes flowing...

RAINER MARIA RILKE, *LETTERS ON CÉZANNE*

Guardi has {black}, of course; it was unavoidable in the midst of the brightness, after the laws against display had prescribed black gondolas. But he uses it rather more as a dark mirror than as color...

RAINER MARIA RILKE, *LETTERS*

There was no painter in that country, but if anybody wished to have the portrait of a friend, of a picture, a beautiful landscape, or of any other object, water was placed in great basins of gold or silver, and then the object desired to be painted was placed in

front of that water. After a while the water froze and became a glass mirror, on which an ineffaceable image remained.
FÉNELON, *LES AVENTURES DE TÉLÉMAQUE, FILS D'ULYSSE*

Silver is a body, cleane, pure, and almost perfect, begotten of Argent-vive, *pure, almost fixed, cleare, and white, & of such a like* Sulphur: *It wanteth nothing, save a little fixation, colour, and weight.*
ROGER BACON, *THE MIRROR OF ALCHIMY*

{Iris} found Helen in her palace, at work on a great purple web of double width, into which she was weaving some of the many battles between the horse-taming Trojans and the bronze-clad Achaeans in the war that had been forced on them for her sake.
HOMER, *ILIAD*

Yes, child: art is the magic mirror you make to reflect your invisible dreams in visible pictures. You use a glass mirror to see your face: you use works of art to see your soul.
GEORGE BERNARD SHAW, *BACK TO METHUSELAH*

If a woman chances during her menstrual period to look into a highly polished mirror, the surface of it will grow cloudy with a blood-coloured haze. It is very hard to remove this stain from a new mirror, but easier to remove from an older mirror... Because it is natural to the eye to be filled with blood-vessels, a woman's eyes, during the period of menstrual flux and inflammation, will undergo a change, although her husband will not note this since his seed is of the same nature as that of his wife...A bronze mirror, because of its shininess, is especially sensitive.

ARISTOTLE, *ON DREAMS*

For of the soule the bodie forme doth take;
For soule is forme, and doth the bodie make.

EDMUND SPENSER, *AN HYMNE IN HONOUR OF BEAUTIE*

There may be raunged among the kinds of glasses, those which they call Obsidiana...exceeding blacke in colour, otherwhiles also transparent: howbeit, the sight therein is but thicke and duskish. It serveth for a mirroir to stand in a wall, and in stead of the image yeeldeth backe shaddows.

PLINY, *THE HISTORIE OF THE WORLD*

The banyan is an octopus insinuating her tentacles.

Pools of light under a cavernous roof, a visiting exhibition from Leiden in the Netherlands, *Ancient Lives*, and ancient deaths, Etruscan mainly, gleanings, terracotta funerary urns, votive offerings of ears, hands and feet, a half-head, and bronze mirrors, jewellery, jugs, glass and enamel. There are massive Roman marbles as well, the work of monumental masons. Among them stands a graceful little white Venus with yellow stains, Aphrodite, coming up out of the sea, a copy of a much-loved long-lost work of

Apelles, naked to the thighs, head bent, her arms lost that were raised to wring out her braided hair, a sprinkle of mica in the marble catching the light all over her like water drops.

A great purple web of double width: μεγαν ιστον υφαινε, διπλακα πορφυρεην. I wonder if her web was silk (and she a goddess, a Valkyrie weaving men's fates not of her making but foreseen, foreshadowed)? In the Aegean they made a *wild silk* from the cocoon of a moth – μια ψυχη, a butterfly or moth, a soul – and a cocoon of just such a silkmoth with wide eyes on its wings has turned up recently in the House of the Ladies in Akrotiri on the island of Thera. The eruption that cored the island and buried the harbour city of Akrotiri in ash was four centuries before the Trojan War; and the women we know from the wall frescoes wore flowing, opulent, finespun clothes. Hundreds of loom weights were found in one house alone; there was a litter of shells of the sea snail, the only source of the rare purple – blood red – dye (also known as αλουργος, seaborn, sea-worked) that meant royalty; and the frescoes have women and girls picking saffron in the yellow fields. A moth emblem with eyes on the wings decorates the bowsprits of the ships in a frieze of the West House, as a trademark, perhaps, no less than a talisman and a sacred sign.

Pliny's 'glass-stone' is *lapis specularis*, 'mirror stone' – muscovy-glass, isinglass-stone, mica, talc, for glazing windows. Or selenite, from σεληνη (on Lesbos, σελαννα), moon.

A bronze mirror filling with a blood-like cloud, νεφελη αιματωδης.

Δεδυκε μεν α σελαννα
και Πληιαδες, μεσαι δε
νυκτες, παρα δ' ερχετ' ωρα
εγω δε μονα κατευδω
The moon has set and the Pleiades, it's midnight, time's passing, yet I'm in bed alone
SAPPHO

At the surf beach on the incoming tide, a swim in the rock pools. Not brave enough to jump in at the outer rim, those darkening depths, I surface there anyway, surged out of the nested pools in a sinuous rush of water. Fish are there, some strung like coins on strings, moving away, and large, blunt black-barred ones burrowing nosedown in weed. The tossing back and forth of the weed, wallowing, water-swept. The image on the sand of water movements overhead, clusters of beads, amoeba shapes coalescing and breaking off, outlined in light; and tangles of white turbulence, a hammock of lazily scrawling openweave, ribbons of rainbow twisting and plaiting, bars of a golden cage and tight rings within rings widening, warping, loose.

Two helicopters, one blue, the police, shuttling and juddering overhead the whole time, once ducking down low, right on top of me holding my hands over my ears under the strap of the mask, kicking down hard. On the news when I get home, a swimmer washed out into the Rip.

On the news this morning – divers have found the body of a drowned swimmer floating close inshore, an overseas student. His name has not been released.

This afternoon, the tide an hour lower and the sea less rough, I set off from the open water into the pools and out along the channel to the surf's edge where the icy water pounds in, and come upon a luminous rain of slanting sand, bubbles, shreds of weed, a shower of fish bolting for the weed beds, cornstalks and tall haystacks of weed, tassels, foxtails, thongs of brown velvet, yellow branchings, pods, leaf clumps as dense as ivy overspun with white fuzz, filament.

Today's tide swings like a storm wind. Swarm, wash, sweep, the sand clarifying under a mesh of light into rocks, crabholes, rooted weeds, ribs of sand. The convulsion of the seaweeds, straps and strands that sweep and then stream out loose with each beat of the sea's pulse, sway, swill. I am vastly clothed in beads of breath, every pore and hair.

{E} come l'aere, quand' è ben piorno,
per l'altrui raggio che 'n sè si riflette
di diversi color diventa adorno,

così l'aer vicin quivi si mette
in quella forma che in lui suggella
virtualmente l'alma che ristette;

e simigliante poi alla fiammella
che segue il fuoco là 'vunque si muta,
segue allo spirto sua forma novella.

Però che quindi ha poscia sua paruta,
è chiamat' ombra; e quindi organa poi
ciascun sentire infino alla veduta.

{A}nd as the air, when it is full saturate, becomes
decked with divers colours through another's
rays which are reflected in it,

so the neighbouring air sets itself into that form,
which the soul that is there fixed, impresses
upon it by means of its virtue;

and then, like the flame which follows the fire
wheresoever it moves, the spirit is followed by
its new form.

Inasmuch as therefrom it afterwards has its semblance, it is called a shade; and therefrom it forms the organs of every sense even to sight.
DANTE ALIGHIERI, *PURGATORIO*

The earliest, most primitive photography – ambrotypes, tintypes and daguerreotypes on metal, calotypes, cyanotypes ('blueprints') on paper – has an unearthly clarity that leaves nothing to be desired, even to our eyes, regardless of any technical shortcomings. At the time it was the accuracy that made such a profound impact. A daguerreotype was reality. Not a work of art, this was a work of life, a true shadow of the sun, a mirror image fixed for all time, undeniable precisely because not made by human hand. Dramatic irony plays its part here, as in life but more sharply. We come to the pictured face with different eyes over time, eyes that know better now what was to be – eyes that know so much more, as well as less, than the sitter ever did, frozen in the past. The picture has stayed the same, it is our impression that has moved on as we have, and we are all retrospect. The face may belong to anyone at all, a stranger, anyone who has taken our eye and held it long enough for us to see inside, or whose story we know, or think we do. Take the arresting daguerreotype, the only one, of Emily Dickinson, doe-eyed and ramrod-backed at seventeen, tensed between sharpness and imprecision, where we are looking at nothing so much, or so it has come to seem, as the chrysalis of a soul.

Of course it went beyond the portrait, far and wide from the very beginning, in search of the picturesque in lost worlds, antique lands, remote wildernesses and cities – those early streetscapes where the necessarily long exposure abolished whatever was moving, figures, animals, carriages, to record only what was fixed, in an extreme case of the blend of fidelity to fine detail and blatant falsehood intrinsic to the new medium. Leaving aside whether it was art or craft – if this is not a false distinction to begin with – photography would, at times, and in some hands, effortlessly deliver a fragment of everyday reality into the realm of high art. At first glance a daguerreotype taken by a Frenchman, Gros, in 1851, for example, is a postcard view of the Thames, milky with the light just breaking through a morning mist. In the foreground is the earthy darkness of the rowboats moored tightly along one bank, in the middle distance a light bridge looped with arches and, off-centre and almost afloat on the skyline, to where the eye is taken at a slant, the pale dome of St Paul's. It is all so distilled, so matter-of-fact, so out-of-time that it has a Dutch feel to it, something in monochrome of the limpidity and composure of *A View of Delft*.

When it came to clarity, the first ever *sun picture* or *photogenic drawing* made on paper, an impressionistic snapshot in the dark by Henry Fox Talbot in 1835, beautiful as it was, and unearthly, was a mere smudge by comparison to the daguerreotype, but a luminous smudge, of a lattice as soft as charcoal – a vision, as much as an image, of the oriel window in the old abbey where he lived.

Caught on silvered and salted paper in one of his mousetrap camera obscuras was a negative still clear enough to print after all this time – it does seem only right and proper, not to say far-sighted, that this vision made solid, made of light, was a window.

My dearest Miss Mitford, do you know anything about that wonderful invention of the day, called the Daguerrotype? – that is, have you seen any portraits produced by means of it? Think of a man sitting down in the sun and leaving his facsimile in all its full completion of outline and shadow, stedfast on a plate, at the end of a minute and a half! The Mesmeric disembodiment of spirits strikes one as a degree less marvellous. And several of these wonderful portraits... like engravings – only exquisite and delicate beyond the work of graver – have I seen lately – longing to have such a memorial of every Being dear to me in the world. It is not merely the likeness which is precious in such cases – but the association, and the sense of nearness involved in the thing... the fact of the very shadow of the person *lying there fixed for ever!*
ELIZABETH BARRETT

There was the heart of the matter for Barthes, the past whose light *will touch me like the delayed rays of a star*: the reference being to a passage of Delacroix that Susan Sontag had quoted, a note – from 1850! – about a daguerreotype of the star Vega that had been made at Cambridge, a pinpoint of light that had been twenty years reaching earth and *had consequently left the celestial sphere a long time before Daguerre had discovered the process*...It is why *Camera Lucida* has been described, wonderfully, by Martin Jay as *a chilling lament, a thanatology of vision.*

One nineteenth-century myth held that if a murderer let himself be seen by the dying victim he would leave his image caught like a photograph on the corpse's retinas, and an ophthalmoscope could detect it. So at least one murderer had the foresight to put out the victim's eyes.

Emily Dickinson hated her daguerreotype and never sat for another one; she wanted *no mould of me*. Balzac was the same – out of fear, as the great photographer Nadar reported, that *every body in its natural state was made up of a series of ghostly images superimposed in layers to infinity, wrapped in infinitesimal films...each Daguerreian operation was therefore going to lay hold of, detach, and use up one of the layers of the body on which it focused.* He would be losing one skin to the machine, one of his images, close kin to those primitive (Pre-Sokratic!) 'husks' long since banished by science. What, then, might he have thought of the magnificent, rearing, dressing-gowned bronze statue of him by Rodin? – who worked, Rilke tells us, by drawing countless poses and fining them down, combining, fusing them until they solidified into the one last possible and perfect form – a process of proliferation followed by elimination?

Chrysalis, χρυσαλλις, from χρυσος, gold, is the insect as a nymph, νυμφη, 'bride', in the Greek dictionary, on the threshold of metamorphosis; and in the time of Aristotle, a golden embryonic *psyche*.

In a Greek story of 1881 from the island of Skiathos, 'Μια Ψυχη', 'A Soul', a young girl has just died. Her body is in the graveyard, το κοιμητηρι, the sleeping place. For her soul's sake the 'unsleeping lamp', το ακοιμητο καντηλι – a glass of water with a wick floating in a little wheel on a layer of oil – will be kept burning by her deathbed for forty days. Her mother is just adding more oil when a moth flutters in the window. She holds her breath in amazement, because this is her daughter, all that's left of her, her soul – to this day you will hear Greek mothers calling out πουλι μου, my bird, ματια μου, my eyes, ψυχη μου, my soul, χρυσο μου, my golden one. Ψυχη μου! But this is her very soul.

Before the mother can utter a word the moth is gone; but the next night it is back at the lamp, gilded, fluttering and then vanishing, not caught in the flame, simply absent. And on the third night it circles the mother's head over and over until the mother cries out, *Don't go, my soul!* Μη φευγης, μη φευγης, ψυχη μου! And to her joy the moth dips down to the lamp and takes a sip of oil before vanishing – this time for good.

The title was a play on words, winged words with a double meaning, 'A Soul', or 'A Moth'. The story, in the literary, neo-classical 'Purified' Greek of its day, turned on the point that ψυχη was still 'moth', or 'butterfly', as well as 'soul', making every ψυχη strike a chord of meanings. Not any more. It has taken time, but the vernacular, 'Demotic' Greek, has won the day. Now 'moth', 'butterfly', is πεταλουδα, from 'petal', and ψυχη is no more or less than 'soul', and the point, like the moth, is lost and gone – lost in translation. Or is it? For the reader maybe. Not for the mother, a woman of the people, for whom all figures of speech are beside the point, which is presence, epiphany, the living metaphor that is folk memory. Loosed from the flesh, haven't the dead always taken shape as aerial beings who for a time are still so human that they are drawn back to their old home as to the flame of life? Since before languages, before words, in the cave days there were *Fire, and sleete, and candle-lighte* and moths at the lyke-wake.

And farther on the flowers in the bed that have nothing to bear, that are only lighted for a while and burn like candles...(it occurs to me, don't night butterflies think lights are flowers?).

RAINER MARIA RILKE, *LETTERS 1892–1910*

John Donne as he lay dying posed in his shroud for the marble memorial that stands in St Paul's, rather as one might sleep in it, as a penance and a memento mori. Upright on a singed urn he came through the Great Fire when the old St Paul's was gutted. Clothed in fire, shrouded, unscathed.

Of Munch's painting *Twilight*, shown in Paris in 1896, his close companion August Strindberg wrote: *The sunlight fades, night falls, and twilight changes mortals into ghosts and corpses as they return home to envelop themselves in the shroud of their beds and to drift off into sleep.*

Death is all we see when awake; all we see when asleep is sleep.
HERAKLEITOS, *FRAGMENTS*

The most basic equipment – more or less any old box with an eye in it – will do, in the right hands. Pinhole cameras without lenses take either film or photographic paper, black and white or colour. They can have more than one pinhole, and take multiple images. Their depth of field is always infinite. Incapable of low contrast, they draw a surreal intensity of impact out of high contrast.

I once read an article on islands *as places and resemblances* that had among the illustrations an extraordinary pinhole image by a Danish (and Greenlander) photographer, Pia Arke. She had built herself a shed big enough to hold only herself and a dark silence – a makeshift camera the size of a shed, like the one in Rilke's first sonnet to Orpheus that is *hardly even a hut to receive the song, / a shelter put up out of the darkest yearnings, / with shaking doorposts*... She had had her shed transported to the bare site of her first home in Greenland, and there inside that dark space and simulacrum of the past she made – she allowed to accumulate like slow dreams – eerie images of the craggy shore of her childhood, a flat sea, a sky threaded with grey, an ice floe adrift in its own luminosity.

An American in a photography magazine, Abelardo Morell, has been working on another variation, setting up a conventional camera in the room he will turn into a pinhole camera – a camera within a camera. The room will be part of the shot, taking a self-portrait as one element of a compound image, the other being the chosen image from outside, the two together making up a complex and mysterious vision where everyday banal objects – subjects – fuse with a reflected world.

He finds himself a large bare room, one deep in the mountains, or high over Manhattan – large, so that the pinhole can be relatively large and still throw a sharp image inside. First he lightproofs the room with black plastic sheets and pricks a single pinhole just the right size, through which the light seeping in hour by hour will distil into an image of whatever is in its visual field: the crowns of trees, a tower, an avenue of skyscrapers flecked with windows. The travelling sun, delayed, will move the shadows across the image. In the pure dark of the room the pinhole burns, a distant star, a water bead. What does he see if he puts his eye to it? – the bright world of surfaces, angles, depths, set in a rim like a porthole. This is what will come fanning in on to the black sheet, upside down, invisible to the naked eye: the latent image that will in turn enter the lens and be imprinted, absorbed drop by drop into the emulsion on his film.

In his absence. Unlike Pia Arke in her shed, Morell does not keep inside with the picture. Having set up his camera in the right spot facing the back wall, he opens the shutter, goes out, locks the door. In the long hours of his absence – exposure in such cases is pure trial and error – the sole occupants will be the camera on its tripod and maybe a chair, a door, a standard lamp, which will come out in sharp silhouette on the film – a white silhouette, on the negative. Behind them will be the fully distilled image from outside. It will still, of course, be upside down, with the sky at the skirting board, and the ground, or the avenue, overhead. Developed and printed, it will come out in soft greys, perfectly distinct all over and yet ethereal, a mirage on fog, bent halfway at the angle of the wall and ceiling, and darker in the bent half, as if under glass or shifting water. The other way up, the chair, the lamp, will be as if suspended from the floor, now the ceiling, and the outside image will be the right way up.

But for the image as a whole there is no right way up, and that is half the beauty of it, more than half, the way the two images, the one sharp and spare, the other smokily intricate, are in perfect equilibrium. The effect is more dislocating than a double exposure, almost beyond grasp, another world that is in this one, a dreamscape, a city brought to light in all its shadows and incandescences.

The soul is a stability; the shifting and fleeting thing which body is can be a cause only of its forgetting not of its remembering – Lethe stream may be understood in this sense – and memory is a fact of the soul.

PLOTINOS

The human body, wrote Ludwig Wittgenstein, *is the best picture of the human soul.* Which is to say, its showing-forth, epiphany – ειδωλον. More, its only conceivable form.

In an installation and a book, both called *Another Water (The River Thames, for Example)*, the American photographer Roni Horn shows close-up shots in murky colour of what might be the river of almost any great modern city, the ruffled opacities of a surface, its eddies and glints and furrows one long smacking of lips. In the book they are laid out in double-page spreads with, running underneath by way of captions, notes, prose poems and shreds of quotations, words redoubling; now and then broken by the bridge of a white page, the transcript of a Dead Body Report, stolid, heavy on fact, with the baffled imperviousness to despair of an angel, reduced to the one flat police voice and the bare facts of another body fished out whole or in part. The surfaces of this other water are like mud, like lava, skin, a thickness that absorbs light, that draws in and down. Lean over any bridge in London and you will see for yourself.

Pure was the light and pure were we from the pollution of the walking sepulchre which we call a body, to which we are bound like an oyster to its shell.

PLATO

Plotinos, deliberating on whether and how soul is in body or body in soul, speculates that they interweave, warp and weft, the soul passing and repassing uncontaminated throughout the body, *just like light.*

What does he mean, exactly, by *the wisdom of the apparition* – τη σοφια του φαντασματος?

Whosoever enjoyes not this life, I count him but an apparition, though he weare about him the sensible affections of flesh.
SIR THOMAS BROWNE

A one-day workshop in the city on making salt prints, sun prints, by Talbot's original method, taught by a modern master of the art. I took rough wisps and threads of seaweed; others had enlarged negatives, lace, flowers. We had to soak a sheet of paper in salt water first and let it dry, then lay a wash of invisible ink, silver chloride in solution, on the good side with a brush and let it dry again. Then we clamped our negatives or arranged our objects in a wooden frame between the coated surface of the paper and the glass and took them out to the courtyard in the noon sun. It took less than ten minutes for the paper to go from white through indigo to sepia – no further though, not black. For once we could see our images form in the open air instead of the firelight of the darkroom. Back inside we could either wash and fix and wash the prints the usual way or dip them in a salt bath. While they dried we made our second print. My first one was fixed and it dried true; the second came out of the salt bath with all its pale arabesques fine and clear on a russet ground. But neither will last, it seems. Fixed or salted, sun prints change colour over time much like oil on dark water, before fading away to nothing – look on it as an alternative pleasure to the usual permanence, the master said, one more like life.

I wonder if the moon will print them as well and how long it will take.

The end of the day, a brewing sky with thunderstorms on the horizon, a slow swell on the surf beach, and a furtive flickering here and there, just above the sand, of jellyfish, a *feu follet* of cold light behind the only other people at the beach, three bearded young men slouching beside their propped-up rods. Passing behind the first of them I nearly trip over his catch, two mullet shoved headfirst in the sand, tails in the air with their swallow-fins down. Short tails, dimmer than the flaky silvery fish-skin on the blunt backs, the blue grey of the heavy sky – the smaller tail still, the other one still moving, beating, a faint and steady constant thudding of the tail.

In the Swedish summer of 1904 Rilke's companions shot a large seagull.

You ought to see it...maybe you would draw one of its wings. They are magnificently constructed, so sure and compact and all of gray silk; but you should draw the under side which is more beautiful by far; everything is more delicate there and as ineffably untouched as a young cloud. And those contours: so sure and necessary, feather upon feather, and yet as delicate as in a Rodin drawing. Or in Japanese prints; of them the color of the whole too reminds one. There is white and gray. But from the last white to the gray's first beginning there is still a world of color, a thousand transitions that have no name. There is hesitant white that, hard before the gray, turns back into itself again, and gray that flashes and wants to turn white. There is the gray of fish scales and the gray of water and the tremulous gray of damp air – : as though the mirror of this outspread pinion had preserved everything that happened below it.

RAINER MARIA RILKE, *LETTERS 1892–1910*

No sooner were the daguerreotype and the calotype invented than alongside the painters with their easels flocked the photographers with their friar's hood and long-legged box of tricks, apparatus, *appareil.* The public was in love with the camera. Was it art? Who cared? Not they. As for the artists, it was a threat and a fraud – an optical aid – a revelation. Nearly a hundred years ago Edvard Munch owned a pocket Kodak he used for studies and, above all, for a series of self-portraits, setting up the shot, the pose, and controlling the exposure with his black hat. In these *Fate Photographs* he sits huddled eternally alone, facing a light that filters as if through bars into the narrow room.

Some display a mutilated hand, the *hand of fate*, harking back to his 1895 painting, *Self-Portrait with Skeleton Arm*, where the arm rests its twin bones along the bottom of the frame as on a window sill. *I was born dying*, he wrote. In some of the photographs his dark outline has blurred with movement, in others he frays with a spectral glimmer or bulks translucent in the foreground so that a wall, a painting, is showing through. Some are double exposures of him alone with his own image, the *dobbeltgjenger*. He in his black hat. Time is an element here, the dimension of time in the slow distillation of a solitude.

Shortly afterwards, in September 1902, Munch had one of the fingers of his left hand shot off and another damaged, during the definitive ending of his love affair with Tulla Larsen. An X-ray taken at the Christiania Röntgen Institute shows the bullet in his finger. In his notes from that date one can read with what desperation he viewed what he later called his hand of destiny *after the operation:*
– the bandage on the hand was taken off
– a shudder went through him
– a monstrosity
– a terrible stunted limb
– was his previously well-formed hand
– his previous helper in his work
– stunted, hideous and useless
ARNE EGGUM

The camera had seen more than the eye could. It had seen though a milky nimbus of flesh to the bone. Why not the inner soul? Why not the aura, the fringed enveloping mantle of the soul, for that matter? – the outer soul? Since there are always those for whom, following Plotinos in Plato's wake, the body is in its soul.

Already established in the 1880's, spirit photography *is now an almost forgotten photographic tradition, which both Munch and Strindberg were excited by in their time. It was often a question of showing a medium sitting in a chair; and behind or beside her the deceased appeared as a light, more or less identifiable shape. It was believed that the spirit of the deceased could be* 'seen' *by the photographic plate. Strindberg, for instance, had a picture of Paul Verlaine on his deathbed, at which he could see a series of spirit-like figures. Munch had probably been fascinated by the phenomenon of* spirit photography *in 1886, when he was working on the painting* The Sick Child...*As late as 1907, Munch gave Gustav Schiefler the impression that he saw aura-like shapes around people, and at the time when he took his most experimental photographs in Warnemünde, he was constantly absorbed by similar thoughts, as the following notes prove:*

Are there spirits
We see what we see
because we have eyes that are so made
What are we?
A collection of moving power – a light which burns –

with a wick – now the inner heat – now the outer flame – and still an invisible flame-ring – If our eyes were made differently – we would like X-rays see only our wicks – The bone system – Were our eyes of a different nature – could we see our outer flame-rings – and see other human beings of other substances.
Why then should not – other beings made of more-easily dissolved molecules be round us and in us –
The souls of the deceased –
Our dear souls – and evil spirits
ARNE EGGUM

In their years as companions in suffering and self-exile between Berlin and Paris, Strindberg experimented with photography and *celestography*, long pinhole exposures he made of the stars, whorls of white light. Munch found his way out of his own dark night on a German beach, by painting bathed in the summer sun and incidentally recording in photographs his own manly nakedness, stalwart at last and impregnable. By 1908 he had admitted himself to a mental hospital in Copenhagen. Rilke would recoil from the thought of treatment to rid him of his devils – his angels might leave him too. (How might Gauguin have chosen? How might van Gogh?) Munch's angels, his black angels, were his devils, they would be the death of him. Treatment, even shock treatment, might keep them at bay. Munch had chosen life. He would live to a wintry old age, a master of his craft to the end, while the blood flow of his art thinned and ran dry. Home in Norway in his house on the Oslofjord he would have his paintings for company, for family, year in, year out, standing them out in the open all winter to toughen them up, taking their photo in space and a white silence, bare black trees, a yard kneedeep in snow and a row of blood splashes frozen against the wall in their frames, more at home than they would ever be in the Munch Museum which was to house them on his death. And there were the murals still to come, for the great hall of Oslo University where, strung up on the scaffolding like a spider on a clockface he would paint the sun, *Solen*, enclosed in lines of flaming red – a clockface with no hands – no midnight sun dripping like a candle but the great sun of a new day bursting in the prism of the eye, a tissue of light spun from cliff to cliff across the bay, a fractured crystal ball.

OSWALD. {Sits in the arm-chair with his back towards the landscape, without moving. Suddenly he says:} *Mother, give me the sun.*
MRS. ALVING. {By the table, starts and looks at him.} *What do you say?*
OSWALD. {Repeats, in a dull, toneless voice.} *The sun. The sun.*
HENRIK IBSEN, *GHOSTS*

Solen. Solen.

The fact is that the sun has never penetrated us people of the North.

VINCENT VAN GOGH

On the back cover of a manuscript of jottings, Gauguin as he lay dying would stick a print of Dürer's *Knight, Death and the Devil*, whose figures ghosted his own pale riders to the Marquesan shore.

His Vincent rises up forever in a passion of yellow, a fiery apparition.

This poor Dutchman was all ardour, all enthusiasm. Reading Tartarin de Tarascon *had made him believe in an extraordinary Midi, to be expressed in jets of flame.*

And on the canvas the chrome yellows surged up, flooding the mas *and the whole plain of the Camargue with sun.*

...In my yellow room, sunflowers, with purple eyes, stand out against a yellow ground; the stalks soak their tips in a yellow pot, on a yellow table. In one corner of the painting, the painter's signature: Vincent. And the yellow sun, passing through the yellow curtains of my room, floods with gold all this coming into flower, and in the morning, in bed, when I wake up, I imagine it all smells very nice.

Oh yes! He did love yellow, did this good Vincent, the painter from Holland, glimmers of sunlight to warm his soul, in his horror of fog. A need for warmth.

When the two of us were in Arles, both insane, continually at war over beautiful colours, I adored red; where to find a

perfect vermilion? He, with his yellowest brush, traced on the suddenly violet wall:
I am of sound mind,
I am Holy Ghost.
PAUL GAUGUIN, *OVIRI: ECRITS D'UN SAUVAGE*

Je suis sain d'Esprit,
Je suis Saint-Esprit.

A day in the snowbound silence of Oslo. No silence like this silence of snow. At first my boots pinch, a cold constriction, then a throbbing warmth free of pain, almost pleasurable, one heel raw in a blood socket – a childhood memory of my feet in the shoe shop X-ray machine, long, pale green, a thick-knuckled crawl, a vision, my bones jiggling, in a *danse macabre.*

In a big city you adopt a particular way of regarding the world. A focused, sporadically selective view. When you scan a desert or an ice floe, you see with different eyes. You let the details slip out of focus in favour of the whole. This way of seeing reveals a different reality. If you look at someone's face in this manner, it starts to dissolve into a shifting series of masks.

With this way of seeing, a person's breath in the cold – that veil of cooled drops that forms in the air in temperatures under 8° C – is not merely a phenomenon fifty centimetres from his mouth. It's something all-encompassing, a structural transformation of the space surrounding a warm-blooded creature, an aura of minimal

but definite thermal displacement. I've seen hunters shoot snow hares in a starless winter night at a distance of two hundred and fifty metres by aiming at the fog around them.
PETER HØEG, *MISS SMILLA'S FEELING FOR SNOW*

In tissue paper veils the relics of strangers have come down to me. The pathos in old photos all haze and mildew, speckle and tarnish and silverfish tunnels, their soft corners crumbling, the embodiment of decay. Material and immaterial, the blind gaze out of the husks of faces no name can ever be put to, ghosts in a mirror unaware of their death.

I watch my hand through the lens, grey fingers loose and swollen like a glove taking their slow steps in this element apart from me, as through a diving mask.

With *The Sick Child*, a painting in memory of his sister, Munch finally scratched away all the background to isolate her milky profile and red hood of hair in an aureole, a heat-crackle, of fever, hope – in a *spiritual shell*, as a fellow artist observed.

Flat gold of the sky and sea in the slide of Swan Bay, with one low tilted bird. The bird is sharp. The reflection under the bird is a frayed brushstroke, the soft pull of the water slowing to a blur.

Do not the Rays of Light in falling upon the bottom of the Eye excite Vibrations in the Tunica Retina*?*
ISAAC NEWTON, *OPTICKS*

Rete, net, as if the eye were a glass buoy on the face of the sea, with a tunic for good measure. A website of etymologies says the Vulgar Latin *(tunica) retina... may be a translation of Ar.* (tabaqa) sabakiva *'netlike layer,' itself a translation of Gk.* amphiblestroeides (khiton). Αμφιβληστροειδης (χιτων). Such sumptuous names to dress the eye in (as is only fitting).

The sense of sight was a great mystery and source of speculation among the Greeks. There were those, like Empedokles and Epikouros, who held with the Pythagorians that the element of the eye was fire and that the eye shed rays of light out into the world, unseen eyebeams apprehending what we see. Others thought that all objects constantly shed images, idols, husks of themselves, *lumina*, brightnesses, filling space at the speed of thought, and these, entering the eye, were what we see. For Demokritos the eye's element was water, and the eye itself a watery mirror, sight as reflection – although in that case, Aristotle argued, why would the eye, among all the other mirroring surfaces there are, alone have the power of seeing? Plato took the view that the light of the eye is firelight, as in a lantern, the soul's light issuing in a stream and mingling with the subtle fire of daylight, like to like, the inner and the outer fire, to produce vision (and not a husk in sight); and the night, the dark, extinguishing it. Aristotle was scathing about all this, especially the 'extinguishing'. He said light was instantaneous. (Alhazen would know better when his time came, and not even Kepler would believe him.) Vision, unlike the other senses, involved no movement. Light by its very being alone brought about vision. (But how?)

The visual rays, a mystical projection, had at least served to bring optics into the field of practical geometry, there to lie lapped for centuries, however, in a visual field swarming with husks. Lucretius, distilling Epikouros into sheer poetry in *De rerum natura*, saw them as images, *simulacra*:

*which, like films {*membranae*} drawn from the outermost surface of things, flit about hither and thither through the air; it is these same that, encountering us in wakeful hours, terrify our minds, as also in sleep, when we often behold wonderful shapes and images of the dead, which have often aroused us in horror while we lay languid in sleep; lest by chance we should think that spirits escape from Acheron or ghosts flit about amongst the living, or that anything of us can be left after death, when body and mind both taken off together have dissolved abroad, each into its own first-beginnings. I say, therefore, that semblances and thin shapes of things are thrown off from their outer surface...as often when cicadas drop their neat coats in summer, and when calves at birth* *throw off the caul from their outermost surface, and also when the slippery serpent casts off his vesture amongst the thorns (for we often see the brambles enriched with their flying spoils): since these things happen, a thin image must also be thrown off from things, from the outermost surface of things...Lastly, whatever similitudes* {simulacra} *we see in mirrors, in water, in any bright surface, since they are possessed of the same appearance as the things, must consist of images thrown off from those things.*

Even the gods cast off their constant stream of idols, only theirs were too fine for earthly eyes, unless in dreams, in visions. As for the sun's idols, they murdered sight.

Bright things moreover the eyes avoid and shun to look upon. The sun too blinds, if you try to raise your eyes to meet him, because his own power is great, and the idols from him are borne from on high through the clear air heavily, and strike upon the eyes, disordering their texture. Moreover, any piercing brightness often burns the eyes for the reason that it contains many seeds of fire, which give birth to pain in the eyes, finding their way in.

Idols are all things to all men. In these profusions of metaphor is there any substance? In the common mind a 'husk' is just a hull, a pod, and 'idols' – ειδωλα to the Greeks – are images. In Homer an ειδωλον is an illusion pure and simple: as in the *Iliad*, where the ghost of Patroklos evades the embrace of Achilleus; and in the *Odyssey*, where Odysseus, sent to the underworld to consult the shade of

Tiresias, the blind seer, and spilling blood on the dark shore of the River of Ocean, sees his own mother hovering to drink. He has thought her safe at home in Ithaka; now when he throws his arms around her in an access of grief, only to have her slip away, like a shadow, a dream, wavering, again and again, he is cut to the quick and wonders aloud if this really is her soul, ψυχη, or nothing but an ειδωλον sent by Persephone to make a fool of him. (And when the shades come swarming over him like cave bats he will flee back to the ship in case Persephone has armed them with a Gorgon's head which, catching his eye – in the absence of all deflecting mirrors – will turn him to stone.) But his mother says this is simply how it is with the dead and not Persephone's doing. *The sinews no longer hold the flesh and bones together; these perish in the fierceness of consuming fire as soon as life has left the body, and the soul flits away as though it were a dream.*

Το ειδωλον του νεου σωματος μου,
απ' τες εννια που αναψα την λαμπα,
ηρθε και με ηυρε και με θυμισε...

The shade of my young body, since I lit the lamp at nine, has come and found me and reminded me...
KONSTANTINOS KAVAFIS

Images, idols, *simulacra*, *species*, ειδωλα, spectres, shades, ghosts, revenants, spirits, doubles, *dobbeltgjengere*, phantasms, phantoms, fetches, spooks, wraiths, *reflets*, apparitions and emanations, jinns, *lemures* and *larvae*, in Rome, as in Montaigne – *Larves, Hobgoblins, Robbin-good-fellowes, and such other Bug-beares and* Chimeraes.

Vincent dreamed of portraits so intense as to appear to people living a century on *like apparitions*.

A grey-pink face and green eyes, ashen hair, a wrinkled forehead and, around the mouth, stiff and wooden, a very red beard, a bit unkempt, and sad; but the lips are full; a coarse blue linen smock and a palette with citron yellow, vermilion, Veronese green, cobalt blue, in short all the colours on the palette, except for the orange of the beard, all the pure colours. The head against a grey white wall. You will say it looks a little like the head of death...
VINCENT VAN GOGH

He had bought himself a mirror to work from, using his own image for want of a model, going for a deeper likeness, though, than the placid old style of portrait (let alone the *photographer's colourless phantoms*): getting his colours, *citroengeel, vermiljoen, veroneesgroen, cobalt blauw,* to bring out all the expression, the passion, in the people of his times, and that aspect *like a waiting, and like a scream – et comme de l'attente et comme un cri*.

If, that is, the word is *cri*, and not *cru*, as it is in *Verzamelde Brieven van Vincent van Gogh*, his collected letters, printed exactly as he wrote them. In his sister-in-law Jo's footsteps it has usually been taken as *cru* and translated as 'growth'. But *cru* in this sense only applies to plants; 'raw' is the dominant meaning. There was a usage in his day, *d'un cru*, which takes this in, so that by *d'un cru* he could mean having a rawness, or coarseness or simply an openness, barefaced, straightforward, down to earth, and this fits the context. The letter, the last ever to his sister Wil, goes on to describe Dr Gachet's *expression de mélancolie* as *triste mais doux, mais clair et intelligent*, 'sad but gentle, but clear and intelligent': no scream there, not even implicit, a silent scream. (Even so, doesn't it all come down to the handwriting? *Cri*, *cru*, the one inside the other, no more than a whisker, a flick of the wrist is all.)

To the Sokrates of Plato, the artist is by definition a dealer in secondhand goods, in fakes – the great Homer himself is only ειδωλου δημιουργος, a creator of phantoms, and his world of characters nothing but shadows. By the same token the written word is a shadow of the living and breathing word: and what man of sense takes up a pen to write in water or sows his seed in ink rather than earth? (But what is Sokrates to us if not the ειδωλον of Plato's making?)

Skia, *skiagraphia*, *skiasma*, *photoskiasis*

σκια – shade, shadow
σκια – 'dark idol' (σκοτεινον ειδωλον) of a solid body

σκιαγραφια – sketch; black and white drawing; silhouette
σκιαγραφια – in Plato, painting that creates an illusion of reality, *trompe-l'œil*
σκιασμα, φωτοσκιασις – shading

Jinns may look human but they are all fire, not clay, and have no shadow.

Jack a Lantern, Friar's Lantern, Will o' the Wisp, corpse candles, *feu follet*. Saint Elmo's fire. Fata Morgana.

Greek witches draw down the moon and milk her for potions. Pliny knows of some who *with their very eiesight can witch, yea, and kill those whom they look wistly upon any long time*. They can be known by their double pupils – *in either eie they have two sights or apples* – and their inability to weep or to drown. But he draws the line at a screech owl, *strix*, of folklore that with evil intent gives the breast to babies: *None that lay egs have paps*. Nor does he swallow the story that the dripping heart of a screech owl laid to a woman's heart in her sleep will make her disgorge her innermost secrets, on the principle of like to like, heart to heart. In Ovid these *strigae* – Greek στριγξ, Latin *strix* – are either witches in bird form or true birds of prey who spirit themselves inside locked houses to gorge on babies who then, spellbound, waste away in real life. The eighth century Greek father, John of Damascus, nicknamed Chrysorrhoas, 'he of the flow of gold', for his eloquence, knows them as the στριγγαι who break in after their prey *in bodily form or as a naked soul*, μετα σωματος η γυμνη τη ψυχη. Στριγγλα is the current Greek incarnation of the *strix* – as a scold these days, a fury – and her στριγγλια is her scream, screech, shriek.

In lands where the Evil Eye is rife, a mirror on a ring or sewn on the clothes may deflect it. And yet a bride is not only veiled, she is kept away from mirrors. Nor is a woman in childbed safe with a mirror in her room: even after the birth until she is churched she and the child must stay behind closed doors and windows between sunset and sunrise. The Evil Eye is latent in mirrors – all mirrors, including water, and other eyes – and in those other eyes of the night, the stars.

That this venenation shooteth from the eye, and that this way a Basilisk may empoyson, although thus much be not agreed upon by Authors, some imputing it unto the breath, others unto the bite, it is not a thing impossible; for eyes receive offensive impressions, from their objects, and may have influences destructive to each other; for the visible species of things strike not our senses immaterially, but streaming in corporall rayes, do carry with them the qualities of the object from which they flow, and the medium through which they passe: Thus through a greene or red glasse all things wee behold appeare of the same colours; thus sore eyes affect those which are sound, and themselves also by reflection, as will happen to an inflamed eye that beholds it selfe long in a glasse; thus is fascination made out…
SIR THOMAS BROWNE

Nor do the shades, dead souls in Hades, have a shadow. Nor do they blink.

Still they lingered on, these old *similitudini*, in that dust of old beliefs that we all take in with every breath. They got into the mind's eye even of Leonardo. Got into his bodily eye no less – though only as far as the aqueous – upside down through the pinhole of his dark chamber.

Every body in light and shade fills the surrounding air with infinite images of itself; and these, by infinite pyramids diffused in the air, present this body through space and in every part.
LEONARDO DA VINCI

Those Englishmen who saw the first photographs ever made were reminded of the fool and his detachable shadow in the German folktale. As if by magic the *infinite images* that met the eye could now be caught on paper and bought and sold over and over.

Like the mind's eye – the inner, spiritual, *gostly* eye – the eye of flesh will see what is not there, and unsee what is, straining to see clearer, deeper, further than it can. The keenest eye, free of all flaws – the best of all possible eyes – is fallible.

Not so the lens. The lens is revelation on revelation. How did it begin? By analogy, perhaps, with raindrops and dew, jellyfish, crystal bowls, veins of crystal still embedded in the mother rock. By patient trial and error it was found that slivers of this pure crystal, polished into a solid meniscus, would infallibly enlarge or reduce, refract and burn. When? Before the invention of *lumina* or *simulacra*, let alone glass, lenses of rock crystal were ground in Troy, in Egypt and Greece, Carthage and Rome and beyond. Some are gathering dust in the drawers of museums, classified – we see what we believe – as mere jewels.

And yet all over Europe well into the Renaissance the lens had sunk to being at best a dangerous toy and at worst, black magic, a tool of witchcraft; and the stench of heresy hung about any experimentation in optics – the stench of the rack and the stake, anathema. The astronomer took his life in his hands with his telescope. Bruno was burnt. Galileo was forced to recant. It took Kepler, trying out a telescope made by Galileo, to affirm him once and for all in a letter of August 1610 with a splendid pun – *Vicisti, Galilaee!* he wrote, *Thou hast conquered, Galilean!* – and close the door on the old optics.

Galileo went blind in old age, in the dark with four years to go.

As for Leonardo, he was an open secret: an acknowledged genius, but only for his paintings. Whatever else he had known or guessed lay hidden for close on three centuries in the notebooks, in the page on page of crabbed and rusty mirror writing, diagrams, drawings, that were scattered on his death like autumn leaves. They are still kept in the dark today, for safety's sake, these translucent relics of the life of a mind, they are so parched and frail, so beautiful in their own right, illuminated like a Celtic gospel with his drawings. But they played no part in the story.

Darkness, therefore, is the first stage of shadow
and light is the last.
LEONARDO DA VINCI

Among other matters Father Francesco Maurolico, working alone in Messina, had exposed the open secret of the pinhole; he had seen how it solved the ancient problem of the dapple of little eclipsed suns under the trees. He also made diagrams of the patterns of light rays in curves, including the *caustic* – καυστικος, burning – curve, an envelope of the rays reflected by a given curve as in a concave mirror. And mirrors, incidentally, are backed with a tain of lunar caustic, also known as lunar nitre, lunar crystals and crystals of silver – the *lapis infernalis* of the alchemists. Lunar caustic is silver nitrate, fused: in alchemy silver was to the moon, *luna*, as gold was to the sun. Silver, of course, tarnishes; and it was this quality – this lack of quality compared to immortal gold – that was to make silver the founding element of photography: silver in its salts in gelatin, on surfaces part shaded, part open to the light, was the trick of it.

The secret of making – but not fixing – sun prints on paper or leather coated with silver nitrate was discovered as early as 1802 by Thomas Wedgwood, Coleridge's friend: an ephemeral art, his delicate laceworks of leaves and insect wings, white on black, no sooner exposed to the light than lost to the dark.

Latent in the beautiful shapes and names of curves, *caustic*, *evolute*, *involute*, *cochleoid*, *limaçon*, *cardioid*, *conchoid*, *nephroid*, *serpentine*, *astroid*, *spiral*, *clothoid*, *Witch of Agnesi*, fire, shellfish, snails, vital organs, heavenly bodies, mythic beings, fossilised in abstraction.

We saw rays coming through the bottom of the clouds. Then, for a moment, we saw the sun sweeping – it seemed to be sailing at a great pace and clear in a gap; we had out our smoked glasses; we saw it crescent, burning red; next moment it had sailed fast into the cloud again; only the red streamers came from it; then only a golden haze, such as one has often seen. The moments were passing. We thought we were cheated; we looked at the sheep; they showed no fear; the setters were racing round; everyone was standing in long lines, rather dignified, looking out. I thought how we were like very old people, in the birth of the world – druids on Stonehenge; (this idea came more vividly in the first pale light though). At the back of us were great blue spaces in the cloud. These were still blue. But now the colour was going out. The clouds were turning pale; a reddish black colour. Down in the valley it was an extraordinary scrumble of red and black; there was the one light burning; all was cloud down there, and very beautiful, so delicately tinted. Nothing could be seen through the cloud. The 24 seconds were passing. Then one looked back again at the blue; and rapidly, very very quickly, all the colours faded; it became darker and darker as at the beginning of a violent storm; the light sank and sank; we kept saying this is the shadow; and we thought now it is over – this is the shadow; when suddenly the light went out. We had fallen. It was extinct. There was no colour. The earth was dead. That was the astonishing moment; and the next when as if a ball had rebounded the cloud took colour on itself again, only a sparky ethereal colour and so the light came back. I had very strongly the feeling as the light went out of some vast obeisance; something kneeling down and suddenly raised up when the colours came. They came back astonishingly lightly and quickly and beautifully in the valley and over the hills – at first with a miraculous glittering and ethereality, later normally almost, but with a great sense of relief...How can I express the darkness? It was a sudden plunge, when one did not expect it; being at the mercy of the sky; our own nobility; the druids; Stonehenge; and the racing red dogs; all that was in one's mind.

VIRGINIA WOOLF, *A WRITER'S DIARY*

It all began with fresco, back in the cave days of the great herds with their pelts of charcoal, fat and ochre brought back to life by firelight and the power of the spirits. The refinement of fresco known as encaustic – εγκαυστικο, burnt in – reached its peak in the Egypt of the Ptolemies in lifelike portraits of the dead on coffin lids. The pigment was mixed with beeswax and stippled on and then heated until the wax fused into skins of paint so flawless and luminous that after more than two thousand years they look modern, almost alive, under the glass of the museums. In the tradition of the Pharaohs, they are ideal faces, put there to affirm the life of the soul above the swathed and shredding reality of the corpse; and at the same time they make a striking departure. They are nothing like the great gilded, smiling masks of the mummy cases. They are everyday Greeks, in exile in Egypt, whose olive eyes meet your own under a black double arch of brow; and so clear and lustrous of flesh, so red-lipped they could pass for Renaissance figures. As in a way they were, and are – reborn, over and over, to rise up before us like loved ones. Souls. Waxen apparitions.

They fell to painting ships also with wax and fire, Pliny noted, wooden ships, to seal them. *And this kind of painting ships is so fast and sure, that neither sunne will resolve, not salt water eat and fret, ne yet wind and weather pierce and chinke it.*

As for the black-figure, μελανομορφη, earthenware of Attica, with the gods and mortals caught in eloquent attitudes like jointed puppets in a shadow-play, it was not so much painted as developed: and the secret was in the firing, carried out with all the precision of a master baker juggling the nature not of the living yeast but the iron in red clay.

The raw clay had to be soaked in water and strained and left to thicken before it was ready to knead. Then, once the pot was thrown on the wheel, the artist would lay each figure on the wet body in the same red clay, only more finely sifted and blended, brushing it on so that it left no trace, working blind, trusting more to the inner eye and the familiar hand. Then came the firing, a threefold firing: once with the kiln hot and the vents open, turning the pot a deeper red, deeper still in the patches of fine clay; next with the fire damped down, the vents closed and the heat raised to the melting point of glass, so that lack of oxygen would turn the whole pot black, while the quartz particles in the patches of fine clay fused into a glaze. Finally the heat was turned down a little and the vents opened, the body of the pot went back to the original deep red and out of the kiln, the cocoon of the fire, it emerged with the figures intact – they were there all the time! – and crystallised in a new black skin by a subtle alchemy of earth, water, fire and air.

Unbearable painful silence.
Black and angelic Attic day.
GEORGE SEFERIS

A dark basement at Munchmuseet houses the artist's relics, photographs, books, diaries and sketches in glass cases around the walls, his black hat on the hatstand, his brushes and palette, a candlestick, a death mask, and lastly, shockingly, burrowed in a coil of panels, an apparition, a room, the bedroom of his house on the Oslofjord. On the wall is his own painting of old age among these very belongings, *Self-portrait. Between the clock and the bed.* There he stoops, hands at his sides, sunlight flooding the walls at his back, his face shrunk to a mask, an old man in dark blue pyjamas staring out into the dark – at you standing by the single bed, brass painted white, with the linen cover appliquéd in pink and black stripes, the very bed he was to die in, quietly one winter's day in 1944, Dostoyevsky's *The Possessed* in his lap. Here is the wicker chair, and the grandfather clock, which has been ticking all along, and has hands, and eyes, while in the painting it has a blank yellow face. Mirrored in the blue shadows of a doorway beyond the bed is a standing, flowing nude. Here is where he spun himself out in the space between Eros, Thanatos and Hypnos, *Selvportrett. Mellom klokken og sengen*, a stage set, a still life, an absence – you blundering in, casting your shadow, you are in his shoes.

Photography brought a new alchemy into the world, the embalming of the shadow, a kind of immortality. The substance might be fading before your eyes, but, once caught, the shadow would last forever. The mourning portrait of the dead, alone or with the mourners, had entered family life with the daguerreotype. When spirit photography came along it went one better, by showing the lost loved one after death and yet miraculously still alive in a body of light: now the camera caught more than the eye could! In its nineteenth-century heyday there were plenty willing to believe; and in the new century the Great War saw a brief revival. A photograph of the bereaved, taken in a bare studio, that when printed would reveal a luminous haze of presence at their side, quietly haunting them – in the slaughterhouse of Europe such photographs made up in a way for the leavetaking that had never taken place, the body trampled among millions more somewhere in the mud of a foreign field. They were the paper equivalent of those Greek steles where the dead and the bereaved, one flesh and one spirit, join forever and part forever in stone.

There was no quiet even in the stones of still older civilizations. The hieratically retained gesture of very ancient cults contained an unrest of living surfaces like water within a vessel. There were currents in the taciturn gods that were sitting; and those that were standing commanded with a gesture that sprang like a fountain out from the stone and fell back again causing many ripples.
RAINER MARIA RILKE, *AUGUSTE RODIN*

Jack Kerouac saw in Robert Frank's book of photographs taken on the road, *The Americans*, the soul of America and of a photographer *with the agility, mystery, genius, sadness and strange secrecy of a shadow.*

In the new Centre for the Moving Image in Melbourne is a black and white video installation, *Tall Ships*, inspired by an old photograph the filmmaker, Gary Hill, came across in Seattle where he lives, of a masted ship in full sail looming unsteadily in the fogbound harbour of the past. You step inside a darkness, a silent passage. Only an icy flare of moonlight shimmers here and there along the walls, low as a pilot light, each one spindling up at your approach until there are eleven living figures of men and women lined up in two rows, milky apparitions, loose and fluttering at the edges, adrift in space as if in water, magnified; and one at the far end, a little girl who raises and lowers her arms like a doll and waits to be gathered up. Young or old, dogged or playful or anxious, they come up one by one out of the depths of a dark world of their own as if to a window, a mirror, and dangle there eye to eye with you trying to see out. But you pass on and they give up, turning away and spindling back down, only to look up and advance all over again – ghostly, or you are the ghost passing in the night, naked souls caught somewhere in time midway between the still and the moving image. All in the dark and out of reach and so lonely you can hardly tear yourself away.

Our sea has the same influence on the moon as the moon has on us.
LEONARDO DA VINCI

'Sail' in Greece is πανι, 'cloth', no longer φαρος. So a ship under sail, μια βαρκα με πανια, is a ship with cloths.

Wave on wave falls flat in a mirror as its own foam overrides it.

In the Sculpture Garden by the lake at the National Gallery in Canberra are two garden sculptures where the seen and the unseen are interwoven in a stand of native trees.

Fujiko Nakaya's Fog Sculpture runs along one side of the reed pond, serried rows of rusty pipes and jets that sizzle alarmingly just before noon and puff out billows of white mist. 'Gas!' scream the schoolchildren in its path, bobbing their heads in the jets and shaking off a spray of waterdrops. 'Poison gas!'

Fingers of mist drift into the trees, which are not cedars – they look so like a Japanese print – but casuarinas, dark she-oaks, supple and furry. Sunlight and fog together, shadows and moss in scaly armpits, spangles, a pad of fog low over the pond and in the reeds, wavering. I kneel to focus on a frond as it moves under a bird, in a moment of breeze, or mist blanks it out. One swoop and a bird pierces the pond with beak and talons and flaps off with a fish – too late I have snapped not the bird but its imprint of whirlpool. One bank of the pipes is above a path with its back to a ring of frail wooden posts on raked earth, old Pukumani burial poles going dark with wet. Soon their bed of brown needles is spangled and the path striped in shimmer and shadow and you are hooped in rainbow as you go, a full circle of rainbow, and come out with your skin slick with wet and your hair in cold clumps.

Two hours later the fog is turned off and fades over the water like a ghost at daybreak, and the view sets solid.

Two women, two gardens. Fiona Hall's Fern Garden is a small courtyard that you keep glimpsing from upstairs windows and yet on foot it is as confusing as Alice's garden to get into. Once you do, you are among dozens of tall tree ferns with slender dark brown bodies husky to the touch, each with a green crown of fronds in the sky and smaller coils of frond unfolding like hands. Hemmed in as they are by walls of windows, they give this block of space another atmosphere, dark and dank, with an old rainforest density, although they are young. On plaques inlaid in a spiral path are as many of their names as are still known in the language of each of the peoples belonging to the ancient homelands of this tree fern, who are the hidden presences here.

fern seed, the spores of ferns, formerly supposed to have the power to make persons invisible.

Adelard of Bath in the twelfth century saw light as a *visible breath*. Six centuries later the Swiss scientist Leonhard Euler saw it as a pulse throbbing. Space was not a vacuum, and nor was it full of what would have to be clashing whirlpools of shed 'husks'. The ether, *incomparably finer and more subtile* than air, filled the universe and earth and everything in it, not only space; and pure light, radiating through this ethereal sea, shed nothing of itself on the way. *Do certain portions, inconceivably small, of the sun himself, or of his substance, come down to us? Or is the transmission similar to the sound of a bell, which the ear receives, though no part of the substance of the bell be separated from it...?* The latter, Euler concluded. *As the vibrations of the air produce* sound, *what will be the effect of those of ether? You will undoubtedly guess at once* light. *It appears in truth abundantly certain, that light is with respect to ether, what sound is with respect to air*...so that his sun hung in the ether like a universal bell *ringing continually*, uttering light.

Between the spring equinox and the autumn equinox
here are the running waters here's the garden
here are the bees humming in the branches
and ringing a bell in a baby's ears
and here's the sun! and the birds of paradise
a great sun greater than the light.

ενας μεγαλος ηλιος πιο μεγαλος απ' το φως
GEORGE SEFERIS

Among the more amorphous enemies of bees in Pliny's great book are gloomy inertia, *tristitia torpens* – the monkish accidie – and echoes, and fog. *Inimica et echo...inimica et nebula. Moreover, the sound made by the reverberation of the aire, which men call Eccho, is hurtfull unto them: for they feare mightily that resounding noise, comming with a double stroke.*

Dead bees would *revive and be quicke againe* if they were kept indoors over winter and then put out in the hot spring sun and kept warm with figwood ashes, in Pliny's day. If there were no dead bees to be found, new ones could be bred in the paunch of a freshly slaughtered ox in a dunghill *by a certaine metamorphosis which Nature maketh, from one creature to another*. Like the human soul, the bee flew out of the carrion on invisible wings. Or the bee was a soul herself. Born of air, *apis ætherea*.

Live bees, for that matter, can be kept alive indoors in the coldest winter if they are fed. Syrup is good, or *drie Raisins of the Sunne, and Figges,* or wool *soked in honied wine, for them to settle upon and sucke*, or barley sugar to lick – the bee is a lambent insect – or a dish of ale syrup is good too.

Lambent?

lambent...1. Of a flame (fire, light): playing lightly upon or gliding over a surface without burning it, like a 'tongue of fire'... 2. In etymological sense: Licking, that licks...1826 KIRBY & SP. *Entomol.* (1828) IV. 492 The Hymenoptera generally lap their food with their tongue and may be called lambent insects.

And so they may, in both senses. The tongue is thin, sheathed and hairy, and red, a tongue of fire with a spoon on the end. She dusts her fur with pollen as she goes, brushing it into the baskets on her hind legs. Her compound eyes, myopic eyes, a mosaic of facets like honeycomb, see in all directions, the image appearing right way up on the retina, not upside down as on ours. There are thousands of facets, every one a true eye with its own lens, and under the microscope, laid out among reeds like a stone garden, a quilt, dried beans – *lens* is 'lentil' of course. She also has three simple eyes, ocelli, on the top of her head. Blind to red light, which is black to her, in compensation she sees ultraviolet: many bee flowers have petals inscribed as if in invisible ink with a map of the nectar we only see under 'black' light. The older the bee, the more sensitive to light and the more strongly drawn to it.

The nectar is sucked not into the stomach but the honey-crop, the crucible, where it is well on the way to honey by the time she gets home. *Apis mellifera*, honey-bringer, is also *mellifica*, honeymaker, no mere vessel or handmaiden. She belongs to the order of the *Hymenoptera*, which sounds monastic, as indeed it is, the workers all being sisters, virgins, thriving at their devotions in a hive of cells. With one proviso: that the hive is 'queenright'. Without a queen they will slowly succumb like so many Desert Fathers to the sour gloom, the accidie, ακηδια, of monkish life, and die *en masse*.

The *Hymenoptera* by definition have fine wings of membrane. The honeymaker has two pairs, *deux paires d'ailes translucides et membraneuses* on which to fly backwards and forwards and sideways and hang in a glaze of whirr, and fan the hive, and hum the honey dance.

A bee larva melts in its wax pot, fermenting – as the grape turns into wine, the nectar into honey into mead, into poetry, transformed into alcohol, *the fire*, the spirit – until it crawls out in fur and wings to peer with new eyes at a new self. Lambent! A bee of the Invisible in the visible world. Shape-shifting, transitory – and yet who else on earth lays up a treasure half so pure and durable, so nearly immortal, out of so little, with so little harm done, as the bee does?

One fine day a new bee finds herself airborne, a *butineuse*, a forager. On the threshold she falters, as well she might. Until now all the light she has known has been a buttery maze of layer on layer of shadowy wax, a Plato's cave. This is her moment of truth. Flooded with sun, she is ready for a second hatching out of the chrysalis of the hive into flight. *Le soleil d'artifice*, the sunburst, the catherine wheel, French beekeepers call this moment when she rises in a sizzle of gold, in one step attaining a voice and a world.

Not that she can afford to lose her head. No giddiness, she is on a mission here, risking her life for it. Although their sight is dim, as Charles Butler noted, bees take *paines at the doore in rubbing and wiping their glazen eies* and so she does, this and every other time; and once in the air she makes very sure, hovering, taking her bearings by the visible or invisible sun, that she will know her way home. Then and only then does she take flight. Only so far, no further, mind, flight costs honey. She is flying blind, out in the open on a course laid down for her in the hive by a sister bee, never having seen a flower in her life. As she makes her way home that first time rich in nectar and experience, does it feel as if she has come a long way, is the hive smaller somehow? Once there she in turn does a dance on the combs for her sisters, the steps of which are a precise mapping of the way, showing how abundant her source is, how far away and where in relation to the sun. She turns, she waggles and beats her wings and hums, a subtle choreography of signs; now and then one of the audience will stroke her fur to release the scent of the flowers she has rummaged in, or scrape on the comb for her to stop and give them a taste. Then each in her turn takes off into the sun.

The little dancer in her nest of honey – does she pride herself on the precision of her performance, every turn and waggle and glassy purr of her wings? Does she know if she has done well? She may stumble at first and get her song and dance map wrong, but she learns fast. How? Wholly by instinct, involuntarily? Is learning, I wonder, by definition ever wholly involuntary? And is what she has just done – the bee lore of millions of years – so different in kind from the theatre of sticks and stones in the sand where the Stone Age navigators taught wayfinding? She must retain the memory of her flight, to dance it; out in the open the others must bear her dance in mind and turn it back into flight: *memory*, remember, *is a fact of the soul*.

No time to lose, she has a hive to feed, she will forage till she drops – milking only one kind of flower on any given day, favouring all the days of her life the first one she tried.

As for the bee we know as the queen, she keeps to the hive. All she does is breed. After Aristotle, to a man the natural philosophers for two thousand years would regard her as male, the king bee (and the drones, by the same token, as female). It stood to reason. In fact what she is, no more, no less, is the mother. In his scrupulous way Aristotle, while unconvinced, noted how the country folk referred to the 'kings' of their hives as μητερες, 'mothers'. On the edge of the known world in Britain they were wise to her all along: they knew her as *mam gwenen* in Old Cornish, 'mother of bees', and *béomoðer* in Old English, and in Old Welsh, *modrydaf*, 'hive-mother' and *gwrach*, 'old woman', 'hag', or 'witch'.

Be that as it may – the whole hive is in her thrall – this bee alone of all her brood never ventures out except on her mating flight when she soars up tailed by drones, one of whom must seize and impregnate her, and die, while she flies home, laden with his sperm and his torn member, to a lifetime of laying eggs.

Any queen hatched in the hive must face the old one. The one time a queen ever uses her sting is on a new virgin queen in a duel to the death. Occasionally a defeated old queen may live on as a dowager in a daughter's hive; more often, giving way, she will lead out a breakaway swarm and start a new one. Their passing makes a hot rent in the air, a fabric that moves throbbing and singing, to enfold her wherever she may settle in one pulsing, shimmering mass in a tree, a chimney, a boat hull, taking off again and again in search. Although the swarm is gorged with honey and not on any warpath, the sight is enough to strike panic. Death is in the air. The old bee books have their stories: the gentle old horse nodding and swishing its tail too close to an unseen hive and dying in agony in a blanket of bees; the girl out in the fields, a maidservant, a novice, smothering in bees, blinded and transfigured as if in living fire, only to be left standing when the whole mass lifts away in the wake of the queen, unstung, immaculate.

And at last one angle declines, another is lifted; the radiant mantle unites its four sunlit corners; and, like the wonderful carpet the fairy-tale speaks of that flits across space to obey its master's command, it steers its straight course, bending forward a little as though to hide in its folds the sacred presence of the future, towards the willow, the pear-tree, or lime whereon the queen has alighted; and round her each rhythmical wave comes to rest, as though on a nail of gold...
MAURICE MAETERLINCK

Gauguin was blessed with a remarkable visual memory, as he said himself, *une remarquable mémoire des yeux* – a photographic memory. Whatever had caught his eye was his. A biographer commenting on the photos the artist took to Tahiti and nailed up on the wall of his hut – a bas-relief from Borobodur, an Egyptian frieze, figures he was to bring back to life in a new golden Polynesian skin – compared him to bees who, in Montaigne's words, *'pillotent de çà de là les fleurs et en font miel qui est tout leur: ce n'est plus thym ni marjolaine.' The Bees doe here and there sucke this, and cull that flower, but afterward they produce the hony, which is peculiarly their owne* (only the French is in monosyllables like a chime of bells, and rhymes), *then is it no more Thyme or Marjoram.* Gauguin travelled light; the photos he took along for company, as he saw it, were samples of the visible, elements of a private image hoard in what Rilke would one day name *the great golden hive of the Invisible.*

A French lieutenant who had made friends with him when he first landed in Papeete and caught up with him later, around the coast in Mataiea, found him living *an enclosed life as if his brain was sealed in a glass jar.*

His early childhood in Peru with his mother's family was the happiest time of his life, his exotic lost paradise. He was born a savage, he insisted, an Inca of Peru – descended on his mother's side from Montezuma himself, according to her own mother, that woman of fire, *cette femme de feu*, Flora Tristan. All dead and gone but for a handful of memories, and a mummy he had found on display in a glass case and sketched in his notebook, an Inca of Peru washed up on the tides of fate, like himself, in Paris, and destined to haunt him and his work for as long as he lived. The mummy is so much more than a corpse – the mummy is already art. This one sits naked in the case roped up knees to chin in the foetal position, its skull propped on both chalky fists, the eye sockets bare, one with a membrane over it like dried egg white, the lantern jaw in a gape of desolation. Like the soul, the mummy is what dwells inside, unseen, buried, waiting to split the papery flesh and fly free. The mummy is the ancestor, androgynous, and Eve and the tiki with the iridescent eyes of paua shell, the savage soul and the spirit of the dead watching, *manao tupapau. Plus thym ni marjolaine* – he had made it his own.

A flare like a line of bubbles bounced off the lens, enlarging as they go – a technical flaw that may give a photo more balance, depth, sparkle – is a 'ghost'.

So many phenomena that had to be invented to make sense of the world! The husks were the phlogiston of optics, motes in the mind's eye, with a long half-life under a whole litany of names, as Roger Bacon observed: 'similitude' and 'image', 'species', 'idol', 'phantasm' and 'simulacrum'; 'form' (Alhazen's *sura*), 'intention', 'shadow of the philosophers' – *umbra philosophorum* – and 'virtue', 'impression', 'passion'. Unlike the sun of the philosophers, with its orbiting earth, their shadow had slipped in under the guard of the new absolute religion. In Europe throughout the Middle Ages and beyond the husk was an article of faith. The Church Fathers found in the husks, by way of Plotinos, a spark to fuse the Trinity with the Good of Sokrates, for whom *the Sun not only makes the things we see visible, but also brings them into being...And so with the objects of knowledge: these derive from the Good not only their power of being known, but their very being and reality*. For Plotinos, the Good, the One, the All, the quick of being, was constantly seeding the universe with its own substance in proliferating self-images. Augustine's God shed himself likewise as light and was one with the light; three in one and co-eternal, and the Light of Lights.

Be that as it may – and such an image might well have the power to burn on in a vacuum – out with the old optics went the husks in the long run. Between the truth of the retina and the truth of the lens they vanished into thin air. These days we believe in a radiation without light or colour, in a physical world that is dark and blind. In essence, light has gone on being a mystery, essentially the same old mystery; so that a scientist of our day like Vasco Ronchi can arrive at the end of his *Storia della Luce* to find himself back in our beginning, and our physics of light and its earliest counterpart, its mirror twin, at peace in each other's arms.

Nothing exists which flows between psyche and phantom to which the name of 'light' could be given. To the word 'light', therefore, only one meaning remains, namely 'absence of darkness' the very same meaning attributed to it by philosophers two thousand years ago. That 'there is light' simply means that the psyche is not idle but produces phantoms, even if only in a dream.

VASCO RONCHI

Light at sundown, coppery, so finespun it catches on surfaces.

Light…is the presence of fire or something resembling fire in what is transparent.
ARISTOTLE

Not fire but the presence of fire…His light is φως, and his πυρ, fire, is in transparency. But πυρ has died out now. Fire these days, φωτια, comes from φως.

The eye may be said to owe its existence to light, which calls forth, as it were, a sense that is akin to itself; the eye, in short, is formed with reference to light, to be fit for the action of light; the light it contains corresponding with the light without.
GOETHE

So there are colourblind people who live in 'grayscale', a world without colours! They have a congenital defect of the retina, achromatopsia, found, though rarely, all over the world. On one remote Pacific island, Pingelap, however, one child in every twelve is born with it. The victims are unable to focus, besides, and are painfully sensitive to light, dazzled and blinded, so much so that they must cover their eyes in the sun and shun the daylight: they are lovers of the twilight, moonlight and the night sea and sky – out fishing at night they come into their own. Theirs is a parallel world of depths and movements, textures, lustres, surfaces of grey, as we see it, though no concept of grey exists where nothing is not grey, where grey is the air they breathe. One account of their affliction is that they are children of the ancestral god of the island, begotten on their mothers under cover of night, and that their ghostly eyes have come down to them from the spirit world.

Golden fire on a lighthouse at sunset, red fire in a heart of glass.

The caves in this honeycomb of cliffs change their shape over time and tide.

At last I have an enlarger of my own, portable, secondhand, in good order, that my son found for me. It will go in the laundry with its tall head in a veil, a dustcloth, since the laundry, for all its chinks and cracks and keyholes, has a surface, the washing machine, and running water in the troughs, and will do very well, if only at night, as a darkroom. A room in a dark house silvery under the moon; my films will hang, wet snakeskins, in the shower recess; a door ajar against a lamp will be a negative in a rim of light; I will wake to my last night's work of prints pegged up to dry on the clothes horse. Printing will be all nightwork from now on, winter work in the dark of the year. I will live in a house of black and white and my night will be my day.

My friend has undergone massive surgery for breast cancer, and is better now, she says, although still in shock, and pain: better enough, anyway, to come for the weekend. She arrives with a present wrapped in black tissue opening on inner sheets of white, a death mask. No, a solid head, a cemetery angel by the look, severed at a slant across the neck, and I catch my breath.

For the garden, she says. I fell in love with it and got two. One each. Twins.

Thank you, I say – who is it?

She shrugs. The goddess.

Which – ?

Aphrodite.

(A severed head?)

You don't like her?

No I do! Of course! Thank you.

I do. Of course. After I have seen her off I have another look. The head has a rusty hook embedded in the flat underside – a girl's head tilted to one side, yellowing like ivory in the folds of the skin and the stranded, braided hair swept off the forehead. The face is set in a half-open, placid smile that tucks in the eyelids and the corners of the mouth. The eyeballs have shallow rings etched in for irises. A fly rests on one cheek and zooms off, opalescent. The cut edge of the throat is like a biscuit with white icing.

If the back of the head is flat, I suppose, still at a loss, she must be lying down. She has cheeks as smooth as river stone, eyes all shadow, and between the lips, glistening, the poke of a sly tongue. So opaque, so cold, the flesh sunken the way it is in sleep even in the very young, sharp over the cheekbones, unless it's the light. The anonymity of all young faces, in the eyes of the old. But no, not asleep, those eyes are watchful under the heavy lids. Half awake, half asleep.

But why the bloodstained hook? – of course, for hanging her upright on a wall or a post outside where the sun and rain can work their changes, scab her with moss and lichen, grey green and yellow, a slime of mould, a veil of cracks and snail silver, spider thread, until she is taken in, barely visible, at one with her surroundings. Our garden angel.

Having nowhere to hang a severed head, I take her clamped in both hands to the front room and lay her down on the mantelpiece under the lamp, where she has been ever since, a stone queen on her tomb, face to the face in the mirror on the wall, gathering dust.

She is writing again, she tells me over the phone. A story in the present tense, maybe a novel, a saga, even the goddess comes into it, pulled up off a seabed or buried, scarred, broken. That makes two of us, I say, because by now I have scenes, images, vague storylines roughed out in which the goddess appears only to disappear, and in the meantime photo after photo of the goddess. She is pitted like bare rock, steeped in shadow, ripples of leaf shadow and water light bar her skin, she is ice, translucent, I tell my friend, promising samples when I see her.

Her hair has fallen out and is growing back in tight

curls. She can no longer walk. Months have passed. I have come home to a shaky phone message explaining that she has been struck down. The doctors who have shrugged off her blackouts all along as stress have done the proper tests and scans and changed their tune now. She is riddled with tumours, all inoperable, the spawn of the missing breast, even in her spine, her brain – four in the brain alone. (What if I lose my mind? You won't. How will I know?) They offer guarded hope, with treatment. She will take everything on offer and go on as usual for as long as she can until she can barely open her eyes, simply to be alive. As she still is, in my head, even now that I've seen her in a coffin like a giant crib, a bassinette, the pain gone from her with the life, surfacing in my sleep from time to time, in dreams, where drifts of weed and sand float up like dust in the sun and coat the inner mirror of the surface, a story in the present tense. Ripples radiate and intersect and wash her smooth, her young self again, worn down by long immersion, adrift with unseeing eyes, wobbling at the edges, uttering water. Wet shoulders, a halo of hair, a dead and living face.

Life is also an Act, the Act of the soul…
PLOTINOS

Wayfinding, wayfaring, seafaring, landfinding. For thousands of years of prehistory a people with no written language, no metal, no contact with what we know as the known world, built canoes and sailed them across the open Pacific by memory alone, the mind's eye. Nothing was left to chance, they had to know their waters. All the islands had their hereditary navigators whose training began in childhood, the work of many years at sea, and on land, mastering the maps drawn in the sand and stick and pebble diagrams of the constellations of stars and islands, the swells and landfalls, the star alignments in all seasons from every other known island. They learned by rote the long skeins of chant in which the lore of the sea and sky had been woven and handed down. The way to steer a course was ingrained in them over a whole lifetime of watching for zenith stars and horizon stars, bearing in mind the behaviour of cloud, wind and water. None of this is speculation, the ancient craft of wayfinding has been handed down from father to son – and daughter – to our own day: the same goes for the Aboriginal tribes who have worked the shorelines, waters and reefs of tropical Australia over thousands of years and who know themselves as the 'Saltwater People'. Nothing is lost on the navigators. They keep a weather eye out for the ocean swells, whether smooth or refracted and reflected in a pattern that means land, leaving a shadow of turbulence; and for the loom of land, the faintest glow reflected in the air or on the belly of rainclouds over an invisible atoll, sunglare or moonlight the colour of sand and surf, or a dry reef, a lagoon; and the deep phosphorescence that sparks and shoots under the hull, always pointing to some far-off island or reef; seamarks, landmarks, shoals, currents, whirlpools, sea spray on the skin, homing and migratory birds, sea life, sighting stones set up on islands.

In a TV interview the poet of the Aegean, Seferis, now long dead, speaks of being taken over by the day, the light; and of Homer having needed to be blind. The dark chamber, the need to retreat, narrow the aperture.

How are we to gain the open sea? For Odysseus is surely a parable to us…

What then is our course, what the manner of our flight? This is not a journey for the feet; the feet bring us only from land to land; nor need you think of coach or ship to carry you away; all this order of things you must set aside and refuse to see; you must close your eyes and call instead upon another vision which is to be waked within you, a vision, the birth-right of all, which few turn to use…

Withdraw into yourself and look.
PLOTINOS

Nous choisirons Ithaque, la terre fidèle, la pensée audacieuse et frugale, l'action lucide, la génerosité de l'homme qui sait.

We will choose Ithaka, the steadfast land, audacious and frugal thought, lucid action, the generosity of the man who knows.
ALBERT CAMUS

Platon, the beloved disciple, is not there on the day. His *Phaedo* will be written from hearsay, put into the mouth of Phaidon who is there with the others for those last hours in the prison cell, on the threshold, while Sokrates puts the case for the immortality of the soul and the life after death and in between. His shackles are hacked off. He remarks how strange a thing pleasure is, how inseparable from pain, how like life and death in that respect, and so the dialogue is away, the weaving of a web of argument in which his companions will be as helpless as flies. Is death anything to be feared? There is a brighter world, a pure land beyond our ken. The misfortune of the soul, shackled to the flesh here below, is to have a knowledge of the true world which is as flawed as that of some creature confined for a lifetime to the seabed, knowing no better than to take the murk and barrenness, the faint shattered sun and stars overhead, for the whole world. Like the prisoners in the parable he once told them, the one about the cave full of shadowy fire, such a creature in its great cave of water, seeing through a glass darkly, could only assume there was no more to be known. Yet he need only have put his head out once, the way even the fishes do, to be bathed in the sun of truth. So it is for the enlightened soul. Why then should the philosopher fear death? The image cuts both ways for us today, who have only to put on a mask to see a whole other shimmering blue world in pane after pane of water that he, Sokrates, could have no inkling of: unless he was ever out on a boat – not he, a stonemason by trade who kept both bare feet firmly on the ground! – to see a fisherman lean over and pour out a window of oil over the sea. Not that it matters. At this moment of leavetaking, his whole being is a window into the afterlife. His soul, unseen, deathless, is bound for Hades, no less *unseen*, the *good and wise god* who takes in all the dead. The shackles are gone, he is in fine form, and if there is any flaw in his vision for once his companions are in no mood to argue. Nor will he let them weep. Sokrates rallies them. He must be allowed a swansong. As always he will have the last word. Mildly he reaches for the bowl of hemlock.

Certainely there is no happinesse within this circle of flesh, nor is it in the Opticks of these eyes to behold felicity; the first day of our Jubilee is death…
SIR THOMAS BROWNE

The physical world is a dark matter. Radiation, dark forces. Our life cuts a path through like a river in its own dark. Our light is all a construct of the eye's mind.

Can darkness ever be loved with the love that casts out fear? Pure darkness? *Du Dunkelheit*, Rilke begins his poem, as he might address a dog he is fondling, a large grave black dog – *You darkness that I stem from* – beginning and ending with night. *I love you more than the flame that fences in the world*…While the communal flame draws us all in, the darkness is where an unseen power may heave into – not sight so much as a blind awareness, a shifting balance, a knowledge. *I believe in nights*.

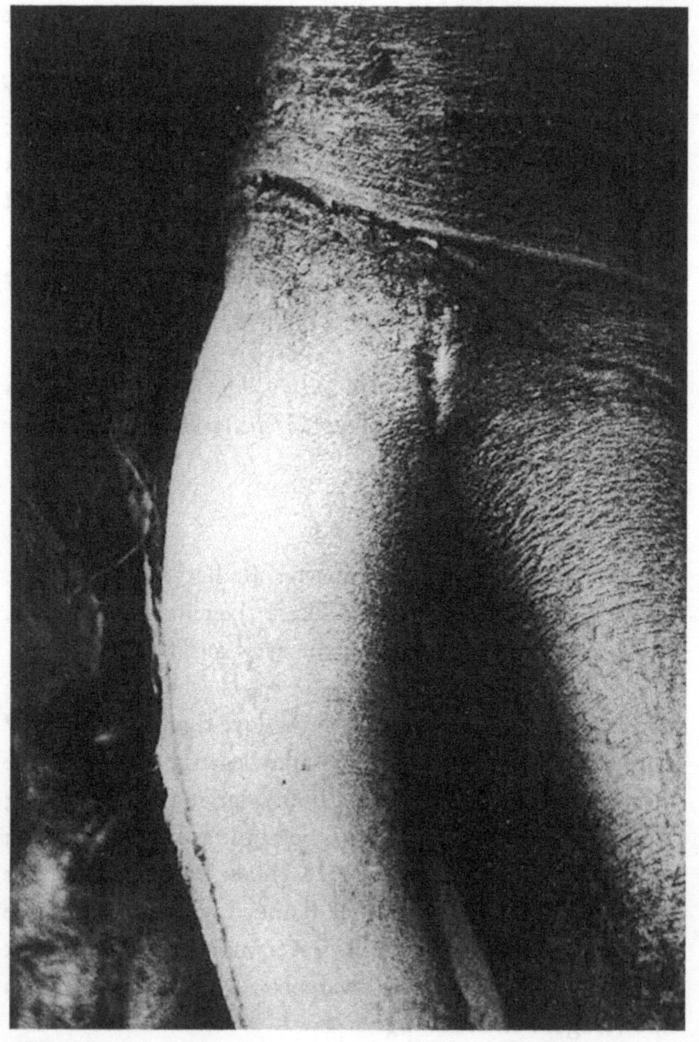

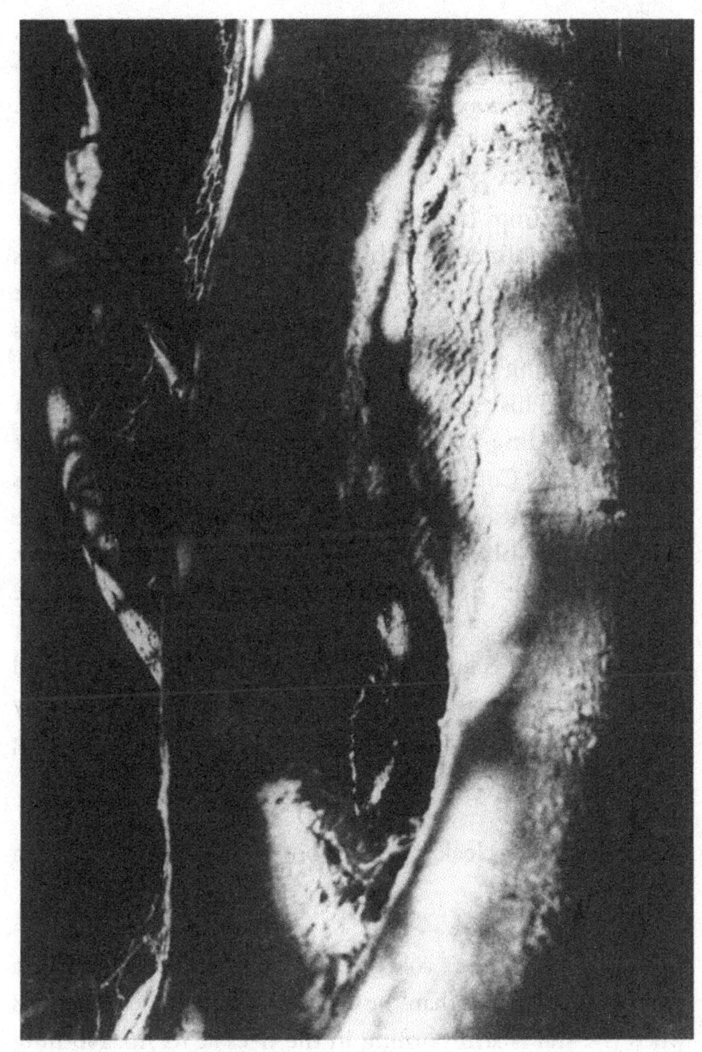

Annie Dillard: *The planet spins, rapt inside its intricate mists. The galaxy is a flung thing, loose in the night, and our solar system is one of many dotted campfires ringed with tossed rocks. What shall we sing?*

Those blind from birth – what are their dreams made on? Was Homer blind from birth? (Do we know if he was blind at all? Or blinded, as quail are blinded, to make them sing? – ομηρος means 'hostage'). He brought his epics into being in the act, his whole body the instrument, his voice and his twanging lyre, and his whole mind intent on the unfolding of a long memory, wayfinding over vast invisible seas. Could anyone have done that with his eyes open? Asleep, at least, he must have dreamed – dreamed he was no longer blind – seen his dreams. So the Greeks say. They see their dreams. Ειδα ονειρο, they say in the morning, always 'I saw', not 'I had' a dream, and at night he saw his islands and ships at sea, city walls, warriors and women and gods rise up before his very eyes like fire, only to be woken to the dark of day. Or was his a life of singing aloud by the fires all night, and sleep by day?

Death wears a cloak of invisibility, you don't see him coming.

The gorge is inland, a cold slit in the rainforest. It lives by a more southerly time than the coast. Down here the night falls when the sun is still burning in the trees at its lip. Nothing of the sea's presence, so near, makes itself felt. Below the waterfall the gorge is in shadow for most of the day, a speckled stretch of rock and water and air, shining, steeped, splotched with pallor, rumpled, or as invisible as glass – treacherous water threaded through, fractured, inlaid with slime, white with its own fall and disturbance or running loose and black under a string of fat bubbles. Smooth rocks dam it, and fallen trees are alight with flamy tongues, fungi, black trunks as if charred in a bushfire, in a ripple of fire. Drifts of scum bank up behind them to bake hard as egg-white, until a flood dislodges them. The tree ferns that spread roots to the river and overarch it in a fan vault of light are of a tall race, slender, with a springy blackish-brown husk of hair as warmly alive as a dog's, pricked with starry green moss. Underneath, even in a dry season, the air is dank. The pools sink under a weight of shadows, reflections and fragments of the green sun-glow through the ferns and feathery dead brown fronds. Lichens, leaf meal, a fungus like a plate of jelly on a thin stalk, others that poke out of a log, grey wingbuds of a dark body. A long fluency in the course of change, written in ink on water, in a cleft of place. The township downstream at the sandy mouth is where my son's life began and my mother's ended, both arduously. These days I come back down into this underworld as from a long way off.

Facets of breaking water, faceted fish, shadowy dragonflies.

Why, then, is the eye-jelly of the eye, water?
PRISCIAN OF LYDIA

Now my right eyeball has an eyelash stuck on it late one night that is no eyelash, that no light in the house is strong enough to isolate or flood of saline wash out. I sleep in fear and wake to a black knot like an ant with trailing feelers that twitches with each blink, then swims loose. My regular optician is away. I find a new one and explain about the other time, in case the aqueous has come adrift again. Taken aback, she uses the word once herself, out of politeness, clearly, and from then on she says 'vitreous'. And I knew that. I knew. The vitreous humour is between the crystalline lens and the retina, and the aqueous between the lens and the cornea. And yes, it has come away. Now this eye as well will have to work out for itself how to unsee floaters, *muscae volitantes*, common enough to have a name, *flies in flight*. Vitreous. Then again, isn't aqua always vitreous, and glass aqueous, liquefaqueous?

Les chambres de l'œil, entre le cristallin et la cornée, the eye's aqueous chambers.

In his sixties Edvard Munch suffered a haemorrhage in his better eye, the right one – a *musca*, a blood clot in the vitreous that left him as good as blind. The shadow it cast on the retina took the shape of a bird with a curved beak and wings held out, a shag, drying off. So he made drawings of the bird standing small and stiffly fluffed up in his crystal ball.

Vitreous humour, υαλοειδες υγρον. Aqueous is watery, υδατωδες υγρον, but in the past it was ωοειδες, like egg, white of egg, the 'albugineous' humour. The waters of the eye. And the whites.

O, let me not O, let me not be O

Ορασις is sight. Ορασις, and ερως, love, the δαιμων, the two words so close they must come from the same root, Plotinos speculated, as they do in life, love at first sight, Eros coming into being *as an eye filled with its vision*. And φως is light, light and long life to the screen in the pit of the eye, woven in blood, placental, silken, damascened, the fragile retina, enfolding sight.

Hydrophane – a translucent opal – that goes clear as glass in water.

Iridescence as unstable as water, a flow. Ιρις and the French *iris* sound the same, with twin 'i's between a soft roll and a hiss. French even has a verb *iriser*, to rainbow, and *s'iriser*, to be rainbowed. *Irisé*, rainbowed! *Verre irisé, pierre irisée, quartz irisé*, glass, stone, quartz.

The sea wasp in a photograph trailing its blue strands from

a diaphanous blue bell – the pale shape upright at its core, as if in a pane of ice, is a fish being digested. The sea wasp has eyes that are themselves invisible but they see clear, they even have a lens. Its sting is lethal. Its whole being is so clear that only a shadow on the seabed gives it away.

As an external sign of the dissolution of the eye sense power, one cannot open or close the eyes.

As an external sign of the dissolution of the visible forms included within one's own continuum, the lustre of one's body diminishes and one's strength is consumed.

The internal sign of the dissolution...is the arising of a bluish appearance called 'like a mirage'. It is like an appearance of water when the light of the sun strikes a desert in the summer.

Mode of exit from the body after death. *One who is to be reborn as a hell-being exits from the anus; as a hungry ghost, from the mouth; as an animal, from the urinary passage; as a human, from the eye...*

Colour. 'The *Sutra of Teaching to Nanda on Entry to the Womb* (*Ayushmannandagarbhavakrantinirdesha*) explains that...the intermediate state [*bar-do*] of a hell-being is like a log burned by fire; of a hungry ghost, like water; of an animal, like smoke; of a god of the desire realm or a human, gold...'
YANG-JEN-GA-WAY-LO-DRÖ, *LAMP THOROUGHLY ILLUMINATING THE PRESENTATION OF THE THREE BASIC BODIES*

Frozen on film, stripped of colour, depth and scale, aspects of the riverbed come to light unlike anything I thought I saw through the viewfinder in the pools of scum in crusts and pelts and furrows, swirls of bubbles, rushes, combs and wings of water, diaphanous, the rocks in a black skin of slime, and fern fronds inked on water where even in real life it can be hard to tell what is solid matter from reflection or shadow. This is water disembodied, taking shapes on the paper that I had no hand in, as if the lens had seen through the veil of this world into a deeper one.

Full moon and the first fog of the winter has fallen, the lighthouse horn hooting all night and far into the morning. I am the only walker out so early in the milky silence of the wharves. My slicker is quickly soaked, fingers cramped with the chill, the lens as dim as twilight. I focus in turn on masts and angled grey spars each fainter than the last, on becalmed boats squat and dark on their shadowless mirror images, on a scaly track of light spilt between rows of hulls. No sound but the hooting, owl-soft at this remove, of the foghorn, and now and then an outboard motor that raises a rhythmic wash of pale water and the solid shape of a boat and crew deepening in grey as if on a sheet of paper in the developing bath, tugging a long wake. Around the muddy shore are rocks, reed clumps, gulls, a heron, a line of ducks. At eleven the fog warms. A white hole forms, small and silver like last night's moon, sears along the water and burns off the last low wad. The world remains a monochrome, bleached in the noon glare. Gulls lifting off on black glass wings.

If you are on your own you will be all your own.
LEONARDO DA VINCI

E se tu sarai solo – this as a mantra, an aria – *tu sarai tutto tuo.* (*Sola,* I say, *tu sarai sola.*)

Printing the fog, print after print, will fail every time to bring out the degree of fade in the whiteness and greyness, the broken water and its fainter and fainter shadows. Not only that, none of the emerging light of the sun will come out. While the glint on the edges of black rocks, the curdle of mercury along the shallows will be clear, the white hole in the fog that was a stab in the eyeball, unendurably bright, its edges juddering with tears, will have sunk back into the fog, an absence. Nothing I can do to make the visible visible. When I try a longer exposure to burn the sky in, the result will be a print so overdone that the fog is smoke. Yet the sun is clearly present in the negative when I hold it to the light, a black sun, high and small, embedded in smoke over a milky shore, white rocks, charred wings.

Away from the harbour the town is still surfacing in half sun, half haze. The banyan tree stands dim, its columns of trunk and leafy branches and the hanks and braids of its aerial roots sun-dappled on the outside only, the bronze of drying bullkelp. No shaft of sun penetrates the inner chamber. The canopy and the panels of aerial roots shield the manifold columns of grey trunk and the knots and prongs of root, sculpted intertwining limbs, here a groin and bony fingers twining, stroking, there a swell of jewelled thigh, moving as the sun moves. Fog and dust and silence. High in an armpit, a beaded veil of spider web sagging under its weight of fog.

Haze, salt and sweet. Water settles on the hair and lips as soft as ash.

Swan Bay, the sun subsiding into the rim and a column of white fire down the water to my feet, pale green in water stained yellow and thick with long shadows, the bottom showing through, rags of weed, broken shells. Circles of water open around me and fill the bay. The shallows, pale over silt, are broken by two long black stilts that are my shadow legs. The edges flicker.

The pomegranate has a woody carapace, its red gloss faded, resistant to the knife. Yet once a slit is made it is a living thing that leaks dark blood on to the breadboard and then the plate, each slice a smear on the white porcelain, scattered with seeds that hold the light like chips of cartilage. The torch, the candle, even the sun, may rim it with fire but penetrate no further into the open flesh than through a hand held to a flame. I take a seed in my red fingers. A bead of ice in a red mouth.

Death appeared in a sort of transparency, as the sun appears through the blood in the living hand, between the bones that draw the shadow.
GEORGES BATAILLE, *VAN GOGH PROMÉTHÉE*

Does the sun lose its fire in the blood of a dead hand?

A spill of waterdrops down a pane – as the angle of sight changes they go from balls of mercury to leaden grey and back, now swollen with reflections, now dense like ball-bearings: positive, negative, hollow, solid. The same goes for underwater bubbles of breath as they rise, fuse to the glassy inner skin of the surface.

A silver gull keeping ahead of me, walking and gliding by turns along a shifting water line over wet sand and dry. Now its dark shadow and now its dark reflection meet its feet, shrinking, and float apart from it, long wings balancing, blurring strictly according to the degree of magnification, the height at which the gull is gliding.

Not once, for all the intensity of my gaze, can I be sure of having caught the point of transition, shadow over to reflection, or back again.

STONE AGE

Love winter when the plant says nothing

THOMAS MERTON

Accidie of midwintertide. Dormancy of the longest shadow, stillness at the furthest pole from the dozy torpors of midsummer. Emptiness, the spread sea. The sun a yellow smear. Earth holding its breath.

Flow, ebb, and in between, here at the still point, slack water, dead water.

Rock pools and sunken overhangs. A place to put life, which is to say, death, in the sea's hands. Wade in and stand there marbled in sea light, naked, gripped in water so cold it will turn flesh to stone, white, numb, transfixed, hugely swollen, a colossus, and once and for all go under.

A track winds through scrub on to the shore. Here the water is shallow, bare, still, nothing but surface apart from a tall white shell standing a little way out, or two shells, interlaced in their reflection, that catch the blurred sun like a lamp. Up close they are wings on a neck of bone, struts of rib, a bone harp snared in a bag of feathers. On the sand the sun picks out seaweed holdfasts laid open and whiskery, a glitter of mica and bottle shards, pipi shells like blue moths. In the distance two people walk out wide apart over the water shine, a black dog splashing from one to the other stitching them together. Saltmarsh, shoreland. Two shrill birds take off one after the other into the haze, their prints flattening on the water, shadows keeping track.

Piles of the jetty, russet and rosewashed velvety bark, grizzled, flaking softly off, sink and rise again dripping with the tides.

The Cyclades are floating islands full of light, or so they can seem from out at sea, volcanic islands incandescent in daylight and moonlight, as hollow as bone: above all, Thera, sunk over and over and risen, this burnt-out spine of rock curled around a deep cold pit of water, the caldera, the cauldron.

The Cyclades are the stone circle around the stone circle we know as Santorini these days, or Thera.

The first Thera, the first child of the volcano that was to swallow it alive, was round and fresh, a green apple of an island veined with waterways, until like an apple it was cored through, slashed – in a day and a night a great wound of fire opened and the sea ran in and sent a pillar of steam and ash and poisonous fumes high into the air to rain down on land and sea. A series of tidal waves surged in high walls of dark water over the shores of Crete and the mainland – the Acropolis of Athens was stripped to the bone overnight – and as far south as Egypt, in prehistory, around 1600 BC, before records were kept in Greece (but they were in Egypt): three tidal waves all told, it seems, or four like Krakatoa in 1883, in the space of a few hours; there are those who argue that one of these enormous throbs of suck and backwash may even have emptied and filled the Red Sea at the Exodus in the very nick of time. Was Thera the pillar of a cloud and of fire? Was there a blood red sunset over the world? The ash cloud of Thera may well be what darkened the skies from China to Ireland and inflicted the yearlong winters imprinted in the bog bodies of trees, in growth rings dating back to the eruption. A dusting of Thera's distinctive glassy ash was left deep in the Greenland icecap – and, in the myth and folk memory of Hellas, a sunken golden bubble, the lost Atlantis.

Villages and towns on the outer shore sank, as did those on the inland waterways, to the deep seabed of the caldera. The harbour town of Akrotiri was built high on a headland, a cape – ακρωτηρι is 'cape' – on the south arm of the torturous wasteland that was Thera, and for thirty-six centuries it would lie not in water but in ash, like an egg in a nest, almost intact. What hatched there at last in 1967 was not another Pompeii – not a 'mummified city' as Goethe saw Pompeii – so much as a ghost town. Akrotiri was deserted. The people, it seems, had enough warning, premonitory rumblings, ash falls, to get out in time, for they left no skeletons, no moulded bodies in the tall houses, no belongings to speak of and no writing, only their images in skins of paint.

It was a town in the Cretan spirit, both like and unlike Knossos in its heyday. The stone houses two and three storeys high that came to light still had their frescoes clinging in patches to the walls. In some they had sloughed off in a shower of scales on to the floor to be sealed in ash, τεφρα, leaving a jigsaw puzzle of daunting complexity and fragility for their discoverers. Over time – it took whole years – patches and bands of colour turned into a harbour and ships, and red lilies, a wild cat, a jackal, a deer, and hunched and leaping monkeys, coloured blue, and geese and swallows in flight, cattle, sheep and goats; and black-haired men and women, the men coppery, the women chalk white, seen in profile in the flat Egyptian style if not the mood, they are far too supple and sensuous for that, and lively, more like Persians, perhaps, or Etruscans. Here a young woman in robes bears a lamp full of embers or beads of incense or pomegranate seeds; there out in the fields among tawny clumps a woman and a girl are picking heads of saffron, κροκος, while elsewhere three more advance in a swaying line, carrying offerings, but one has plumped herself down with a pout, look! – she has stubbed her toe.

Ribboned black hair, earrings, long white breasts with rosy nipples under their gauzy blouses, an ebb and flow of banded skirts for the morning of the festival. More girls and women arrive with baskets of saffron for a goddess enthroned, Artemis, Our Lady of the Animals, Ποτνια Θηρων. She smiles down. A snake coils its tongue in her rich hair; she wears two strings of beads, one strung with ducks, the other with dragonflies, and is flanked by a blue monkey and a griffin with its broad wing flared.

Life was sweet there on the lip of the furnace. If, as they must, they have the look of tombs to us, these few gaily painted foursquare houses, empty shells, there is no taint of death in them. They were for the living. Atlantis, Minoa, Thera – the sun of a lost world glows on the walls, a limpid world without volume or shadow.

A green ghost hangs over Thera today, the vision of a young self. Ghostly sails shimmer out at sea, wraiths slither up the cliffs out of the icy cauldron, heroes in bronze armour shine out in a tomato field. Within living memory in this or that village a vampire, βρυκολακας, has been known to rise in the flesh, monstrously bloated, and walk the night. Long notorious all over Greece as the chief haunt of vampires, the island itself, the shell of a volcano, is of their kind, not dead and gone, biding its time on the seabed. Earthquakes, the handiwork of the god of the sea, strike like thunderstorms all around the Aegean, sporadic, harsh. The smith god who blasted Thera out of the earth's core was harsher by far. He took shape *by day in a pillar of a cloud...and by night in a pillar of fire.* He was uproar and fire, with lava for blood and sulphur fumes for breath. He turned day into night, he made islands and sank them. Thera in his hands gave birth to a new Thera hot from the forge, a misbirth, lifeless, a water island.

The signs had been there a hundred years before, when French vulcanologists came to observe a new eruption, and diggings were cut in the pumice to supply cement for the Suez Canal. Under the grapevines out by the fig tree on the donkey path to the cave poked a bony shoulder of rock, a drystone wall, and a shard of pottery, a gold ring or two, that went all the way back – had they but known – to the Minoans; but not even Knossos had been unearthed by then. The remains of one man were dug out, only one, who was still reaping, perhaps, or so old or sick or stubborn that he stayed, when everyone else put to sea, and laid his meagre sprawl of bones in the ash.

On the north wall of a room in the West House at Akrotiri the image of a young man emerged flake by flake, intact and in the flower of young manhood. All of seventeen, his whole life ahead of him. His arms are bent up as if for a round dance, lifting two long sheaves of fish, mackerel, blue and chrome yellow, strung up by the mouth. He is smiling with his head coyly ducked, naked but for a thong around his neck, his cock nestled against his thigh. He is sway-backed in a strut, ruddy brown all over but for his blue scalp with two long black locks at the temples – the blue head of a god, it might be, except that here it means newly shaved skin, blue grey, like pale skin underwater. No blue on his face, no beard shadow, no shadow to the fisherman at all and no darkness, he is as naked to the light as a god.

Like a god as well, in being on the very point of breaking free. But for the eye – which, as always, looks straight out at you, long and rimmed with kohl, an Egyptian eye – the head is in profile. As are the legs, though the shoulders face forward and from the waist he flows with a sinuous warp down to the hips, a liquefaction, impossibly prolonged: a mistake, to the anatomical eye, a clumsy flaw, a malformation. But what the inner eye sees is a quiver of life as if in a skin of water around his loins, as if the flaw were a crack he is slipping through, between the elements, between worlds. He is all but alive, if only because where the two halves of him meet there is this lovely improbable refraction, this afterimage of movement clinging to him like salt.

In a dado all around the four walls of the same room in the West House – surely a captain's house, if not an admiral's, or a king's – appeared patches of a battle, thronged harbours, fleets of low-slung ships with a mast and banks of oars, lionesses, birds and moths, dolphins painted along the sides (no black ships here), tall brown men in them and dolphins in flight all around, the same half blue, half chrome yellow as the fisherman's mackerel, in a blue sea fading to invisible, so that they float by in midair, the ships and the wrecks and the drowned sailors, naked and long-limbed, who go tumbling head over heel as if they were there for the fun of it and might burst their brown pods of skin any minute and be dolphins.

In the tombs we see it, throes of wonder and vivid feeling throbbing over death. Man moves naked and glowing through the universe. Then comes death: he dives into the sea, he departs into the underworld.
D H LAWRENCE

Underworld. Undertow. How far did they get, choking and jostling in their panic with what they could carry down to the harbour? Surely they took ship in time. Unless there were not enough ships, or the tidal waves overwhelmed them and they sank underwater, or washed up on the rocky beaches of other islands, or else they were still boarding when the cone blasted, spurting up a column of fume and fire and ash over twenty miles high, and are bone of the island's bone.

The archaeologist who had brought Thera to light over summer after summer, Spyridon Marinatos, fell and broke his neck in the excavation and lies buried in a grave in the ruins.

Some say they sailed west, the lost Atlanteans and others, leaving their stripped and buried cities of ash all over the Aegean, an exodus out along the Atlantic seaboard as far away as Britain – like the Fir Bolg, sailing from Greece to Ireland in leather boats speckled like seals to pull good farmland out of the bog with their bare hands – and may have had a hand in the building of Stonehenge. Others say Stonehenge was built in Adam's lifetime and wrecked in Noah's Flood, or floated through the air from Ireland under a spell cast by Merlin, or was the work of giants or Druids, those navigators in earth time who claimed descent from Dis, Pluto, Hades, the dark god.

Build then the ship of death, for you must take
the longest journey, to oblivion.
D H LAWRENCE

The rawboned old red sandstone cathedral of St Magnus the Martyr at Kirkwall in Orkney, that forest of glass, has a Sailor's Loft where a painting used to hang, of a three-masted ship with blown sails on a dark wave, chrome yellow cloths on old gold as in a Byzantine ikon. In Scandinavia a church within reach of the sea may even have a real ship hanging in midair, sails furled in the shifting half-light as if sliding in between worlds, bringing to mind the drowned cathedral, the city of Ys off Brittany, and Hy Brasil, Lyonesse, Ile Verte, 'Green Isle', Lemuria and the lost Atlantis, a chiming of bells washing in on the tide and, whenever the waters are as still and glassy as oil, a spire wavering on the seabed, the play of a green sun in the wreckage of a nave.

Throughout the Ice Age the Northern Isles of Scotland, Shetland and Orkney, the Norse islands, were icebound, bodies of sandstone sunk deep in the icecap until the coming of the thaw.

In Greek folksong there is a harbour where every journey ends, and Charos is the captain of a black ship sailing into the dark, less a ferryman than a pirate. Or the corpse itself, all dressed up, is the ship dressed up for her maiden voyage in sails of silk, oars of silver and masts and yards of gold. The singers ask the ship where she will cast anchor and where she will moor. Στην Κατου Γης το σιδερο, στον Αδη παλαμαρι, comes the answer. *In the Under Earth I will cast anchor, in Hades I will moor.*

The great voyage home of Odysseus, the last but one, ended when he made landfall on a beach on Ithaka where there was (and is) a cave by an olive tree, the cave of the Nymphs, the Naiads. Inside in the gloom were stone jars where the bees wove their combs for the honey of generation, and looms of stone where the water nymphs wove crimson webs, tissues, φαρε' υφαινουσιν αλιπορφυρα, cloths of sea-purple – *the tenacious vestment of body*. The cave ran with spring water and had two doors, one facing south, one north, and a path for people and another for the immortals, gods, and souls; on all of which grounds Porphyry the disciple of Plotinos glosses it as a womb of genesis, incarnation, rebirth.

For the flesh is generated in and about the bones, which in the bodies of animals may be compared to stones...But the purple garments plainly appear to be the flesh with which we are invested; and which is woven as it were and grows by the connecting and vivifying power of the blood, diffused through every part. Besides, purple garments are tinged with the blood of animals; and flesh is produced and subsists from blood. Add too that the body is a garment with which the soul is invested...Thus according to Orpheus, Proserpine, who presides over every thing generated from seed, is represented weaving a web; and the ancients called heaven by the name of πεπλος, *which is as it were the veil or tegument of the celestial gods.*

PORPHYRY

Now launch the small ship, now as the body dies
and life departs, launch out, the fragile soul
in the fragile ship of courage, the ark of faith
with its store of food and little cooking pans
and change of clothes,
upon the flood's black waste
upon the waters of the end
upon the sea of death, where still we sail
darkly, for we cannot steer, and have no port.

D H LAWRENCE

The great stones, megaliths – the *menhirs*, 'long stones' in Breton and *tursachan* or 'mourners' in the Gaelic – have stood like dead trees for thousands of years alone or in lines and rings all along the Atlantic seaboard, on headlands and shorelines, seamarks perhaps, and inland around the big-bellied stone mounds. In the myths they are dropped or thrown there by the Bone Hag, the Cailleach, the Black One who broods over the land. Deep-rooted in a long socket, from the air they gape like the jaws of a buried monster, an embedded scream. They are figures on a giant clockface. They are night dancers, giants, trolls who shambled to a standstill in the heather one daybreak and might come back to life yet: stones of power, many transported from a long way away over the years by a people who loved and knew stone through and through. Was it caves with their frozen fountains of stone that inspired them, and groves of winter trees? Like trees, no two stones cast the same shadow. Like trees, they house a spirit and like trees they sleep standing up in the fields as horses do, liable to be split and felled by a lightning strike. The survivors, whether they stand straight and smooth, manlike, or brood womanlike over the earth, hold fast on a long taproot. Their heads are domed or flat or splintering half dissolved in light. They grow blisters and scabs all over, and lichen, the subtle flower of stone, in splashes of white, grey green and ochre, in marigold sunbursts: standing stones, kin to each other and no two ever the same, whether naked or gowned in stone and hooded, rugged or smooth, gravid, spindly, in the wind and rain. Even the drystone corbelled roof of the passage grave is a ring of stone in its own self, wound ring over ring into a beehive. Rings were written in and on them, signs, coils and snakes and cups, waves, zigzags and lozenges, triangles, rings around rings, single and in pairs like owl eyes; and in some passage graves a swirl of three spirals like swollen breasts and a belly that may or may not stand for a goddess of life, of death. In Brittany there are menhirs that have pairs of breasts, either young and full or withered, passage stones etched with a naked guardian or a masted ship. Were the stonemasons also the shipwrights, there on the edge of the ocean? Voyagers were few in those times. Only famous prophets and healers, bards and builders, as the godly swineherd of Ithaka points out in the *Odyssey* – this in defence of the hero himself, that seafarer amd dire man of craft in his beggar's rags – were *bidden all over the boundless earth*. The earliest seafarers had to make themselves at home in the night sky, inching from star to star of the great web, as the earthbound kept time to the seasons. The stones themselves, and the images pecked in them, had a bearing on the sky – here a sunburst, there a crescent, a fan of lines along the fall of a shadow like a sundial, sinuous lines tracing seasons of the sun and moon, a coil for the sun's path, a snake for the moon's, eclipses, a comet, a bright star. Cup-and-ring marks, the wave shape that a raindrop or a flung stone leaves on water, may stand for a ceremonial basin, or a spring or well, holy water. Islanders in the west of Scotland within living memory

filled the cupmarks in flat rocks with milk in spring, to keep the cows in milk; and why not, when one reading is as good as another and for all we know the stones had more than one meaning all along, a cluster of lost meanings, open to everyone and kept dark from the very beginning. They are the fossils of their meanings.

mor (dialect *moder*) – mother
perlemor – mother of pearl
morsmål – mother tongue
mål – language, voice; meal; goal, intention, purpose
maler, dialect *målar* – painter, artist
morsliv – womb
liv – life
fra mors liv an – from birth on
morsmerke – birthmark
morsmjølk (dialect *morsmelk*) – mother's milk

Wood circles and henges came before stone. For that matter, in the north the first couple, Ask and Embla, were trees uprooted and washed ashore, where the gods made flesh of their sodden trunks, breathing new life into them. *Ask* is the ash tree; *embla*, maybe the Greek αμπελος, grapevine.

Naked in all weathers, at times the stones would be robed in fire kindled from the sun, on those days and nights foretold by the stones themselves in conjunction with sun, moon and stars, when the men and women danced in the furrows in between and inside and around the rings of flame and stone, gravely in tune with the gravity of stone, or uproariously arm in arm, tented in fire and breath in a time out of time, singing aloud. On midsummer eve a man or animal would be roped up as an offering to the earth or sun, the throat slit, the body drowned or burnt, broken up and shared in circles laid out stone by stone by yardsticks or a rope and peg or outstretched arms, fingertips touching. *Have not all races*, wrote Yeats, *had their first unity from a mythology that marries them to rock and hill?* Did the dance go widdershins with the moon, or clockwise the sun's way, or both, spiralling in and out? And which came first – round dance or stone circle?

A filmy scatter on the brick path like a moonstone bracelet – the snail trodden on blindly last night, a wet crunch – catching the sun for one moment, the never-before-seen mother of pearl lining of the spiral shell.

We are the spawn of fire, the universes.

The beauty of stone, great and small, and its prism of names – plutonic stone, meteoric and metamorphic stone, all the great metaphoric families of the stones, ancient names, many of them lost now along with the human worship and desire embedded in them. Pliny's great book, *The Historie of the World*, ends in a long stone poem, a litany of all the gemstones with their provenances and their numinous powers. As always he offers what he has mined in the authorities, suspending judgment but for his regular swipe at those frauds and liars, the Magi, Greeks and Druids, always preying on the gullible. How, though, are even the wise to know what to believe? *Neither are we to argue and reason how and why Nature hath done this or that? sufficient it is that her will was so, and thus she would have it* – an exclamation torn from him by the idea that the diamond, the hardest of all stones, can be cut if you first soak it *in Goats bloud*, of all things. As for how stones came into being, this is a mystery not even Aristotle throws much light on, except to suppose that they are liquids, more or less pure – rock crystal is pure ice and has the same name, κρυσταλλος – that have become compacted under pressure over the years in either a hot or a cold exhalation of breath, πνευμα, underground. Stones live and go on growing, Plotinos was convinced, *as long as they are embedded*. Sir John Mandeville in his day would go one better, having seen for himself how diamonds *grow together, male and female. And they be nourished with the dew of heaven. And they engender commonly and bring forth small children, that multiply and grow all the year*. The stones take on their multiple forms of crystallised flesh and blood, of scales, bark, fish roe, mould, flame, constellation of stars – images, microcosms – according to the laws of their being; and a magic to match, a power for good or evil over us and our human fate, by rough analogy, the rule of thumb that is sympathetic magic. *As above, so below.* The *galactitis*, for example, the 'milk stone' – from γαλα, milk –

leaves a milky smear and smell on the fingers and gives the nursing mother milk in abundance; just as the blue bead, the ματι, will do, now that the word for blue is γαλαζιος, or γαλανος. Also for mothers, *the gems Pæantides...are said to conceive and to bring forth other little stones: but a singular vertue they have to help women that be in travell of child-birth. Such bee found in Macedonie, neare unto the monument or sepulchre of* Tiresias, *and that which they bring forth, seemeth like unto water grown to be congealed into yce... Heliotropium,* green with *veins of bloud doth represent the bodie of the Sun, like unto a mirroir: and if there bee an eclipse of the Sun, a man may perceive easily in this stone how the moone goeth under it, and obscureth the light*; the Magi even claim it has the power, together with the *hearbe Heliotropium*, a sunflower, and with mumbled spells and charms, of making you invisible. The 'tongue stone', *glossopetra*, has the appearance of a human tongue while not being of this world at all, only ever falling to earth in the wane of the moon, endowed with the power both of divination and of stopping storms. The *Gorgonia* coral, 'Gorgon's stone' – it is fleshy in the sea, but hardens in the air – wards off thunderbolts and whirlwinds. The *Hephaestitis*, named after the smith god of the volcano, is a red mirror stone that cools boiling water poured over it and out in the sun will set tinder on fire. Amber is variously the tears shed into the river Po every year by nymphs turned into poplar trees; or a resin shed by the trees on an Adriatic cliff at the rising of the Dog Star; or it flows from crags in Britain or from the setting sun in the sea congealing in drops like toffee, and elsewhere it is lynx urine petrified, *reddish and of a firie colour* if male, *whitish* if female. The crystal *dracontias* forms in the brains of snakes and the *sauritis* in the bellies of green lizards. The *chelonia*, 'tortoise-stone', the eye of an Indian tortoise, when placed on the tongue after washing the mouth with honey confers the power of prophecy, or so say those swindlers, the Magi. The tawny *lychnis* is so called from the kindling of lamps; the *melichrysus*, 'honey gold' is like honey in a clear film of gold, the *crocallis* a honeycomb in stone; the Arabian *selenites*, 'moonstone', is *white and transparent, yeelding from it a yellow lustre in manner of honey, and representing within it the proportion of the Moone, according as she groweth toward to the full, or decreaseth in the wane*... Then there is the 'iris stone' or 'root of crystal' found on an island in the Red Sea, which throws shifting veils of colour on the walls of a dark room, by taking in the ambient light as some lenses do, and magnifying, splitting, projecting. *As for the diverse colours which they cast forth, it never happeneth but in a darke or shaddowie place: whereby a man may know, that the varietie of colours is not in the stone Iris, but commeth by the reverberation of the wals. But the best Iris is that which representeth the greatest circles upon the wall, and those which bee likest unto raine bowes indeed.*

A whole stone world that is in this one.

And now let us declare that our discourse concerning this All has reached its end. Having received all mortal and immortal creatures and being therewithal replenished, this universe hath thus come into being, living and visible, containing all things that are visible, the image of its maker, a god perceptible, most mighty and good, most fair and perfect, even this one and only-begotten world that is.
PLATO

Ποιητης the maker and εικων του ποιητου, *the image of its maker*, the what-is-made, enfolded in each other in the microcosm as in the great world.

Did we learn to swaddle babies and corpses from the insects who swathe their eggs in a parcel of twig and leaf and spun silk as immaculate as the bud it resembles? We all learn by imitation.

What if it was the banyan, the monumental sprawling Indian fig, that gave rise to those temples of sandstone, now in ruins, covered in a supple, writhing, tangled mass of gods and goddesses? Such bodies are all over the banyan, rudimentary, monstrous and beautiful, clothed in shadow, groping their way into being. They were before us. They are far older and closer to us than any stone god. They wax and wane under the sun, they die like us and the earth eats them.

A flare of spider thread, a flank, a mouth, deep shadows and eyes of light.

As for the handprints and footprints made on rock all over the world, might this have grown simply, naturally out of the far older art of tracking? And painting on rock, out of painting on the body and pecking a tattoo into skin as into stone? The cave animals born of charcoal and spit and ochre (like blood, full of iron) into immortality in the tunnels and halls of caves, wombs of bedrock, and by holy wells, were they meant to ripen as flesh in the upper world, knowing their maker and master, who himself had gone down into the womb of the earth, the dark cave, and risen? They would yield themselves up as prey at his bidding, in the mystery, the sacrifice, flesh of his flesh, while living on there in essence eternally, an unfailing source. An owl engraved into soft grey rock, feathery, staring. Handprints made by breathing a spray of ochre over a hand spread out as if to the hearthfire in the rock, that fit us like gloves.

Unless the impulse to do something with the hand is there from the very outset, nothing will ever happen.
ETIENNE GILSON

Ζωη, life, ζωα, animals, cattle, and ζωγραφος, painter, he who writes life.

There are horses and men, all in dark silhouette, and very fascinating in drawing. These archaic horses are so perfectly satisfying as *horses...that one asks oneself, what, after all, is the horsiness of a horse? – what is it, that will never be put into words?*

For a man who sees, sees not as a camera does when it takes a snapshot, not even as a cinema-camera, taking its succession of instantaneous snaps; but in a curious rolling flood of vision, in which the image itself seethes and rolls; and only the mind picks out *certain factors which* shall *represent the image seen.*

D H LAWRENCE

The dream of the crucible, to give raw matter its ideal self in the refining fire.

Living, of course, is just the opposite of expressing. If I am to go by the great Tuscan masters, it means bearing threefold witness, in silence, flame and immobility.

ALBERT CAMUS

Eye to eye I look into bark knotholes, into rockholes and rock circles. At some sites old trees, wintry trees, and standing stones have grown old together for so long now that they look the same. To go in and see with the naked eye, if I dared to be so helpless, as good as blind among strangers, would be the way – to find myself in among flimsy, stooping, vast shadows, a flock of ghosts, and having come as close as I would have to come to see anything clearly, to have under my nose constellations of pock and grit and pollen mote, knot and driftnet of lichen, of web, moss, flakes and snailslime, the thick chalk of bird shit in the grain, the light and shadow of them falling on my skin and the cold breath.

Jellyfish mantles thrown high and dry, sand grit and amber in a flare.

Engulfed cathedrals underwater, underground, cavernous. And caves as cathedrals, and as tombs, such as the one on Kangaroo Island lit up with lanterns to reveal a high host of white spindles, frets and groins. Some shadow kneels down and shines a torch behind a pane of rock as fine and pale as skin, with seams inside, veins and rusty scribbles. In the torchlight we see wavering, spreading tall wings of shadow at its back, an angel, a graveyard angel of dark fire – gone as another pane burns red, the Rasher of Bacon, our guide proclaims, and not so wide of the mark as all that, since in the early days of settlement a horse once crashed through a sinkhole in the thin crust and landed in an upper hall. The rider clawed his way out. Not so the horse, who was left to die without trace. The cave digested him, blood, bones and slender skull, in a slow fusion. Rock falls and long inrushes of floodwater carved the recesses and columns, the curtains of stone that move through the torchlight like vapour, like frozen waterfalls, but the only water now is the drop on the neb of each tooth of stone and the milky puddle calcified under each neb, water into stone. Candles in dribbles of wax, a bowed monk, seahorses, a squid hung out in translucent drapes of tentacle. In the floor, one blood red eye. In the vault, a web of dark roots, pure stone veined with the tannin of the living wood, and the horse spun into stone, the horseflesh, the essence of the cave horse.

Tropfstein, dripstone, flowstone. How old are the ancient skins of paint on the cave walls of old Europe? Some are occluded, inhabited by organic matter, wasp nests, spiderwebs, lichens, that will yield a minimum age when carbon-dated. Some have mineral outgrowths, cataracts of stone.

But though the Carbon-14 process is of great value it has its limitations. In the first place it is limited to organic material (stalactites are the exception as they take in carbon direct from the air like all growing, living creatures).
FELIX PATURI

Munch once told a friend that, while he found an afterlife hard to imagine, he did believe in *a mysterious force that continues, so that we repeat ourselves like crystals that are dissolved and then re-crystallize again.*

Drops and scales and plates of ice that focus the light hard. Lenses of pain.

In a North Sea dune in Sandwick in Orkney are the ruins of Skerrabrae, now Skara Brae, a Stone Age settlement of seven or eight underground houses linked by stone-lined passageways, huddled together in a midden for warmth, much like these windswept islands themselves in their bays and firths, sounds, lochs, deeps, falls and flows. Skara Brae was abruptly abandoned in a storm, a swill of sea and sand, and lay buried for thousands of years until another wild storm tore the dune open and revealed that the green mound by the sea was man-made, and no tomb either, but a set of dwellings. Householders had lived down here and lived well, in stone crofts furnished in stone, their beds set into the walls around a stone hearth, stone seats and dressers, stone basins for cooking with heated stones; they had crafted stone and bone tools and beads and enigmatic knobbled spheres, some of which they left behind in the rush. They fled in time. No one knows who they were, or where they left their bones in the end, or where they came from if, as seems likely, they were not native to these islands. Not farmers, anyway, since the midden showed that their grain came to them ready for grinding, and their meat slaughtered. They may have been a new race, perhaps the builders of the megalithic monuments, the stone circles, howes, long cairns, barrows and portal tombs and passage graves with corbelled beehive chambers, temples more than tombs, that date from that time – long before the Pyramids – all over these islands, as in Scotland, and Ireland, England, Wales, and in Scandinavia, Brittany, the Iberian Peninsula, Sardinia, Malta, Greece. If so, they were the bearers of new gods, the teachers and shamans of new magic, new arts and skills, a new map of the skies and wheel of the seasons, they being seafarers and navigators – how else would they have found their way west? They may have been from a very long way away, *bidden all over the boundless earth*, uprooted by war or some natural disaster undreamed of in these cold islands where they built the tombs, the temples, to be pierced by a shaft of the low sun in the very dead of winter. From as far away even, perhaps, as the Mediterranean.

Mediterranean, Μεσογειος, Midgard, Middle-Earth.

And behold, in a trance, he was shown two ships upon the river: in one he saw the Holy Ghost sailing together with the abbot Arsenius in silence and in peace: and in the other ship he saw the abbot Moses and the angels of God, and they were giving him honey and the honeycomb into his mouth.
THE SAYINGS OF THE FATHERS

Northbound from Bergen to the Arctic Circle our ship *Polarlys* docks first thing Sunday morning. We passengers have all of an hour for Trondheim, half-walking, half-slithering full of hope in the still streets banked with snow and still rosy under lamps to the cathedral. The town is sleeping in under a sky heavy with new snow and even the cathedral, a battleship rearing in the gloom, is closed. Only at the doorway, a white plume is jetting up from a buzzing snow plough, an old dog dodging from side to side in its wake, his black coat clotted with snow: and we are in luck, the sexton says there is a christening on soon and, yes, we can have a quick look around if we hurry. We tiptoe into a stone cave of candlelight warm as an oven for the child, who will have a font with a Noah's Ark on its bronze belly and a

Baptism of Jesus under a pointing hand of God. We take in a carved organ, a crucifix, a dark rose window of garnet and lapis lazuli, and flagstones, etched and glowing – the bones of old saints and kings are enshrined here. Humbler folk are out in the snow, thin shoulders poking up in rows among the stark trees, names and dates a blur on stone. I kneel in front of one, pulling off a glove to trace the sunken letters. But the headstone fuses to my finger and I jerk back, sucking the pain and stumbling on, only to realise – my glove! Somewhere away back there in the trees, webbings of bough and stone in the blind sky, a scatter of snow thickening and swarming – by the time I weave my way back over my snowprints they and the glove are all but swallowed up and my black hood is a white fur. A blurt from the harbour, a horn, *Polarlys*! – and here comes the young couple with the red-cheeked baby in snowclothes while I flounder on kneedeep here, and blessed be the gravity of stone and the light snow and the dog treading his maze and the glove warm from the grave.

Am I on the way? No footprints ahead if so – no way of knowing.

Polarlys. Among her sister ships are *Nordlys*, northern lights, and *Midnatsol,* midnight sun. The three ships of light. How do you live a life where there is one long day in a year, the summer, the unsetting sun, and one long winter night? Moon, stars and the dark dawns of the northern lights, the *fire-flaught*, as they used to say in Scotland. An island in the far north harbours a rowan tree in the quadrangle of an old turf-roofed fort, the only tree alive in this whole wilderness of ice, trussed like a corpse all winter in snowy tarpaulins, like a chrysalis. The air a grey mist, stinging, smeary with the lamps of ice folk, snow folk. And a wasteland, a border, a blind alley, Kirkenes. Murmansk.

fire-flaught...Lightning; a flash of lightning; a storm of thunder and lightning...The northern lights; *aurora borealis.*

Here is a sun with no heat, only light. But a light that drenches in honey whatever it reaches, the furrows of fresh snow on deck, the plaits of rope rolled up under cover, papery fish hooked up to dry, a bird afloat among the crags, one golden bird, a visitant. Did you see the sea eagle, two young men ask me in English, offering binoculars, see its nest up there. A sea eagle? Where!

So *Polarlys* threaded her way among islands and fjords, the mythic ice and the rockscapes, letting us off in the harbour towns for an hour or so to stumble and slither on our sea legs, ploughing on into the dark and back again. By the time I got the train across the white mountains to Oslo to sleep on land again the spell was over and the thaw well under way. Another year I took the morning ferry from the tip of Jutland, past a scatter of yachts and ferries and lanterns on rocks, laying a snailtrack into the Oslofjord. That time it was Whitsun coming up to midsummer and the long slow twilight of Munch's paintings, those silvery shores with an unsetting sun on a pillar of wet light. Then on a little island ferry I sat up on deck, the rain setting in cold in flapping sheets as harbour after grey harbour loomed and swung away, bound for Hovedøya, 'Main Island', and the *klosterruinen* in its wet heart. The founders were English, White Friars, an abbot and twelve monks who set sail from Lincolnshire more than eight hundred years ago under vows of poverty, chastity, obedience and stability, bringing a stone, a handful of earth, the Word of God from the mother church across the North Sea, nosing their way up the fjord through islands and skerries to build a *kloster* here in the name of Our Lady to live and die in.

The broken walls were black with wet, dripping among the spring green and gold, no sound but birds and water and planes taking off from the other shore. A dark spiral stair in the tower – an improvised coolie hat of planks on shoulders of black stone with a white stripe. A well of darkness underfoot – was there a bell up here? – a narrow lookout, dizzying, dank, and I blundered back down. Beads of rain hung in the green of grasses, leaves, ferns. They would have lived off the land and the sea, these island monks; they were seafarers of old. They had crops in summer, a physic garden and a graveyard, ducks and geese, a flock of sheep or goats perhaps, and bees for honey and candlewax, in bell-shaped wicker hives kept warm and fed indoors in winter, garden beds quilted under straw. *Religious houses are those hyves where Bees Make honey for mens soules.*

A map at the entrance – there was a well – gave the ground plan, the trunk of the church, arms wide for a crossbar: a long cross with an apse, and the shaft of the cross is labelled *skip* – nave, of course, the same 'ship' our own churches have under the Latin veil. *Nef* in Norman French, 'nave', was a ship first and foremost: the great earthbound stone cathedrals of Normandy were the work of Norsemen with a ship in mind as a vessel for souls, a ship of death. The first father of their universe was the frost giant Ymir, killed and dismembered by the god Odin and his brothers to make a sky of his skull, with his brains for clouds, land out of his flesh and bones and seas of his blood; and the wash of Ymir's blood drowned all the frost giants ever hatched from his body except one who got away with his household on a *lúðr*, a word encompassing *cradle*, *coffin*, *bier*, *ship*, and box, raft, ark of salvation. Far closer to the northern soul than homestead or temple was the ship in flight between air and sea. In pagan times the dead were sent on their way in stone bells and beehives, corbels of stone knitted in thick grey rows like fishermen's beanies; and in oval hulls of stone, and in honey, in salt and pitch, in hollow logs and some in the hulls of boats sunk out at sea on fire or in the earth or midway, in bogland.

hull[1], *n* the husk, shell, or outer covering of a seed or fruit. [ME; OE *hulu* husk, pod; akin to *helan* cover, hide. Cf. HALL, HELL, HOLE]

hull[2], *n* the frame or body of a ship, exclusive of masts, yards, sails, and rigging. [orig. uncert. Cf. HULL[1], HOLD, HOLE]

hive...[ME; OE *hyf*. Cf. Icel. *hufr* ship's hull]

Old words keep their secrets as do old ships, old bones, and stones.

The traditional beehive, the skep, was a wicker bell, a basket, a nest, a curragh tarry with age, a cradle – and a mother too, in a manner of speaking, a mother of honey, the way a spring, in Greece, is a νεροµαννα, a mother of water. But getting at the honey took fire and brimstone, an annual holocaust of bees. There came a time when architects of vision put their minds to the invention of more practical, more humane beehives that were also works of art, miniature chapels, temples and lighthouses of sleek wood. The simplest, most covetable of all had one or more lanterns let into the roof, bell jars, kept hooded for warmth, into which the bees would spin a fret of pure white comb. Slowly a stream of these rare and beautiful domes of glass came on to the market, each with a spine of wick as intricate as coral. Lamps of honey, ethereal skeps.

A card in the mail, from the English friend who came with me to the stones, and a pendant to hang around my neck, a crude figurine carved out of bone or horn – a cailleach! – a bone hag of the north, winter mother and barrow hag and

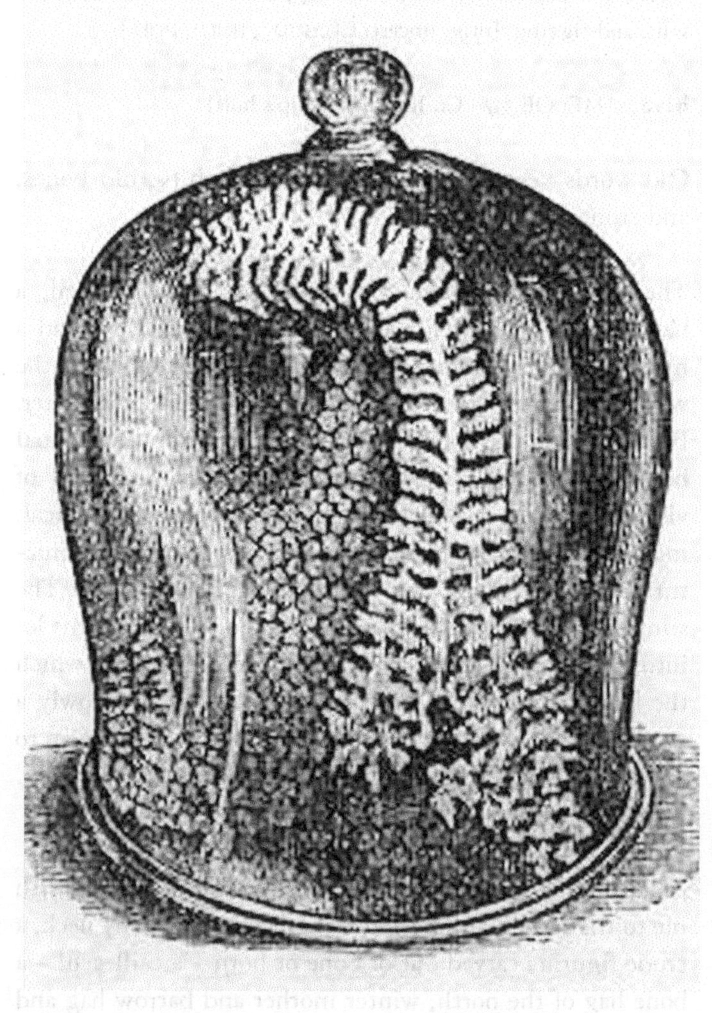

white lady, brown in the folds like an old tooth. She hangs by her pierced hands clasped over her head in a wishbone. Her womb is a pinhole with a double ring around it, a wide eye. Her legs form a beak. She has the blinded gaze of all images, owl eyes, eyes of the *cailleach oidhche*, the night-hag. She is the image of me. She is what I am to live up to, down to. She endures. She knows the way.

She is the Cally, the corn dolly braided to hang up on the wall.

The black ships that went to war on Troy were horned, fore and aft. Just such a horned black ship has haunted me since I touched her in the flesh in Oslo years ago – in the flesh, because the wood, softened and blackened with age and over a thousand years buried, flaky, butter-smooth, was like the peaty skin of a bog body, the past brought to light, patiently put back together from chips and scales of wood in their thousands: the full flesh of a ship on a light skeleton of ancient oak. She was one of two Viking longships – a third was in ruins nearby – that were propped up, as if in the slips, in a great hall like a white hood with lamps in brackets on the walls and loops for windows; pulpits for an overview were reached by a coil of brick stairs, on a grey stone floor like shallow water. Students with notebooks wove around the carved hull sketching a prow, a knotted leafy snake, a dragon. Midday at the tail end of February – the lamps in their niches, a grey glint in the window panes, snow light, and shadow birds flying up from the trees in flurries of snow without a cry. In coves all along the road to Bygdøy and back, tall yachts as still as the Viking ships, covered in snowy tarpaulins, moored in ice.

The silence of the long walk then, through the wooden village of the Folk Museum, no one in sight, only the scrinch of my bootsteps on soft snow and glassy paths past a stave church like a wooden dragon and on to the winding road down to the waterfront, the last of the sun kindling in topmasts and turreted walls. But inland Oslo was still under the spell of winter, the Queen's palace afloat in an ice park, trees like black masts, flowerbeds under heaps of straw, ice-clogged, smelling of ice. And at nightfall in the old university quarter, sour buffets of malt and yeast from a brewery, the smell of my schoolday afternoons in Melbourne.

Ice is its own world. *Polarlys* had followed the Viking searoads north on the tail of longships like these, hugging the shores that gave them birth – and death, often enough, at the hands of their masters, along with their chattels, the Vikings being seafarers whose heroes were sent by fire and water to the otherworld. These black ships in the museum were royal coffins from the Vestfold, the western shore of the Oslofjord. The fragile handcrafted Oseberg Ship – unearthed at Oseberg, Åsa's Mound – had sails as well as oars and rode high in one great curl of hull as light as a paper nautilus. She was never for war but ceremonial, spellbound and spellbinding; not a *drakkar*, a dragon, so much as a black swan of the north. She took to her grave Queen Åsa, daughter of a long line that went back to the god Odin, as the *Ynglinga Saga* tells, daughter of King Harald Redbeard and mother of Halfdan Svarte, Half-Dane the Black, by King Gudrod, who killed her father in a night raid from the sea to get hold of her. Åsa bode her time. It was not until their son was a year old and Gudrod blind drunk one night, lurching on a gangway, that she had him stabbed by a thrall, who was felled on the spot. The blood debt settled, she sailed home with the boy and took up Harald's throne. On her death she was carried on board her ship along with a great wealth of gravegoods, her sculpted cart and sledges, cauldrons, tapestries and bone combs, a yew bucket with a brass Buddha perched cross-legged like a goblin on each lug, crabapples of immortality, bread dough and spices, butchered horses and oxen and, willing or unwilling, a lady-in-waiting. The boy in turn made a good king in a time of plenty – such a good king that when he drowned crossing over thin ice on a lake the people fished him out, cut him up and divided him among four burial mounds – Halfdan's Mounds – for the sake of the whole kingdom.

As for the earth going round the sun: it goes round as the blood goes round my body, absolutely mysteriously, with the rapidity and hesitation of life.

D H LAWRENCE

Late February of another year on Swan Bay, the summer sun is a gong of brass at the rim and the spire of St George the Martyr still alight as the audience files in for the annual concert of the Junge Philharmonie Köln. A full house, a lamplit hive of stone. The young musicians are out of sight beyond the furrows of heads, except for the fern-tip of a double bass tossed up from time to time like the bound head of Our Lady in a procession, or the curled prow of a dragon ship. At interval we pour out shivering into a black sky, silence, stars, an afterglow on the hearthstone of the bay, slow to fade that summer in the wake of the volcano in the East, Pinatubo; and then a quiet whimpering of swans in the lee of the reed banks, black swans a long way out in the dark but their voices carry as if the water holds the sound the way it holds the light and heat, waves of sound and light and heat – holds the note in a high glaze of resonance as never before, or else our ears are so tuned tonight that for once we are hearing it as it is.

A summer's night...

The stones took on life and began to move. In the forest's damp darkness, creatures were born...

The moon turned yellow. A golden column appeared in the water and grew and swelled. It melted in its own glowing light, and the yellow flowed over into the water.

EDVARD MUNCH

A swan is afloat in the fjord, a wild swan, the pulse of

whose paddling breaks in soft waves against him as he wades in unearthly shallows, no apparition, there is a swan out at sea alone, as if a ship in full sail has drifted into Åsgårdstrand, a ship of the gods, weightless, alight, a ghostly ship.

A cloud like a wing of fire joins with its image in midair, wings parting on a rim of silver, lips of a vast wound. The whole fjord to its rim of hills is one skin of glass. He stands stricken on the shore as the two great wings burn out, gold, vermilion, a thick plumage, plunging, crimson turned into ash.

It is 1893, the year of the volcano in the East, Krakatoa. He is standing by a railing on Ljabruveien in Nordstrand where he rents the yellow house in which he will one day paint his mad sister. *Melankoli. Laura.* And looking west across the fjord to a shoreline the shape of a palette, the same as the shoreline that flows west of the lighthouse in the town where I live. The same indented bay and winter sky filling with the sun's blood.

When the winter sun stood near the horizon it shone through the windows, he wrote, *and flamed up red and yellow in my room. The yellow walls became flame and the brownish wooden floor was blood. The light and colours stabbed like a knife into my soul and my body in which the blood flowed sick – Melancholy…*

Skrik. Scream. What is the foreground figure faded against

the sunset, sallow in a black robe, its eyes and mouth round, hands clapped to a bald head? Not a man or a woman, or a child, necessarily (it looks like a foetus): it is a self. Its hands are over its ears to shut out the scream which is in everything. The sky, the sea, the world, the *voice unutterable*. It has become the instrument through which the scream makes itself heard. It hears the scream, knows the scream, is the scream. Pallor and gauntness, suffering. It resonates with the pain of the world. It bleeds with the sun.

Waves of red and yellow, and green threads of light, the sweep of the sea in the fjord and of the streaked land, the inexorable straight line of the vanishing path with its railing lit by the sky. The stiff remoteness of the only other human figures. The downflow of waxen flesh into the darkness of the clothes as if the figure is melting in the last heat of the sun.

Infinity and the surface of the canvas play hide-and-seek in a room where a painting is hung.
JOHN BERGER

At the top of the world, two little black ships with two masts forever at anchor in the skin of blood and pus that is the Oslofjord. Fire of the sunset, as in a Viking funeral, the image in flames of the black ribcage of the hull as the fire slides away dwindling to the mouth of the fjord. Also there in *Angst* and *Despair* – the persistence of two little ships as inconsequential as dragonflies. As if the overwintering boats in the coves at Bygdøy had broken out of their ice husk and rushed, sails loose and flapping, hammering over the water. Charred sails, charred masts.

I was walking along the road with two friends. The sun set. I felt a tinge of melancholy. Suddenly the sky became a bloody red.

I stopped, leaned against the railing, dead tired and I looked at the flaming clouds that hung like blood and a sword over the blue-black fjord and city.

My friends walked on. I stood there, trembling with fright. And I felt a loud, unending scream piercing nature.

Jeg gik bortover veien med to venner –
solen gik ned –
Jeg følte som et pust af vemod –
Himmelen blev pludselig blodig rød –
Jeg stanset, lænede mig til gjærdet mat til døden –
så ut over de flammende skyerne som blod og sværd
over den blåsvarte fjord og by –
Mine venner gik videre – jeg stod der skælvende af angst –
og jeg følte som et stort uendeligt skrig gennem naturen.

Skrik, skrig. Screech or *shriek* is closer than *scream.*

Jeg is a scream. I! Of course, always, I. *Aï! Jeg!*

Jeg is the scream.

It was black-veiled witch queens of Orkney, blood of his blood, who made King Arthur and unmade him at the end. It was the witch his own mother who made a banner for Earl Sigurd of Orkney to take into war, with a raven on it, Odin's raven, flying in the wind. The spell she put on it would bring victory to the man it was carried before, she said, and death to the bearer, and so it was that one after another the bearers lost their lives until no one would take up Sigurd's banner and in the end he carried it himself – *A beggar should carry his own bundle* – to his own undoing.

Over three nights of Holy Week in 1014, as the Viking fleet gathered behind Earl Sigurd of Orkney, the ships of Brodir were drenched with boiling blood. It was Brodir who would be the one to behead the victor, Brian Boru, by stealth at the end of the battle of Clontarf outside Dublin, paying for that with a gash from throat to groin and the living guts dragged out of him and twined round a tree. On Good Friday morning at Svinafell in Iceland splashes of blood wet the stole of the priest, while the priest at Thvattwater saw in the floor by the altar a long abyss of the sea full of such horrors that it was some time before he could say Mass. That same morning a man in Caithness and another in the Faroes had seen the Valkyries ride up to a hut and sit chanting at the loom while they wove a web of all the men, Norse and Irish, doomed to die, a web *as red at the heart's blood, as blue as the corpse.*

Blood rains
From the cloudy web
On the broad loom
Of slaughter.
The web of man,
Grey as armour,
Is now being woven;
The Valkyries
Will cross it
With a crimson weft.

The warp is made
Of human entrails;
Human heads
Are used as weights;
The heddle-rods
Are blood-wet spears;
The shafts are iron-bound,
And arrows are the shuttles.
With swords we will weave
This web of battle.
. . .
It is horrible now
To look around,
As a blood-red cloud
Darkens the sky.
The heavens are stained
With the blood of men,

As the Valkyries
Sing their song.
NJAL'S SAGA

stamen...[t. L: thread, warp in the upright loom]

stamina...2. *Obs.* germinal elements; rudiments. [t. L, pl. of *stamen* thread (specifically, those spun by the Fates determining length of life)]

Blood – subtle, light, swift, pure – is the vehicle most apt to animal spirit: the heart, then, its well-spring, the place where such blood is sifted into being, is taken as the fixed centre of the ebullition of the passionate nature.
PLOTINOS

The Scream in the flesh. Bottled in a human head like the jinn that it is, the δαιμων with a god's voice and no name, the blood red angel.

The Scream is the keystone of *Livsfrisen*, *The Frieze of Life*, the series of anguished paintings that outraged the public, and the critics, who wrote them off as *sexual fantasies, the hallucinations of a sick mind.*

The Frieze of Life *is really about heredity as a curse...*
EDVARD MUNCH

A house wall emerging in the thaw matted with bare limbs, black and ashen grey. The clutch of hundreds of little grey relentless fingers, Virginia creeper, *Parthenocissus*, Munch's *Rød villvin*, where the man's face goes past livid, in a trance of fear – sexual fear, of the red flood up the wall, the menstrual flux, stronger every autumn, draining away to the bare bones, soon to be masked in snow.

Veins in red glass, leaves the red of a full glass of wine against the light.

There was a time when he could only live drunk – the buzzing in the head, the beehum and beedance of the fevered mind, every runnel bursting its banks, every swollen vein: *vin*, wine and vine, *vene*, vein – to be hollow clay on fire with wine, awash in fire.

The mirror is blind, an oval of fog, a wall eye in which she is not reflected. If she were, if it cleared, the visible self shimmering inside would be bloodshot. So Roger Bacon, after Aristotle: *if a menstrous woman beholde her selfe in a looking glasse, shee will infect it, so that there will appeare a cloude of bloud.*

What if the woman you love wants too much of you, marriage, children, only to spawn yet more death into this world of death? – you fight her off, as you must, to live. But she has one last trick up her sleeve. One night a messenger comes to call him to her deathbed. They sail back over the fjord – *the blue-black fjord* – with the moon dipping and spilling in their wake, and walk up the hill to the house where she lies moulded in a white sheet in a room feverish with candles. Mother, sister, lover – faint, his head bowed, he steps up to yet another corpse. At this the sheet twitches, erupts, flies open, beating wings, and she rises up with a screech, laughing, naked, her teeth bared and her hair flowing around her in folded blood red wings, the red woman of the dead of night, the vampire, Valkyrie, angel of death. She has a gun. She will kill herself, she swears, if he leaves her. He makes a grab for it and in the struggle it fires, maiming his hand. His hand! The painter's hand, torn and gushing blood. A thick skein of her hair drips down his neck. He ought to have let her die. Now she has got in first.

Over den blåsvarte fjord

The only bare surface he can find for the lamp is the floor. The peaked hood of the lamp, the slant of it and the angular shadows and patches of yellow it casts up, all take him back to another night, a lamp on the floor of the past. He is transfixed in the horror of memory, unable to move, only aware of a whiteness, a naked presence rearing in the rim of the lamplight. No one is there. No one. He need only move the lamp to breathe again. His hand falters in midair, aflame at the edges, fire, blood, mutilated, one finger off at the joint, his living hand, helpless to save him.

In Japan a miscarried or stillborn, neverborn baby is called a 'water child', *mizuko*. In folk Buddhism even a living child under the age of seven is still more or less water, not yet solidly of this world. But the *mizuko*, not having been through birth into the life of flesh, has not been through death. It is stranded, as fluid and unformed as the primordial waters we all come from, between the worlds of being and nonbeing. The *bodhisattva* of this realm is Jizo Bosatsu, under whose care the water child will haunt the threshold, the bridge and the river of stones, the crossroads, the other shore, in the hope of a mother to bear it safely across. Little stone figures of Jizo abound, all wearing a red bib, layers of red bibs, the offerings of mothers who have lost a *mizuko*.

Blank face. No face, only the lamplight and the head in the way with no face, a ghost mask, a hole in the bloom of the lamplight, a shape and a shadow. He raises his brush to the mirror.

On the Copenhagen train once he met his own self, *dobbeltgjenger*.

What if there were a child conceived, a water child, fathered on Edvard Munch one night by the fierce will of his demon lover, vampire, succubus – how might such a child fare in the liminal world of mirrors and reflections? How might he find his way back into the world he was born to, the landscapes and seascapes of his melancholy?

A water child of Edvard Munch, a fragile soul of air and water, ephemeral as a snowflake, a hailstone, a sliver of ice. Denied entry to life, finding another way in, however, another womb, he comes with an unknowable inheritance, three black angels and the soul of a soft-shelled crab. Wherever he is born he will be drawn back to Oslo, the water child, to the shores and waters of the fjord. His life will be shadowed by a journey he has never made, a spectral journey across water, gliding from shore to shore over the glassy moonlight to a rendezvous at a deathbed. Silent watchers, candles wavering, a graven woman's body under the sheet and he at the bed's foot, grief and horror in his heart, touching the white sheet where it flows in pools and runnels of yellow light, and heaves up, the corpse jerking upright with a scream of laughter, a great shatter of breath in his face, the raddled mouth open, the hair in one great bloodfall down its body and then his and the room a flare of fire.

Here death stares you in the face. Across the Arctic Circle, tall crags to the water's edge, serrated summits fading in mist, the ranges behind them veiled and unveiled. Cliff faces are festoons, pleats, ruffles of black rock, sheeted with white, or transparent, superimposed on cloud so that only the snow runnels and dapples show up. You slip into Risøyhamn along a channel so still and clear that the wake sizzles like skis over snow and the bow wave, the only wave, bulges the mirror into lazy spirals. Painted wooden towns by the water, white-roofed, a fume rising off the snow, hanks of mist coiling up off the inshore waters into the sun path. In the Raftsund, the Trollfjord, sea haze dims the white walls to the faintness of plates in old books under tissue paper. In the dark you leave Svolvær under a lid of cloud glazed with streetlights. Foam at the hull, white mountains and black of the sea in between, a wink and flash, green, red, white, gold, at water level and on white peaks a spark, a flare, a fan of light opening full in your face and snapping shut. At daybreak under the rock of Hornelen, blue rims of mountains over a sea in glassy folds, and then red peaks and black ones in their shadow, and one side of each wooden house red gold, creases of soft water, shadows swelling and strung out, and the glitter of every comb and spear of rosy ice.

Via negativa, the way in the dark, the way of unknowing.

I may have made a home by the sea, in a pine box burnished inside, a weatherboard house made a century ago of old *eastland boards* as they were known in the Middle Ages, Baltic pine shipped from the far north. My bedroom walls may dapple with amber when the sun breaks through the branches, and with ice under a moon, a sundial, a moondial, the whole house a lantern at full moon when the sky is clear. Bays and beaches all around, cliffs and dunes, a lagoon, wild swans, tidal waters.

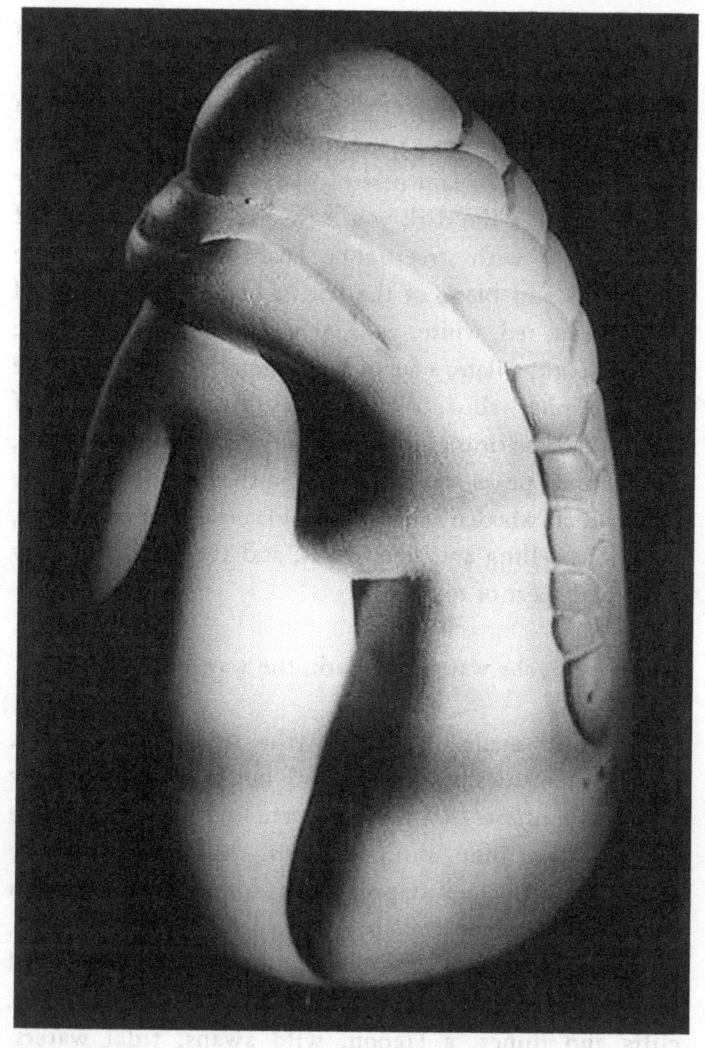

I would still give up the summer on my doorstep any day for the sake of a winter in the ice, out of sheer longing for pure ice, its frets and prisms and translucencies at close quarters and the vast ice to the horizon. How come? Those who are children of the Old World see the light out of season here on the underside of the globe. A midwinter's child is born in midsummer, born – why not? – into another world of snow and ice inside this one, another soul. Why not another soul, after all, a lost twin? – assuming any soul at all, why not two (Plato thought so)? The Egyptians had all of seven: *aakhu*, the one that lived in the blood; *ab*, the heart that was formed out of the mother's heart's blood; *ba*, the ghost that flitted out on the last breath and haunted the tombs; *ka*, the image, the reflection, water-bound; *khaibut*, the shadow, the black shade in the underworld; *khat*, the body of flesh; and *ren*, the secret name.

Which one of these is most likely to be longing for the great Ice? *Ka*, the reflection, who takes shape in water? *La grande Glace.*

High winter in the north, snowbound, icebound. Before there was a Middle Earth there was the world of Niflheim, Helheim, abode of the dead, a fogbound vault of ice with a well, and eleven rivers, and an Iron Wood of frozen trees. Northbound.

How lovely snow is, though, whirring, driven, a white swarm, storm, ice in sparks.

Who will ever know us again as the dead have known us? For our part, we carry them about with us in the pouch of memory, blended in with the ashes of all our lost selves.

Αναχωρησις is departure, retreat, embarkation, a setting out, a word that has the sweep of wind and water in it, of a voyage under sail or adrift. The early Christian anchorites had been hermits in the desert; the anchoress of the Middle Ages in England was a woman who for the love of God departed this life for a living tomb, a meditation cell, bricked-up, in some cases, in an annex of her convent. As a rule she would have three loophole windows: one for her food and drink to be passed in and her bodily wastes out, and her changes of clothes; one for outsiders in need of solace or counsel; and one into the church, for taking communion. The living flesh was slime and filth and loathsomeness, while the spirit was *swetter than hony*. Walled up, even as Antigone was, by her own hand, in the dark space between the worlds, undead, unliving, the anchoress was on an endless journey of self-mortification for her soul's sake; on board her ship of death before her time. The sisters sang the psalm and sprinkled earth on her; and then, having received the last rites she walked in singing her own requiem, *This shall be my rest forever: here will I dwell, for I have a delight therein.* The sisters sang the psalm and sprinkled earth on her. She had weighed, not cast, anchor – although 'anchoress', 'anchorite', αναχωρητρια, has nothing to do with 'anchor' as such, except that by a confusion of sounds this word drenched in movement has come to rest over time in a word that embodies the *held fast* (and is no less fitting, for all that).

{F}or hwet is ancre hus bute hire burinesse?
{F}or what is the anchor-house but her grave?
ANCRENE WISSE

When the man of God had finished speaking, one of the inhabitants of the island was seen to come out of doors...He was very shaggy and full at once of fire and darkness. When he saw the servants of Christ pass near the island, he went back into his forge. The man of God blessed himself again and said to his brothers:

'My sons, raise the sail higher still and row as fast as you can and let us flee from this island.'

Even before he had finished speaking, the same savage came to the shore near where they were, carrying a tongs in his hands that held a lump of burning slag of immense size and heat. He immediately threw the lump on top of the servants of Christ, but it did no hurt to them. It passed more than two hundred yards above them. Then the sea, where it fell, began to boil, as if a volcano were erupting there. The smoke rose from the sea as from a fiery furnace.

NAVIGATIO SANCTI BRENDANI ABBATIS

Awakening after madness after the bushfire, some trees in the garden charred, the lemons and plums baked on them, smoking, and some cool green, the house smouldering around the prow of its brick chimney. The old rowboat still down there where the fence had been, still there! – her joy, reaching out, but at the mere touch of her hand it falls away, like a skeleton on a cave floor, age-old and solid until then, apparitional, falling to ash. Fire night, fire light. At this, something in her that has held firm until now gives way and she falls to air and ash on the blackened earth.

Was that how it was for Munch, one more touch, however light, would be the end of him? The only hope, to grow a new solid man of flesh out of the sun and sea, a tougher, if lesser, man?

Does he dream this? Does he see? Himself huddled in a window corner in a railway carriage furtively pulling his cock. A drop glistens at its slit of mouth, a pearl of semen. *Perlemor*, he mutters, and once it is over he falls gratefully asleep, wet, his hand enfolding the softness of his cock. The skin of his face slicked with the same pallor of mother of pearl.

The face is a blank, lit or unlit, the mirror face under the shine holds nothing but silence. It is wordless. There are no words to put to this face. He puts the palms of both hands to it, clamps it between them because it is so lacking all solidity, a face as it might be reflected in slowly moving water, seeping palely through his hands, a mask held on like a smashed soft-boiled egg.

Once, one day, I am a madwoman. More than once. Never here, never this house of gold. But mad, null, a body of white fungus in the dark behind the hot blind as one whole autumn dies down into amber and the fixity of winter. Day after day I am no more than a skin in a mirror, paper-thin on the silver, mute, the ghost of a self. Life is a matter of lying in bed outlining in ink on the body a hand, another hand and two feet, drawing the extremities, tracing each ridge and crease, the groove around each nail, the fan of bones and the ravels of veins, white, blue, on a cold surface. Not a fungus, then, more than a puff of dust, ash, spores, that can take black ink and brush hands on to skin in lines as clear and solid as the veins and bones themselves. The next step is on paper, tracing each hand and foot, copying in every bone ridge and vein. One day a glass of water spills over the paper so that the lines run and bleed, shrivelling, and dry with a bronze glint in the wash of blue. The hand does not wash off. Held up into the sun it is still the same red and jointed, skeleton hand, translucent, as the hand holding it. Solid hands, and solid feet, talismans, bedfellows, make a way out on all fours.

The funeral flesh, a lantern in its hull of bones, a ship of fire.

A story in the present tense, an imprisoned bride. All one winter she has slept alone and naked under the bedclothes, feet to the window, on a low wooden bed on a floor of bare white wood. Every morning she has woken up in the half-light of the early morning and stood shivering at the window as the sun rose dark red on the skyline. One morning as she turns to go the sun seizes on her. Waxen, she flares, red to the core, her masses of watery flesh woven on bone, irradiated, blind. Her shadow is a hem of black silk that will trip her up if she moves. Head thrown back, her open mouth on fire, she will swallow fire.

Afterlight. Snowy streetlamps. In every pane of glass, an orange lamp.

One February, a new snowfall just as I arrive, and soon a blizzard. Århus is under snow and ice, even the sandy beaches. On Risskov Strand, a little hump of a dune matted with scrub and yellow grasses on Århus Bugt, Bight – how close to twins these languages are on paper! – the stalks in their sand bed are twisted, dark, snow-scorched. Frozen clumps and drifts of snow in marram grass as dry as straw – a ridge of it, a snowdrift eaten away by a high sea or storm. A tessellated pavement of thick ice running down to overhang the shallows, glistening in the sun like jellyfish, sprawls of stranded sea jellies.

Soon after moonrise squares of light slide over my bed. Snow moon, ice moon.

From Bergen I came back on the Oslo train overland, over snow, overnight in the glare of the full moon, wide-eyed, determined to stay awake until moonset, but I must have drifted off because one moment we were threading, two white wings lifted, through long silvery slopes of snow rising and falling into clefts of blue black that were all shade, void, and the next moment halted alongside a row of lamps, a little station. Figures laden with skis moved forward in a cloud of breath. The train stayed moored to the row of lights, breathing, caught without hope of struggle in a web while the silence thickened and a skin of frost grew on the panes. My eyelids were pods of stone.

Then we were sliding through the white night again, the moon full in my eyes as bright as the sun. A woman had got on and was sitting across from me, given away to sleep, her head back and to one side, lips slightly parted against her hood of hair. The black rope of her braid had worked loose to leave fine dark strands of hair draped over the headrest, and I saw it lift like a feather with each breath, and one strand was swirled at her throat, a woman's hair, on the loose, its power to rope in and choke and drown a man.

I was snowblind and she half lost in the rush of the dark. But at last I stole a glance at her image in the other window. Her eyes were open, not on the snowfields – no, as I dreaded, they held mine in a triumphant smile, quivering, her long dark eyes in the pane like still water in a stir of wind.

A sudden bark and I jumped out of my skin, a cough – a man I had not seen was sitting across from us, at the long apex of the triangle we formed. He sat tensely upright with his jaw set hard, and from time to time I caught the look he darted from one to the other in anger, or fear, but his eyes slid away before meeting mine. Insomniac eyes, small and stone pale under the slit flesh of the lids, the white lashes. All his visible skin, even to the scalp under the thin hair, shone red in patches, red raw and tight over the bone. Until our eyes locked, widening, and held. Stiff with shock I fought to tear my eyes away, back to the white window, as the sweat drenched and chilled my flesh and I felt my heart bloat and shrink back, quivering, a red frog bulging under my hand.

The next thing I knew it was morning, the sun burning in on empty seats. The white slopes had given way to buildings and the train was pulling into Oslo Sentralstasjon.

Clearer by the day than the moon under the black clothes the shine of bone.

A snowfall at daybreak and by the milky afternoon I am deep in the beechwoods of Moesgård following the path along and around the frozen millstream, the little *å*, to the sea. A clogged tongue of grey green ice with a fishy mottle and speckle, patches of melt, holes where the water runs dark underneath. On the snow, trees written like runes. The birches come first, white birches with sooty notches and new red limbs springing out fine and jointed like lobster feelers, tentative, blood red, growing wild. A bare wild tree where I come from is dead more often than not, burnt or ringbarked or stark with salt, the clarity of the skeleton. Here the clarity has no taint of death, the trees are gravid, birch and beech burn on a low flame in the snowbound woods. The beeches have a green skin of moss, rough and smooth, and a white stripe like a finger of sunlight all down one side, fresh snow. Branches of papery brown leaves here and there are caught in a shaft of sun that makes the little tree-skeleton inside each one stand out like the core of a flame. After the forest come hazy fields of pasture ribbed in snow, long dry grasses and brambles and matted grass laced with sheep droppings; twisted apple trees and sawn tree trunks, golden brown inside the rind; dolmens, mounds, leaning stones in a dreary flat light against a sea that has been a rim of ice all winter and now is mush, turbulence.

Aa, *å*, is a creek, and was the same in English at least until 1430, the date of a manuscript from Saltfleetby in Lincolnshire; its forbears are Old Norse *á*, Old English *éa*, Gothic *ahwa*, Latin *aqua*. I am keeping a wordbook, *ordbog*, grappling in vain to pin down a language that is too much akin and at the same time not enough. *Elm. Arm*, *trawl*, *flag*, *blind*, *blizzard*, *skunk*, *under*, *over*, *top*, *topflag*, *toplanterne* (masthead light). *Orm*, worm. *Silkeorm*, *silkegarn*. By midnight the street-lamp has grown a thin beard of ice.

The red brick cathedral, *Sankt Clemens domkirke*, has a leper window in one wall, a hooded niche in the white-wash painted like fancywork with daisy petals and ribbons, faint clear frescoes showing in patches through Lutheran coats of whitewash as if in melting snow: a hovering angel, a wall with turrets overlooking the seat where the priest celebrating the mass would sit, and a tall Christ in a monk's robe looming in the niche so that the pane is his body. Not that the lepers waiting out in the street could see it or even know that the hand holding out the bread and wine, shrinking in horror, came out of Christ's body, unless they had been inside the cathedral before they were known to be lepers. The window arch is bricked in now on the outside.

The Christmas snow is thawing. Slabs as thick as concrete, grubby ice, but whiter than the sand, are melting down to ledges of frilled and spotted glass, disgorging fishheads, torn wings, messes of red bone. Rowboats are hauled up face down under a keel of snow. Here and there in the shallows a raft of ice has broken off to run aground or go bobbing a little way out, worn thin and bubbly. A frail sun picks out the amber in the broken boat ramp kneedeep in a diaphanous sea that is all sky, and in the breakwaters, piles of sealskin boulders. Even the seaweed pods and dog turds are amber. Gulls wade by with black eyepatches and tailfeathers. A horizon of sea in a frame of low purple hills, sun on the masts of fishing boats and one red sail, a city skyline of chimney, spire and tower, silvery flashes of a tower, and smoke coiling up like a reflected mast.

In a dream I sit on the seawall eating hot fish in batter out of a bunch of white paper spread out in flapping folds and the gulls have got wind of it, landing and gathering around, running at each other on red feet, angry heads lowered, uttering their red squawks, lifting off and fluttering aside. I am throwing flakes and crumbs, and how I am laughing, wildly, hoarsely with my hands open, hands that burn red and sprout wings.

Far out against the low hills tonight Århus Bugt was a luminous, deep, heavenly blue – polar blue. All the edges of the ice glinted. You could wipe off the coating of snow as if wiping the steam off a window, ice like rock crystal, clear to its depths, cracked, iridescent. Kayakers sliding back and forth, a freighter out on the horizon, gulls and ripples and sandbanks, children and dogs. The tide out, barely rippling, turning shadowy. A sliver of moon.

Anchored to the pillow, a spirit of the dead, a *tupapau* of Gauguin's Tahiti, where I once sailed away to – robed in the black of night, her blind eyes fixed, eyes inlaid with mother of pearl, black pearl shell.

One morning the window is red in the Danish sunrise and I am waking riven to the heart for the gulls' cry of home, silver gulls, not this yowl of the northern breed, our own gulls raucous on the bluestone seawall. Bluestone is a black stone, not basalt, a clayey sandstone, ledges and pedestals moulded in shallow rings of flow on flow, and soft sand gathering in whorls and pleats and fans. The landslide of rubble, the breakwater, further around the neck of the bay at home is chunks and boulders of this bluestone, dry and coke grey or wet blue black, pocked and grizzled, ashen, hacked old surfaces, a sky blue scatter of tight periwinkles, a flow of rust.

Weaving my way is the only way I can go. Sidetrack to sidetrack snakewise and if I wear out my skin I will have to shuck it, a papery twist of stocking in the grass.

Ebb and flow of the day and night, waves, tides – tides and all are waves – of the sea in and out, and of the snow and ice, throwing up their dead and gulping them back in. Now that the sun has come out the ice is a shimmer of cold, an ice shelf of caves and fissures dwindling out over the shallows. Icicles, prisms, dissolving castles in the air. A shag of white like a sheepskin caught in the sun at the mouth of a dripping ice cave is plumage, a vaulted cape of feathers and a long mask, hollow-eyed, starting to stink, one great draggled, broken wing, a swan. Held fast in the ice a whole season out of the sea's reach, a white princess in a glass palace, a Viking queen run aground in a longship.

Swans are black where I come from, like the first peoples of the land – who, if they had songs from the time before time where men and women were turned into swans, gave them sleek black skin and plumage.

There are ships' figureheads stacked high and dry on an upper floor in Århus Old Town, from the days when ships were still crafted, human, with a sense of life about them, like the wide-eyed Mediterranean ships. They are all individuals, these scraggy mermaids, paint peeling, hair stiff with salt, each one as stiff and unblinking in the dark as an Egyptian mummy.

A milky night. The moon pushes round and wet through a hole in the cloud.

Now the whole jut of ice shelf has broken off into a raft. Boat ramps of thin planks jut out over grey water, a clear shell and pebble bottom, no wave breaking the surface, only a steady cross-wave of swell nudging the ramp, the quickening tremor in the planks, of the life of the water.

skrig – cry, scream, shriek, screech
skrog – hull; (*skelet*) carcass
skrog is – shell ice, cat ice

In Rilke's poem about the swan, the struggle he has to make his way on land is like our struggle in life as if shackled, whereas dying is like the swan's anxious, *ångstliches*, way of *letting himself down into the waters, which softly receive him*, and sliding away on sliding wave on wave, ever more noble, calm, silent. Cumbersome at first, the words, the lines smooth out correspondingly in a long flow of sibilance. So simple, see, we let ourselves slip away, as simple as falling asleep. But the consolation is, alas, of course, false. If falling asleep is simple, dying is not. Dying is Mallarmé's swan anchored in the ice. Death is his rags and bones encased in ice.

From Moscow in the May of the first year after the collapse of the Soviet Union came a newspaper report of a strange crop coming to light with the spring thaw, hundreds of babies, far more than in any other year, hidden in the snow all winter, snow children made in one playtime and lost in a snowdrift when the bell rang. Were they white still, and fresh as the day they were born, or blue with cold? So solid, so light to lift, the ice children, water children, black and blue, so cold they scorch the cupped hands that bring them to light.

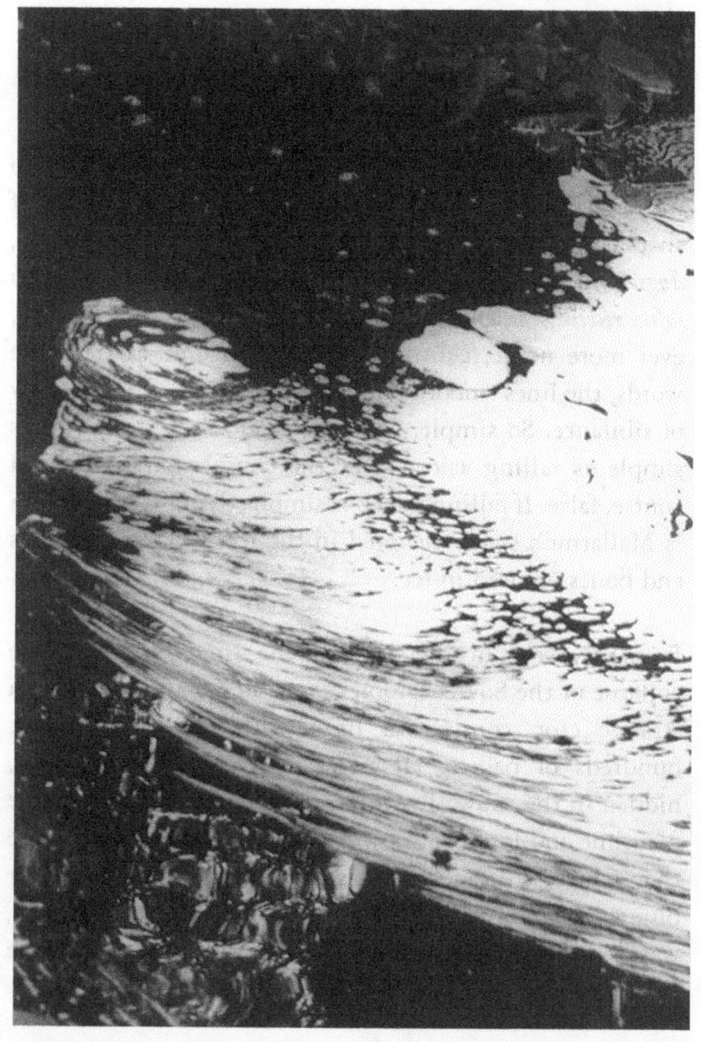

Long after sunset, the red glow like a lamp on in an empty room. Otherwise, flat grey sky and water, the city lights coming up like a print in wrinkling water. Boulders, jetties, a black figure here and there in the filmy expanses. Distances, melancholy.

Århus, *bán-hús*. Bonfires in the neighbourhood for *valborgs-nat*, Beltane. The witchburning crackle of bones from next door, thick smoke flattening in the wind and a high flap of fire in the bushes – no, a reflection, a window pane.

Last night I slept with the window open and was not cold. I had inherited an old house of many rooms. In the dark depths of one I found a child in bed asleep surrounded with bay branches and stalks of some tall, knotty, dark blue flower – the quilt a rolling wave, his face going under. I woke him – Don't sleep here, it's wet – and suckled him, only from the one breast, left hanging as empty as a stocking, but he went smiling off to sleep. It was the child I was looking for. In another room I found my mother on a high bed asleep and crept away so as not to wake her.

The brand new glass and steel bank by the cathedral above the ice canal in the dark heart of Viking Århus has a headless man in its bowels, murdered, like in the olden days of the blessing, the blood offering. Dug out of the mud, he is preserved under glass now with other relics, in a small Viking Museum in the basement, open during bank hours. He is crossed-legged, missing one foot, a sprawl of opalescent bone on a bed of dark soil, light as a dragonfly husk, and headless but for the bottom jaw on a plate at his side. Not buried – he was thrown down in haste. Was he beheaded so no one would know who it was? Or so if he came back to life he could never find and murder his murderers? Glass like creek water, floating reflections and his long spine on the bottom, shoulder blades like folded wings, blades of ribs like armour, the hips a knot of lap and fold, a ruff of bone, shards of a clay bowl. The soil under him is sooty, as if he has been on a low flame all this time and it was fire, not earth, eating him down. He shod horses here by the ramparts of Aros of the sagas, or he sold skins or meat or carved combs out of bones and antlers while his wife cooked and span and wove wool by the hearth in a pit house half underground, snug as a shepherd's hut – like the one on show down here, firelit – under a shag of thatch, earthen beds boxed in with planks, and deerskins, sheepskins for bedclothes, the loom taking up all one wall. Now he is the hoard in a bank vault, their fallen angel. The city is one long hush under the snow. Schoolchildren come trooping downstairs and start roaming and peering, teasing, shoving elbows. Who's afraid of the headless once-man? Who spares a thought for the bone child growing under the skin, biding his time? The teacher makes a quick face across at me, eyebrows raised. They still think it's a history lesson, she says.

I think that we are sailing with a corpse in the cargo.
HENRIK IBSEN

Gauguin had a wife, a Dane who, finding herself stranded in Paris, went home to the family in Copenhagen, taking the children. He, who loathed everything about Denmark and made no secret of it, had a fraught stay there in 1884, at the Hotel Dagmar, in a forlorn bid for reconciliation. While there he made her a little oblong box with a lid on hinges, the kind all the seamen used for their belongings in his seagoing days. This one was of pear wood with carved sides and two netsuke masks, stained red. In the floor of it he carved a naked corpse, so that with the lid up his ship's box – a miniature, a netsuke sea chest – was a coffin. A jewel box for a castaway wife, a memento mori for a marriage.

Since 1875 in the National Museum in Copenhagen – where Gauguin saw it – there has been on display a coffin of oak, dug out of the Bronze Age mound of Borum Eshøj, in which lies the skeleton of a young man with a face and tangled fair hair. He was one of the Mound People, *Højfolket*, who worked the low hills behind Århus within sight of the sea: an old man and woman unearthed from the same mound were evidently his parents – hard-working folk, dogged, frugal, one ear to the ground, for whom every grain counted. Whoever had laid him out, and replaced the precious sword in his wooden scabbard with a dagger, had shrouded him in his woollen cape and an ox-hide for the winter journey. Great stones were planted in a ring at the base of the mound.

Bronze Age grain production had its roots in Stone Age agriculture with its cultivation of single-grained wheat, emmer (triticum dicoccum), *dwarf wheat, ordinary wheat, six-rowed barley and millet. No doubt the descendants of the old Stone Age peasants continued to till the soil for the Mound People. In the Bronze Age, barley, both naked and awned, was the most important grain, though several of the old kinds were still cultivated, while oats, peas, beans and the oil plant, dodder, gradually appeared as new field crops.*
P V GLOB

Barley, both naked and awned.

awn *n. Bot.* 1. a bristle-like appendage of a plant, esp. on the glumes of grasses. 2. such appendages collectively, as those forming the beard of wheat, barley, etc. 3. any similar bristle. [ME, t. Scand.; cf. Sw. *agn*, Icel. *ögn* husk] – **awned**, *adj.* – **awn'less**, adj.

glume *n.* [L. *gluma*, a husk, from *glubo*, to peel, akin to Gr. *glypho*, to hollow out.] The husk or chaff of grain; the palea or pale.

Art is a water child of a kind, the child of the union of the artist and the δαιμων, never coming fully to life, suspended in a liminal realm, always more or less botched in the making. Not that perfection is the answer. To be perfected is to be dead.

We take our bearings as we go. A journey may turn into a pilgrimage before we know it, a spirit journey alongside that of the everyday restless body, and end up fused with other journeys, remembered, or only imagined, dreamt of, in multiple exposures, shifting overtones, nostalgias for places we have never been. It was the land I went back to, stemmed from – my ancestral place, as well as others that might be mine, on a long taproot into the past – that drew me north late in life, in the polar opposite of wanderlust. So I was taking and losing my bearings in familiarity, knowing these fens and lowlands and islands on sight, the watery landscapes inland and on the shores, the stones, the green graveyards, the yew trees already ancient before my people ever heard of a Great South Land.

In Orkney where a lost race once lived underground in a stone maze, all too close to the sea, I walked the bounds of the stone rings they had raised up in the singed heather. I crawled into the mound they built, Maeshowe, Orkahaugr, at Stenness, beyond the Stones, in a cold sweat of close-woven stone into the dark, down a passage angled to take in the last red shaft of the midwinter sun. Vikings broke in through the dome for shelter and treasure and here were their runes among the Stone Age markings. On a raid once Earl Harald, a kinsman and rival of Earl Rognvald Kali Kolsson, sat out a snowstorm in Maeshowe and two of his men went mad, as the *Orkneyinga Saga* says. Earl Rognvald himself with his followers, wintering with their ships before setting out for the Holy Land, or safely back home afterwards perhaps, by way of Byzantium and Rome, also took shelter in there and he was a great carver of runes.

Rings of stones around heather, in a mirror of rainwater. One day on a windswept cliff in a sun glare I slid inside a tunnel into a chamber stalled like a cowbyre, the Tomb of the Eagles – sea eagles, in bones among the picked bones of the people – and later on, in Ireland, I lay in the dark lap of a dolmen half sunk under a massive capstone and another staggering in the sun, four long legs and a low-slung shade full of cold. In the depths of a brown bear's cave I made my way to a river of darkness, a living waterfall. And at last by the smooth waters of the River Boyne I was inside the dark stone hive of Newgrange under the mound, watertight for over five thousand years, where the rising midwinter sun – and once every nineteen years, the full moon also – shafts in and kindles with firelight – glazes with ice – the inner chambers, the apse, the nave, so long as there is a sun and a moon.

bedendom, bedenskab – heathendom, paganism
bede – moor, heath; heat
bedemor – heath peat
bedemose – heather moor, heather bog
gå beden – depart this life
bedengangen, *bedenfaren* – deceased, dead

A deathfaring, wayfaring, seafaring life. Earl Rognvald Kolsson, the Viking Crusader, was always two men in one, at least two, and a poet, a skald, a visionary. It was Rognvald who vowed into being the red stone cathedral on the foreshore at Kirkwall to house the bones of his uncle Earl Magnus, butchered by another uncle, Earl Hakon, for the earldom. It was Rognvald who one day by Sardinia on the way to the Holy Land set fire to a Saracen merchantman the size of an island, only to look on as a stream of honey poured from its hull, molten gold, into the sea. Every battle a poem.

First aboard the black
boat, the unbending
Red Audun, rampaging,
that stern ravager.
Christ helped us crimson
the carrion, the dark-
blue bodies, piled
black on the deck.

Another day he walked into Jerusalem.

A cross on this bard's
breast, on his back
a palm-branch: peacefully
we pace the hillside.
ORKNEYINGA SAGA

Orkney is stone land, bedrock, and not as I had always foreseen it, grey all over, 'grayscale', like the sagas themselves. There were whole days, and more twilights, when it was grey, but mostly even when overcast it was blue, one wash of blue from top to bottom, shallow to deep. When the sun was out it was a white glare, tawny at sunset. In any light at all there were the flamy lichens and a green velvet of grass and moss, the auburn of the heather moor, a lazy wobble of red and white hulls along the harbour and the deep warm earth colours of soil and peat and faces of stone, worked and unworked. What looks to be blue stone in one light or shade, dry or shiny in a water slick in the cold sea-fog, the *haar*, will be ochre, yellow, brown or baked red in the sun. Up here, as in the far south, the look of things is as much a matter of air, of light and shade, as of substance. There is the yellow sandstone and the red, russet red or the burnished red of a skun rabbit or at sunset the hot scarlet of heart's blood as in the hulk of St Magnus on Mainland, once the Norse island of Hrossey, 'horse island'; and the blue-grey slate and granite of Stromness, a stone town of houses turned end-on to the salt wind, and cobbles and piers and, behind a stone wall on Hoy Sound, gravestones that face into the sunrise and take their colour from the wind and rain, sky and sea. There is a finely hewn slabby, buttery brown stone in the mound of Maeshowe, where the midwinter sun burns in at sunset and not sunrise as at Newgrange, and the same stone underground in the Grain Earth House, not a tomb but a cellar; on the brochs and cairns, fretted stone with the lichen on it as lush as the seaweed at low tide on the rockshelf; and anywhere, everywhere, wild black rock. On the windswept Atlantic side of Hoy, 'high island', is a wet valley of sheep and drystone walls and stone crofts with their turf roofs weighted with slabs: this is Rackwick, 'wreck bay', on the mouth of a black burn that has worn its way in the path of an ancient glacier down through the black cliff to the sea. Here the light is always on the wing. A path along the cliff with steps in the heath, and peat stacks, goes to the rockstack called the Old Man of Hoy, black and indigo cliffs with dashes of green ledge and a white scatter of seabirds defiant in every crack, as is the Old Man himself, icy and immense in this wind. The sharp nose of land that points to him is a seabird graveyard, bones, feathers and fluff and one bright curl of orange peel that is a puffin beak. Skuas harry and dive on the stone path through the heather, and back in the hollow of Rackwick the burn runs black with seaweed down through a nest of pale round pebbles and boulders, brindled and speckled, that trundle underfoot, every one of them, large or small, as smooth as an egg.

The *haar*, they say here, a white breath of a word on a cold morning. Is it from the Norse *haar*, *hår*, 'hair', for a spun white veil of fog drifting in low off the sea? No, it seems 'hoar' is at the root of it, hoarfrost. A cold sea fog is a *haar* – *harr*, *haur* – on the east coasts of England and Scotland, from Lincolnshire up. A further Norse echo lives on in *haaf*, the fishing grounds of the sea, the high seas, the ocean – *le large,* ο πελαγος – in Shetland and Orkney. *Haaf-eel* is conger-eel. *Haaf-fish*, great seal.

The mariner, astronomer and geographer Pytheas of Massalia, Marseilles, in the last days of Alexander is the first we know of to circumnavigate Britain (so he has seen the stone circles for what they are, he being Greek and knowing a temple of the sun when he sees one). In the North Sea in the high season of no sunset he is close by an island he calls Θουλη, Thule, probably Iceland – that volcanic island on the flight path of the whooper swans, the singing swans – a six-day sail north-west of Britain by way of Hoy Sound when, as he will write in his lost work, Περι του ωκεανου, *On the ocean*, he bursts into a clotted world that is *neither earth nor sea nor air but a slurry of all three, like sea lungs*, πλευμων, sea jellies, blubbery heaves and sucks of drift ice and fog that stop him dead in his tracks. A likely story! As if any man of sense will swallow that back home.

The Old Man burns in the sun with the sear and hiss of a gummy log.

After three days and three nights the wind dropped and the sea coagulated, as it were – it was so smooth. The holy father said: 'Ship the oars and loosen the sail. Wherever God wants to direct the boat, let him direct it!'

NAVIGATIO SANCTI BRENDANI ABBATIS

The hearth is the core of each one of the stone burrows of Skara Brae. The people hugged the fire down there under the turf in the dead of winter and the roar of the wild Atlantic; they sang songs and told tales and crafted stone tools, and balls that fit the palm of the hand, some granite, the hardest stone they had, raked with spirals or clustered with grapes, pods or mounds, all perfectly smooth and regular: 'Platonic solids', carved for who knows what purpose. Were the spiral ones, as some believe, a map of the coiled entrails of pigs and lambs used in divination?

In snow Maeshowe is an igloo from the air, a blown egg, a cocoon.

All along there have been those who hold it to be a truism that the earth is alive, an immortal being, goddess or daimon: *firm earth, eldest of Gods, that nourishes all things in the world*. The Greeks never began it; they handed it on, in the word, spoken, sung, breathed, and in clay, in stone and paint. For Plotinos, the earth has a lucid soul that feels and sees: *the soul in the earth has vision*, he reasoned, and after all *it is the soul of no mean body*.

To have been mad once and to have sat all one night by a moon and its dangling self-image in the water, the notations of beacons at twilight on some far shore of the sea, in a rapture of the eyes sensing the structures and symmetries, coherent, incoherent, unfolding witherings of form, the anatomy of the world.

Towards sundown gulls flying from the sun throwing shadows on ahead.

I have come full circle and, along the way, chanced on the reason why they must have laid the dead of Sindos to rest with a seal of immortal gold over the mouth. It was a charm, as spelt out by a Cambridge man who went travelling in Greece in the 1890s when the country was only half out of Ottoman hands, like the statue halfway out of the stone – a lost Greece, risen again only to be lost again – picking up the living and breathing language as he went and seeing for himself how the oldest of faiths lived on in the culture, not as a relic, a fossil, but quick with life, in a language, a folklore, and finally an Orthodox church steeped in the past.

A coin is often used as a charm against sinister influences. In this case then it may have been a prophylactic against aërial spirits. Why then is it generally put in the dead man's mouth? Not, I think, because the mouth is a convenient purse, as seems to be assumed in the classical interpretation of the custom, but because the mouth is the entrance to the body. The peasants of today believe as firmly as men of the Homeric age that it is through the mouth that the soul escapes at death. The phrase με τη ψυχη στα δοντια, *'with the soul between the teeth,' is the popular equivalent for 'at the last gasp'; and in the folk-songs the same idea constantly recurs; 'open thy mouth,' says Charos to a shepherd whom he has thrown in wrestling, 'open thy mouth that I may take thy soul.' Now the passage by which the soul makes its exit, is naturally the passage by which evil spirits (or the soul, if it should return,) would make their entrance; and, as we shall see later, there is a very real fear among the peasantry that a dead body may be entered and possessed by an evil spirit. Clearly then the mouth, by which the spirit would enter, is the right place in which to lay the protective coin...*

Again, in many places throughout Greece, where this use of a coin is no longer known, a substitute of more Christian character has been found. On the lips of the dead is laid either a morsel of consecrated bread from the Eucharist, or more commonly a small piece of pottery – a fragment it may be of any earthenware vessel – on which is incised the sign of the cross with the legend I. X. NI. KA. ('Jesus Christ conquers') in the four angles. Here the choice of the inscribed words of itself seems to indicate the intention of barring the dead man's mouth against the entrance of evil spirits; and as final proof of my theory I find that in both Chios and Rhodes, where a wholly or partially Christianised form of the custom prevails, the charm employed is definitely understood by the people to be a means of precaution against a devil entering the dead body and resuscitating it. Nor must the mention of a devil in this connexion be taken as evidence that the Chian and Rhodian interpretation of the custom is not ancient...{T}he idea of a devil entering the corpse is only the Christian version of a pagan belief in a possible re-animation of the corpse by the soul.

But there is yet another variety of the custom, in which no coin and no Mohammedan nor Christian symbol is used, but a charm whose magic properties were in repute long before Mohammed, long before Christ, probably long before coinage was known to Greece. Again a piece of pottery is used, but the symbol stamped upon it is the geometric figure ☆, the 'pentacle' of mediaeval magic lore. In Greece it is now known as το πενταλφα...

JOHN CUTHBERT LAWSON

I X is ΙΗΣΟΥΣ ΧΡΙΣΤΟΣ, Jesus Christ. NIKA is 'conquers'. A mirror image of I X NIKA is carved into the bread stamp they press on to every communion loaf, the Holy Ghost in the Body. And the mouth-mask was a seal against any other, unholy ghost. Why the name πενταλφα for this symbol aflame with magic since Babylonian times? For its five capital 'A's in a ring. Αλφα, as the first letter, has to do with first things, beginnings, birth, new life. Ωμεγα is the end. Αλφα and ωμεγα, the closed circle, the two thresholds as one.

Still I love the thought that at least one of the mouth masks of Sindos had a ship in profile flying with dolphins in the gold with its owl eyes wide awake, a half-moon boat for a spirit journey. Others had a flower, others an open eye, to ward off the Evil Eye, surely, το κακο ματι, and to keep out the soul, or any other lurking soul, δαιμων or devil, desperate to slip in and reanimate the corpse. At the heart of the Greek rites surrounding death from ancient times was the belief that the dead must be free to rot away – the very opposite of the Egyptian obsession with hoarding the flesh. At need the Greeks might preserve their dead, as when Alexander was borne in *white honey which had not been melted* from Babylon to Alexandria, his godlike rank overriding the usual fear: the fear being that, once reanimated, the corpse in the flesh, neither truly alive nor free to lapse back into the earth where it belonged, was doomed to a half-life, half-death in the form of a revenant, a vampire, βρυκολακας. Such monsters appear in the Norse sagas as well, this or that malefactor who was so evil in life that the grave only fattens him, blackening his flesh and turning him loose, a nightwalker with a troll's strength to kill; or he lives on undead as a shapeshifter, a huge bull seal attacking and dismembering boats. In Homer and Aischylos there are traces of this folk horror of the corpse denied the last rites and therefore trapped above ground, a misdeath, between this world and the next. Any corpse slow to dissolve in its grave was a βρυκολακας in the making. More dreadful than the fear of death was the fear of being stuck in the earth's craw. The ancient curse is still flung out to this day: Να μη σε φαγη το χωμα! *May the earth not eat you!* Anyone who died in sin or under a curse or simply before his time, by violence, wilful or not, was more than likely to turn into a βρυκολακας and an avenger of blood, to the point of turning on its own kin if they failed to hunt down his killer. The only hope was to have the corpse dug up and exorcised and, if that failed, as it well might, then burn it to ashes.

As for the countless other unseen powers of evil in the air, a ματι, eye, a blue stare at the invisible, kept the wearer more or less safe. The velvety watchful ones like donkeys' eyes painted on boats were for far more than finding the way. Even a wine cup had sharp eyes – at least the shallow kind called a κυλιξ, with vine tendrils and a lordly black-figure Dionysos and handles like two black ears – to make sure no evil slipped down with the wine.

Porphyry, the disciple of Plotinos, saw pottery as akin to the grape and both to Dionysos, in that the clay pot holds the wine and that both achieve their being only when fired.

ωυτος δε Αιδης και Διονυσος – *Hades and Dionysos are one and the same*
HERAKLEITOS, *FRAGMENTS*

Dionysos and Osiris, the Egyptian god of death and resurrection, were manifestly one and the same in the eyes of Plutarch. So it was with Eros and Thanatos for Munch, one and the same, to be kept at arm's length. Not that he would go on to live a monk's life, a skeleton's life. Just not love. Another kind of death.

Να σε φαγη το χωμα! – *May the earth eat you!* – might seem more of a blessing than a curse, considering that the opposite is the ultimate horror. Not so. Or if so, a blessing in disguise at best, of a kind we might wish on ourselves. *May the earth – and sea, air, fire – eat us.*

All it took in the old days to lay a curse on any living soul was to pay a μαγος or μαγισσα, a witch, for a written spell and hide it in some sacred cave or tomb or grave or coffin from where it would make its own way to the underworld and into the hands of the black goddesses, the Furies, *fearsome as a dragon-brood*, as they appeared to Aischylos, the ultimate avengers of blood.

ψυχης πειρατα ιων ουκ αν εξευροιο πασαν επιπορευομενος οδον· ουτω βαθυν λογον εχει – *no finding the bounds of soul by travelling however far on any road, so deep is the extent of its logos*
HERAKLEITOS, *FRAGMENTS*

There must be ghosts all the country over, as thick as the sands of the sea. And then we are, one and all, so pitifully afraid of the light.
HENRIK IBSEN, *GHOSTS*

Solen

I lie in the moonlight thinking about the soul's logos and its nature in a world whose logos is fire. My front room looks east through two long panes of glass three feet by six that burn in the low fire of the sunrise. Down the passage my bedroom only gets it slant. I do have a bed in the front room though I never sleep there, winter or summer, facing the rising sun. I will when the time comes.

gravhøj – burial mound; barrow
gravsten – gravestone
gravøl – funeral feast, wake
øl – ale
gravet laks – cured salmon

Soon after the shortest day, overnight the first iris of the year has risen again milkwhite, half-folded over with one long tongue out, golden-feathered.

Barefoot I lug hanks of seaweed the length of the beach, arms high as if for a round dance, stopping to wash off the sand on the way in the rush of water in and out of a rock channel. The rest of the sand and salt I hose off in the garden, holding each hank up for the tongue of the water to lick it out, long, fretty strands with dark teats like olives. In the low sunlight they have translucent rims like amber, like crafted gold, the diadems of leaves and olives that still turn up in the clay of the tombs. The hose has set a leaf spinning in midair, folded on a spider, and then another, wheels of spangles appearing and fading back as they dry and I weave a blanket of dark seaweed, all the gold gone out of it now on the grey of the herb garden.

Like a brass cauldron our bay will hold the heat well into the autumn.

Now and then, these mornings, muted foghorns and the replying lighthouse. A warm breath of mist wreathing up off the ground, gold in the sun. Three times to the lands of the dead and back here for the beginning of my own winter, shadows, a yellow sun, the simmering of crickets like the kettle on the hob, the rasp in the belly of a wood stove. Today I have a bottle of Danish *øl* and stoneground rye bread to go with the smoked fish of memory, a lanky body gilded and crisped, acrid, its fins and tail scorched, its eyes ambered. I cut slits into one leathery mottled flank and peel the skin back in flaps, a lining of grey damask. The pink flesh, rich and sweet, lifts in flakes off the white hairs of the bones and the skin falls back into place. Intact on one side and on the other a fossil, a rock painting, a skeleton in ochre and soot out of the cave days, hearthfire, rack and smokehole.

Where are the lands of the dead? Under foot and ground and sea. Under sky.

Leavings of the sea. Lobes of leathery sponge. Red ball of a sea urchin, hollow, bald. Cuttlebone with a fold at the tip like an iris tongue. Egg case of a shark. Thoughts of salt, of sun, stone.

Midnight. The full moon, so high and clear when I first go out to the sea wall – waves thrown across each other, spills of white froth – hazes over in a film of cloud that makes a creamy aureola inside a red gold ring inside a ring. One bright star at the frayed edge of the cloud and, against the red gold, a rainbow, a moonbow, all the way from purple to deep red.

A blackbird, loops of spray flying in the birdbath, a beak of amber.

Barefoot and fishcold out of the sea I pull off the old black smock I wear over my bathers, rusted at the shoulders and seams and dulling like ink where it has dried on me. I am pegging it up on the line under the fig tree with the last sun hot on my back when I see red gobs, a hanging purple fig in the shifting green gold light, the first fig of the year. It slips off like a glove in my hand, its milk welling, overripe, with a purple stain under the skin but still rose red inside, hollow, as sound as a bell. I rinse it under the hose and lick the torn pulp off the skin, so luscious that I grope up for more, and yes, caught in a slab of sun is another fig already black at the base, with a red gash in its side. And a sudden blue flare, lapis lazuli blue, iridescent on the grey skin of the bough – a bull ant, eating its fill, and I rear back just in time, every hair of my skin on end, as it straddles the gash and throws its spiky shadow down and fire fills it.

The gold dust on grey limbs, in the leaves and shadows, is light, is lichen.

A full moon is iced in shadow on the blind.

Sources

Margaret Alexiou, *The Ritual Lament in Greek Tradition*, Cambridge, CUP, 1974.

Dante Alighieri, *The Purgatorio of Dante Alighieri*, London, Dent, 1956.

Ibn Al-Haytham, *The Optics of Ibn Al-Haytham II*, trans. A I Sabra, London, Warburg Institute, 1989.

Ancrene Wisse: Parts Six and Seven, ed. Geoffrey Shepherd, Manchester UP, 1972.

The English Text of the Ancrene Riwle: Ancrene Wisse, ed. J R R Tolkien, London, Oxford UP, 1962.

Aristotle, *Problems*, I, Books I–XXI. trans. W S Hett, London, Heinemann, 1953.

Roger Bacon's philosophy of nature (critical edition of *De multiplicatione specierum* and *De speculis comburentibus)* trans. David C Lindberg, Oxford, Clarendon, 1983.

The Mirror of Alchimy: Composed by the Thrice-Famous and Learned Fryer, Roger Bachon (1597), ed. Stanton J Linden, New York/London, Garland, 1992.

Elizabeth Barrett Browning, *Elizabeth Barrett to Miss Mitford: the unpublished letters of Elizabeth Barrett to Mary Russell Mitford*, ed. Betty Miller, London, John Murray, 1954.

Roland Barthes, *Camera Lucida*, trans. Richard Howard, London, Flamingo, 1984.

Roland Barthes, *La chambre claire: Note sur la photographie*, Paris, Gallimard, 1980/2002.

Georges Bataille, 'Van Gogh Prométhée' in *Œuvres Complètes* vol. 1, Paris, Gallimard, 1970.

John Berger, 'Go Ask the Time', *Granta* 15, Spring 1985; 'infancy' in *Keeping a Rendezvous*, New York, Pantheon, 1991.

Martin Brennan, *The Boyne Valley Vision*, Mountrath, Dolmen, 1980.

George Mackay Brown, *Portrait of Orkney*, London, Hogarth, 1981.

Sir Thomas Browne, *Religio Medici*, London, 1645; *Pseudodoxia Epidemica*, Oxford, Clarendon, 1981.

Charles Butler, *The Feminine Monarchie*, New York, Da Capo, 1969 [facsimile of 1609 edition].

Albert Camus, *L'Homme révolté*, Paris, Gallimard, 1951; 'Le Désert', *Noces*, Paris, Gallimard, 1950.

Eiléan Ní Chuilleanáin, *The Second Voyage*, Loughcrew, Gallery Press, 1977/1986.

Felix M Cleve, *The Giants of Pre-Sophistic Greek Philosophy: an Attempt to Reconstruct their Thoughts*, The Hague, Martinus Nijhoff, 1973.

Keith Critchlow, *Time Stands Still: New Light on Megalithic Science*, New York, St Martin's Press, 1982.

(John Cumming), *Beekeeping by the Times Bee-master*, London, 1871.

Annie Dillard, *Teaching a Stone to Talk: Expeditions and Encounters*, New York, Harper & Row, 1982.

Christos Doumas, *The Wall-Paintings of Thera*, trans. Alex Doumas, Athens, Thera Foundation, 1992.

Arne Eggum, *Munch and Photography*, trans. Birgit Holm, Newcastle-upon-Tyne, Polytechnic Gallery & Oslo, Munch Museum, 1989.

Leonhard Euler, *Letters to a German Princess*, New York, Arno Press, 1975 [fascimile of 1833 edition].

E M Forster, *Alexandria: A History and a Guide*, London, Michael Haag, 1982.

A G Galanopoulos & Edward Bacon, *Atlantis: The Truth Behind the Legend*, London, Nelson, 1969.

Paul Gauguin, *Oviri: Ecrits d'un sauvage*, Paris, Gallimard, 1974.

Trevor Gett, 'Room With An (Obscured) View' in *Australian Photography*, January 2000.

Helmut Gernsheim with Alison Gernsheim, *The History of Photography from the Camera Obscura to the Beginning of the Modern Era*, London, Thames & Hudson, 1969.

Edward Stewart Gifford, *The Evil Eye: Studies in the Folklore of Vision*, New York, Macmillan, 1958.

Etienne Gilson, *Painting and Reality*, New York, Meridian Books, 1959.

P V Glob, *The Mound People: Danish Bronze-Age Man Preserved*, Ithaca, NY, Cornell UP, 1974.

Johann Wolfgang von Goethe, *Goethe's Theory of Colours*, trans. Charles Lock Eastlake, London, Cass, 1967 [facsimile of 1840 edition].

C F C Hawkes, *Pytheas: Europe and the Greek Explorers*, Oxford, Blackwell, 1977.

Gerald S Hawkins, *Stonehenge Decoded*, London, Souvenir Press, 1965.

J L Heilbron, *The Sun in the Church: Cathedrals as Solar Observatories*, Cambridge, Mass., Harvard UP, 1999.

Reinhold Heller, *Munch, His Life and Work*, London, University of Chicago Press, 1984; *Edvard Munch: The Scream*, London, Penguin, 1973.

J P Hodin, *Edvard Munch*, London, Thames & Hudson, 1972.

Peter Høeg, *Miss Smilla's Feeling for Snow*, London, Flamingo, 1994.

Roni Horn, *Another Water (The River Thames, for example)*, Zurich/Berlin/New York, Scalo, 2000.

Walter Woodburn Hyde, *Ancient Greek Mariners*, New York, Oxford UP, 1947.

Henrik Ibsen, *Ghosts (Gengangere)*, trans. William Archer, London, Walter Scott, 1900.

Martin Jay, *Downcast Eyes: The Denigration of Vision in Twentieth-Century French Thought*, Los Angeles/Berkeley, University of California Press, 1993.
Mette Jørgensen, 'Islands: Literally and in Literature' in *Kunapipi* 2, 1997.
Charles H Kahn, *The Art and Thought of Heraclitus*, Cambridge UP, 1979.
Iosif Aronovich Khalifman, *Bees: a book on the biology of the bee-colony and the achievements of bee-science*, Moscow, Foreign Languages Publishing House, 1953.
The Holy Kur'an, trans. Ali Abdullah Yusuf, Beirut, Dar al Arabia, 1980 [facsimile of 1934 edition].
Lati Rinbochay and Jeffrey Hopkins, *Death, Intermediate State and Rebirth in Tibetan Buddhism*, Ithaca, NY, Snow Lion, 1980.
D H Lawrence, *Etruscan Places*, London, Olive Press; Siena, Nuova Immagine, 1986; *Apocalypse*, London, Heinemann, 1972; 'The Crown' in *Phoenix* II, London, Heinemann, 1968; *Selected Poems*, ed. Keith Sagar, Harmondsworth, Penguin, 1972.
John Cuthbert Lawson, *Modern Greek Folklore and Ancient Greek Religion: A Study in Survivals*, Cambridge UP, 1910.
Leonardo da Vinci, *The Notebooks of Leonardo da Vinci*, trans. and ed. Edward MacCurdy, London, Jonathan Cape, 1938.
Leonardo da Vinci, *The Notebooks of Leonardo da Vinci*, trans. and ed. Jean Paul Richter, New York, Dover, 1970.
David Lewis, *We, the Navigators: the Ancient Art of Landfinding in the Pacific*, Honolulu, University of Hawaii Press, 1972/1994.
Carus Titus Lucretius, *De rerum natura*, trans. W H D Rouse, rev. Martin Ferguson Smith, London, Heinemann, 1975; *De rerum natura*, trans. and ed. Cyril Bailey, Oxford, Clarendon, 1949.
Euan MacKie, *The Megalith Builders*, Oxford, Phaidon, 1977.

James W Mavor Jnr, *Voyage to Atlantis: The Discovery of a Legendary Land*, Rochester, Vermont, Park Street Press, 1996.

Martin P Nilsson, *Greek Folk Religion*, Gloucester, Mass., Peter Smith, 1940/1971.

Njal's Saga, trans. Magnus Magnusson and Hermann Pålsson, London, Baltimore, Penguin, 1960.

The Voyage of Saint Brendan: Journey to the Promised Land [*Navigatio Sancti Brendani Abbatis*] trans. John J O'Meara, Dublin, Dolmen, 1978.

Orkneyinga Saga, trans. Magnus Magnusson and Paul Edwards, London, Penguin, 1981

E Panagiotakopulu et al, 'A lepidopterous cocoon from Thera and evidence for silk in the Aegean Bronze Age' in *Antiquity* 71, 1997.

Alexandros Papadiamantis, *Απαντα* II, Athens, Domos, 1982/1997.

Felix R Paturi, *Prehistoric Heritage*, trans. Tania and Bernard Alexander, New York, Scribner, 1979.

Plato, *Timaeus*, ed. R D Archer-Hind, London, 1888.

Pliny, *Naturalis historia*, trans. H Rackham et al, London, Heinemann, 1938–63.

Pliny, *The Historie of the World. Commonly called, The Naturall historie of C. Plinius Secundus*, trans. Philemon Holland, London, 1601.

Plotinus, *The Enneads*, trans. Stephen MacKenna and B S Page, London, Medici Society, 1917–1930.

Porphyry, 'Concerning the Cave of the Nymphs' in *Thomas Taylor the Platonist: Selected Writings*, ed. Kathleen Raine and George Mills Harper, London, Routledge & Kegan Paul, 1969.

Hilda M Ransome, *The sacred bee in ancient times and folklore*, Burrowbridge, Bridgwater, Bee Books New & Old, 1986.

Rainer Maria Rilke, 'From *The Notebooks of Malte Laurids Brigge*' in *The Selected Poetry of Rainer Maria Rilke*, trans. and ed. Stephen Mitchell, New York, Random House, 1982; *Letters of Rainer Maria Rilke 1892–1910*, trans. Jane Bannard Greene and M D Herter Norton, New York, Norton, 1945; *Selected Letters 1902–1926*, trans. R F C Hull, London, Quartet, 1988; *Auguste Rodin*, trans. Jessie Lemont and Hans Trausil, New York, Haskell House, 1974; *Letters on Cézanne*, ed. Clara Rilke, trans. Joel Agee, New York, Fromm, 1985.

Vasco Ronchi, *The Nature of Light: An Historical Survey*, trans. V Barocas, London, Heinemann, 1970.

Oliver Sacks, *The Island of the Colorblind; and Cycad Island*, New York, Knopf, 1997.

George Seferis, in Philip Sherrard, *The Marble Threshing Floor: Studies in Modern Greek Poetry*, Athens, Denise Harvey, 1981; 'Πρωι', *Ποιηματα*, Athens, Ikaros, 1963.

Snorri Sturluson, *Heimskringla, Part II: Sagas of the Norse Kings*, trans. Samuel Laing, London, Dent, 1961.

Susan Sontag, *On Photography*, New York, Farrar, Straus and Giroux, 1978.

Rolf E Stenersen, *Edvard Munch: Close-Up of a Genius*, trans. and ed. Reidar Dittmann, Oslo, Sten & Stenersen, 1994.

Robert Temple, *The Crystal Sun: Rediscovering a Lost Technology of the Ancient World*, London, Century, 2000.

Alexander Thom, *Megalithic remains in Britain and Brittany*, Oxford, Clarendon, 1978.

Bente Torjusen, *Words and Images of Edvard Munch*, London, Thames & Hudson, 1989.

E O G Turville-Petre, *Myth and Religion of the North*, New York, Holt, Rinehart and Winston, 1964.

Verzamelde Brieven van Vincent van Gogh, ed. J van Gogh-Bonger, Amsterdam, Wereld, 1952–54.

The Desert Fathers, trans. Helen Waddell, London, Constable, 1936.

Virginia Woolf, *A Writer's Diary*, ed. Leonard Woolf, London, Triad Grafton, 1987.

Arthur Zajonc, *Catching the Light: The Entwined History of Light and Mind*, London/New York, Oxford UP, 1993.

The words of Edvard Munch quoted by kind permission of the Munch Museum, Oslo.

Use of the line 'Water has no memory' from 'Family' by Eiléan Ní Chuilleanáin in *The Second Voyage*, 1977, by kind permission of the author and The Gallery Press, Loughcrew, Oldcastle, County Meath, Ireland.

Permission to quote a passage from *A Writer's Diary* by Virginia Woolf, edited by Leonard Woolf, The Hogarth Press Ltd, 1953, granted by HarperCollins Publishers Ltd.

Lines from *Njal's Saga*, translated by Magnus Magnusson and Hermann Pålsson, Penguin Classics, 1960, pp. 349–351, copyright Magnus Magnusson and Hermann Pålsson, reproduced by permission of Penguin Books Ltd.

Acknowledgements

My thanks to the Literature Board of the Australia Council for a Senior Fellowship in 1996–99; and for their hospitality and a support during the writing of this book, Flinders University of South Australia and Århus University in Denmark for residencies in 1995 and 1996, the Hawthornden Castle International Retreat for Writers in Scotland for a fellowship in 2001, and the Eleanor Dark Foundation for a Varuna Fellowship in the Blue Mountains in 2003.

An earlier draft of 'Mouths of Gold' appeared (under the title 'Harbour') in the anthology *Harbour* edited by George Papaellinas and published by Picador in 1993, and a later one in *Fire and Shadow*, HEAT 1, new series, 2001; of 'Seeing in the Dark', in *Southerly*, Spring 1998; and of 'Stone Age' (under the title 'Notes Towards *The Scream*') in the anthology *Risks*, edited by Brenda Walker and published by Fremantle Arts Centre Press in 1996.

This project has been assisted by the Australian Government through the Australia Council, its arts funding and advisory body.